Streaming Horrors

# Streaming Horrors

*Essays on the Genre
in the Digital Age*

*Edited by*
SOTIRIS PETRIDIS

McFarland & Company, Inc., Publishers
*Jefferson, North Carolina*

*This book has undergone peer review.*

LIBRARY OF CONGRESS CATALOGING-IN-PUBLICATION DATA

Names: Petridis, Sotiris, 1990– editor.
Title: Streaming horrors : essays on the genre in the digital age / edited by
    Sotiris Petridis.
Description: Jefferson, North Carolina : McFarland & Company, Inc., Publishers, 2025 |
    Includes bibliographical references and index.
Identifiers: LCCN 2024056264 | ISBN 9781476693118 (paperback : acid free paper) ∞
    ISBN  9781476654249 (ebook)
Subjects: LCSH: Horror television programs—History and criticism. | Horror films—
    History and criticism. | Streaming video.
Classification: LCC PN1992.8.H67 S77 2025 | DDC 791.45/6164—dc23/eng/20250127
LC record available at https://lccn.loc.gov/2024056264

**ISBN (print) 978-1-4766-9311-8**
**ISBN (ebook) 978-1-4766-5424-9**

Front cover image: © Egrigorovich/Shutterstock

Printed in the United States of America

*McFarland & Company, Inc., Publishers
   Box 611, Jefferson, North Carolina 28640
   www.mcfarlandpub.com*

# Table of Contents

# Introduction

## Sotiris Petridis

Audiovisual content has expanded into new ways of production, distribution, and screening enabled by the evolution of technology and the advent of new media. Apart from giving new life to older audiovisual works by making them accessible to the wide public through an alternative way of consumption, streaming platforms are producing original content that is meant to be consumed exclusively via online means.

Older film and television practices are now largely replaced by the technological evolution of the new media, which have drastically changed the landscape of the industry. By defying the classical distinction between cinema and television, the streaming services can blur the lines between the old media and create new ways of narration that adapt audiovisual storytelling to contemporary needs.

Film and television horror is one of the genres that managed to adjust to the digital era and flourish through its evolution that is based on the conventions that the streaming services brought to the fore. New media strengthens the horror genre by introducing classic horror to the new generations and by creating new content that obeys the needs of the digital society.

Audience fragmentation, solitary watching and binge-watching along with narrative complexity are some of the catalysts in the rapid evolvement and reinvention of the audiovisual horror. This edited collection focuses on this turning point of the genre and the fundamental changes that have taken place.

This edited collection is dedicated to a thorough study of the evolution of film and television horror and its adaptation to the features of the digital era. Subscription Video-on-Demand (SVOD) and other streaming platforms initiated a new flourishing period of the horror genre both in film and television. Based on a selection of carefully organized and similarly structured essays, this volume enriches the bibliography regarding the present and future of the genre and thoroughly studies the effects of the new media in the audiovisual landscape in regard to institutions, audiences, and content.

To achieve these goals, the book is divided into two major parts. The first part is dedicated to audiovisual horror and its audience in the digital age. The first essay, "The Horror Genre, Its Brand Community, and the Emergence of a Queer Icon," written by Sotiris Petridis, deals with the complicated relationship between the brand community of the genre and the narratives themselves. Since the beginning of the new millennium, the internet has conquered the promotion of the audiovisual sector, while the audience has acquired a more interactive role in this new landscape. Based on these facts, audiovisual works and/or genres can be interpreted as brands. One of the biggest and best known brands is the horror genre. The audiovisual horror genre boasts a large and vibrant community of fans who actively engage with its works through fan theories, fan fiction, edits, and memes, often reshaping their meanings in the process. One of these cases is the film *Babadook* (2015). Even if the film cannot be strictly categorized as part of an LGBTQ representation, nevertheless the brand community received it as queer in the most empirical sense, since the existence of Babadook is defiance, and it seeks to break down the borders of acceptability and establishment. This essay examines the mechanisms of the horror genre as a brand that led to the creation of a queer icon from a film like *Babadook* that does not include LGBTQ representations. This essay analyzes how the active members of the brand community used viral marketing techniques of unofficial content to change the meaning of the film according to their own experiences.

The second essay, "Beyond the Boundaries of Jump Scare: OTT Platforms and the Discourse of Elevated Horror," written by Sony Jalarajan Raj and Adith K. Suresh, has as its main objective a study of the popularization of digital streaming and its contribution to the reawakening of the horror genre through new possibilities. Digital spaces created by online streaming platforms have decentralized the meaning of the "popular," which is perceived today as not only a measure of quantity but also as a measure of quality. In an era where artistic and capitalistic dimensions of the audiovisual influence content creation, distribution, and reception, new strategies and approaches to horror narratives depend on the platforms in which they find new meanings after their exposure to a variety of audiences all around the world. This essay analyzes how the emergence of over-the-top (OTT) platforms has changed the mode of horror film/series reception by challenging the conventional methods of screening practices. Horror, unlike other genres, has always had a limited fandom. The social, cultural, and moral restrictions frequently dissuade people from watching horror films, and the way such films are censored and banned in many countries speaks volumes about why people could not get access to horror materials in the mainstream media. OTT platforms subvert this historical reality by streaming horror of all subgenres for all people from all places. Transgressing censorship rules and allowing consumers to access content in their private spaces are some of the revolutionary aspects of modern horror in the digital age. Discussing this transformation in detail, this essay examines the discourse of horror and explores how this new idea is celebrated and accepted through streaming platforms like Netflix, Amazon Prime, Hulu, Shudder, etc. It also investigates how this changed scenario gave birth to new experimental horror films and series that refer to the notion of "elevated horror," a category of horror that utilizes the artistic aspects of the horror genre to create a cinematic form that subverts the archetypal jump scare tropes of conventional horror.

The third essay also deals with a horror fandom and the role of villains in the reality landscape. In "Monstrous Morality: Making Unreal Villains Within Reality TV," Neelima Mundayur uses the seminal work of Robin Wood, which explored queer subtext within the horror genre, arguing that monsters present as "Others" who disrupt heterosexual normality. But instead of positing that the horror genre would reinforce a heteronormative ideal alone, Harry M. Benshoff examined the queer legacy of horror, including explicit as well as implicit depictions of undoing gender convention, especially through drag, as well as of homosexuality; the ritualistic overturning of normality could be exhilarating for queer spectators. This is reflected in *The Boulet Brothers' Dragula* (2016), a reality competition show for Drag Monsters, who use gender-play alongside horror, filth, and glamour as a form of art. The series is primarily based on pageants held by the Boulets and often pays homage to iconic moments in horror, reality TV and drag, including *RuPaul's Drag Race* (2009). The two series are often compared, and the Boulets themselves consider *Dragula* a radical alternative to the sanitized and commercialized *Drag Race*; their thesis is that in celebrating the monstrous, the series also attacks heteronormative culture and centers those who are socially excluded within the same. However, Prins suggests that in televising the drag competition, the Boulets unintentionally dilute this ethos; the series came into being after the rise of an online popular culture and is distributed largely through SVOD platforms. Thus, it is deeply embedded within a neoliberal platform economy. This essay examines how the series transforms the idea of the queer, monstrous Other by analyzing the role played by the "villains" of the series in cultivating sensationalism and, subsequently, a fandom online. It closely examines character arcs in *Dragula* and production tools used in constructing them and affective responses shared online, on discussion platforms such as Reddit, Instagram and Twitter or video-edits on You-Tube. Through this, the essay showcases how online fandom resignifies the queer monstrous Other within a normative, moral economy.

The last essay of the first part of the volume is titled "From Page to Screen: *Junji Itō Collection* and Affect." In this essay, Ivan Jaramillo studies Japanese manga artist Itō Junji, who is considered today one of the masters of horror manga among the likes of Maruo Suehiro and Umezu Kazuo. Ito became a renowned horror author since, in the late 1980s, his perhaps most popular work, *Tomie*, was released. His already large following reached an even higher level with the anime *Junji Ito Collection* (Studio Deen, 2018). Having some of Itō's most representative work both in manga and anime provides a good chance to understand how horror is conveyed in two different media beyond the existent live-action adaptations. Through the lens of different (re)interpretations of Deleuze's affect theory, this essay analyzes how affect works in Itō Junji's work across media. Affect has been used as a tool to study horror films, and all these perspectives agree that it is a group of emotions and somatic responses that the viewer has when watching a film. Drawing upon these approaches, the concept of transmedial affect proves appropriate for this essay considering, first, that affective responses might differ in each medium and, second, that Itō's manga has been studied mostly from perspectives related to body horror and Lovecraftian influences. How do black-and-white printed images, panels, and frames convey affect akin to that of horror films? How differently does affect work in Itō's manga and its anime adaptation? By looking closely at the narrative techniques used in five of Itō's horror manga stories and comparing them to their anime equivalents, while considering the medium in which each occurs, this essay analyzes how affect works on the printed page and how this changes, or not, when translated into its animated form.

The second part of this book is dedicated to forms of narration and to its narrative representations. In "Containing the Uncanny: *A Babysitter's Guide to Monster Hunting*," Christina Adamou analyzes how mortal danger is often present in children's narratives, from classical fairy tales to contemporary films. According to some psychoanalysts, its presence can constitute a warning against real dangers, or it can allow children to work through their fears. Yet, very few narratives for children would be placed in the genre of horror. Using methodological tools from genre theory and psychoanalysis, this essay highlights how *A Babysitter's Guide to Monster Hunting* seeks a new audience for horror in the seven-plus age group and maps out the possibilities for a new subgenre in the streaming era, catering to children's desire for and need of horror. *A Babysitter's Guide to Monster Hunting* is a hybrid of teen/high school films, fantasy, and horror. Although it employs numerous clichés in regard both to characters (the underdog that becomes the hero, the ice queen and the imprisoned boy) and the monsters (coming out of the closet, spider-like shadows, cats as the helpers of a witch), it is also innovative both in its choice of an Afro-American girl as the lead character and in its use and containment of the uncanny. The film's spooky elements are based on rendering familiar objects unfamiliar, blurring the lines between the known and the unknown, the inanimate and the animate—a technique that has often been used in the horror genre. At the same time, the uncanniness and horror are contained by preparing the audience for scary scenes, timing that does not prolong suspense, costumes and acting that stress performativity and the implicit promise of a happy ending.

The next essay, written by Anna Rufer Bílá and Klára Feikusová, is titled "*The Hauntings* on Netflix: *Hill House* and *Bly Manor* as the Forms of the Serial Anthology in the Binge-Watching Era." In this age of peak TV, a program with a clearly defined ending may be the solution for audiences who are oversaturated with content. This is where the serial anthology seems to be an appropriate strategy. By serial anthology, we mean an anthology where the transformation of setting, plot and characters is not limited to single episodes, but seasons. Examples of this narrative form include *American Horror Story* (2011– ), *The Haunting of Hill House* (2018) and *The Haunting of Bly Manor* (2020). It is *The Haunting of Hill House* and *The Haunting of Bly Manor* that constitute the subject of the present essay, where the authors discuss the narrative structure of both in the era of plenitude, binge-watching, and streaming services, and why the serial anthology is advantageous to it. It is a closed narrative that does not commit the audience to long-term viewing but allows the story and characters to unfold. Also, this form represents a type of narrative complexity as it works with intratextuality and, in the case of *Hill House* and *Bly Manor*, with numerous narrative devices such as flashbacks, multiple points of view, focalization, etc. The serial anthology is an adaptation of an existing narrative form that was particularly popular in the early decades of television to the current era of increased serialization. For Netflix, this form is advantageous due to their overproduction of original work—it allows these shows to stand out more in the overall lineup of season-long programming. However, through connecting elements between seasons (genre, author, actors, etc.), viewers are compelled to come back. Bílá and Feikusová approach the topic from the perspective of television narratology with respect to the context of digitalization and streaming. The aim is to use the example of *Hill House* and *Bly Manor* to introduce this updated form and to highlight its functionality in the era of plenitude.

"On *Black Summer* and Embodied Spectatorship," by Fernando Gabriel Pagnoni Berns, is another insightful analysis of an important but overlooked narrative of contemporary audiovisual horror. The power of narrative cinema relies on characters who can be empathized with, characters who can carry the audience into any kind of adventure, any kind of ideology, any kind of fantasy. This is especially relevant with TV seriality, where the different episodes allow "multilinear" time and complex storylines and characters, unlike mainstream cinema, which is forced to tell the story in a very limited length. Further, streaming seriality changed the rigid order of conventional TV. Rather than depend on a certain number of episodes for each season, streaming allows a TV series to use only the number of episodes it needs to tell the story without relying (in most cases) on padding and filling. *Black Summer* (Netflix, 2019–2021) successfully plays with this new freedom while, at the same time, disrupting it. Created by Karl Schaefer and John Hyams, the series is a spinoff of *Z Nation* (SyFy), centered on the early days of a zombie apocalypse and those who have to live through it. It adopts an almost documentary style with little verbal exposition about the lives of the different characters. *Black Summer* privileges action and horror, asking the viewers to follow characters presented via brief segments. With such brief presentations and with little exposition, viewers are confused about who exactly leading characters to follow are. Further, almost everyone does in fact die over the course of the story. In his book on horror and affect, Adam Daniel argues that when classical structures of narrative are de-emphasized, such as when emphasis is placed on the moving camera, on what is out of the frame, or on pure action, they activate a distinct, concurrent embodied response for the viewer. *Black Summer* invites viewers to a constant re-evaluation of their ideological and/or affective positions as to pin a particular moral to a particular character becomes increasingly difficult as the series progress. With little exposition, the viewers' sympathy starts to collapse in stories where "evil" and "good" characters shift constantly in their positions ("Card Game," season 2, ep. 3). With the murdered victims becoming murderous zombies in just seconds, this moral shift accelerates even more. The sharp difference between the episodes' lengths (varying from 21 to 58 minutes) further plays with expectations, as the series focuses only on the minimal structures of storytelling. *Black Summer* creates a world where viewers are forced to engage in innovative ways with the different characters using the advantages given by the new system of streaming TV and its flexibility. Through an affective and close reading, this essay investigates the disruptive nature of this (overlooked) Netflix show.

Finally, in the last essay of the volume, "The Many Faces of Thomas Hewitt: A Streaming Approach of *The Texas Chainsaw Massacre*,"

Giuseppe Previtali studies the reboot of a well-known horror franchise. Since its first installment in 1974, *The Texas Chainsaw Massacre* was immediately recognized as a cult horror, capable of articulating a new dimension of horror, more "realist" and connected to everyday life. In almost fifty years, Leatherface's saga was able to reposition itself in the new contexts of horror cinema, as the various prequels/reboots and sequels demonstrate. In so doing, the story of the Sawyer/Hewitt family was continuously rewritten, but the franchise maintained its capacity to show a hidden and disturbing aspect of the so-called "American Dream." The most recent installment by David Blue Garcia (*Texas Chainsaw Massacre*, 2022) was distributed on Netflix and, in its narrative development and aesthetics, reveals a profound connection with the products licensed by the streaming platform. The essay, after having recalled the development and legacy of the franchise, shows precisely how the myth of Leatherface has been re-territorialized in this new context, arguing that the longevity of the series has to do with its ability to "wear new masks," thus adapting to the ever-changing rules of the mediascape.

# PART 1

# Audiovisual Horror and Its Audience in the Digital Age

# The Horror Genre, Its Brand Community, and the Emergence of a Queer Icon

Sotiris Petridis

## Introduction

Since the beginning of the new millennium, the internet has conquered the promotion of the audiovisual sector, while the audience has acquired a more interactive role in this new landscape. Based on these facts, audiovisual works and/or audiovisual genres can be interpreted as brands. One of the biggest and well-known brands is the horror genre. Audiovisual horror has a vast brand community with a lot of active members who, through fan theories, fan fiction, fan edits, and memes, interact with each work and sometimes alter its meaning. In this essay, I will analyze the mechanisms behind an enormous brand community like horror aficionados, and I will argue that their unofficial viral content created a queer icon from a non-queer narrative, like *The Babadook* (2014).

Even if the film cannot be strictly categorized as part of an LGBTQ representation, nevertheless the brand community received it as queer in the most empirical sense, since the existence of Babadook is defiance, and it seeks to break down the borders of acceptability and establishment. This essay will examine the mechanisms of the audiovisual horror as a brand that led to the creation of a queer icon in the face of Babadook. Moreover, I will analyze how, based on viral marketing techniques of unofficial content, the active members of the brand community changed the meaning of the film according to their own experiences.

## Audiovisual Brands and Brand Communities

Before I go any further, there is a need for clarification between two basic terms that I will consistently use in this research: brand and brand management. Brand is defined as the perception customers have about a product or a service, while at the same time it is what consumers think of when they hear or see the brand's name and/or products.[1] Brand is a wide term that distinguishes one's product in order to differentiate it from others of the same category, and incorporates all consumers' experiences and opinions, creating a unique product identity.[2]

According to Daragh O'Reilly and Finola Kerrigan, audiovisual works can be considered as brands, both artistically and commercially, while these values cannot be easily separated. Audiovisual works are brands because

> [they] have a symbolic dimension; are the subject of capital and technological investment; are offered for sale; carry intellectual property rights; differentiate themselves from other films; and are strategic assets for their production studios' brand portfolios.[3]

On the other hand, we have the planning and execution of advertising practices that ultimately want to create a stable and enduring relationship between the brand and its consumers—the so-called brand management.[4] One of the most commonplace techniques that nowadays is constantly being used is viral marketing, a term that describes every strategy that inspires potential consumers to transmit a marketing message to others, creating exponential growth in its exposure and influence, usually via online means.[5]

Marshall McLuhan's concept of the "global village" can help us understand how viral marketing works. McLuhan claims that the globe has been contracted into a village by the instantaneous movement of information from every quarter to every point at the same time.[6] Today, knowledge and information are accessible by everyone with internet access (around 40 percent of the world population, and 88.5 percent of the U.S. population),[7] and a significant percentage of users have become more active than ever. Unlike traditional marketing techniques, viral marketing focuses on a personal experience of the brand and taps into the consumer's power.[8]

A characteristic example is LG's 2012 online promotion of its realistic new IPS monitors. In an attempt to create buzz around the product, their promoters/marketers staged a stunt where they replaced an elevator floor in an office building in the UK with the monitors to make it look like the floor was falling, while they filmed unsuspecting people having hilarious reactions and posted it online.[9] By 2025, this video had racked up more than 53 million views on YouTube.

One of the first examples of such a strategy in cinema comes from the horror genre with the film *The Blair Witch Project* (1999), a horror movie about three film students who disappear in a forest while filming a documentary on a local witch legend. At the time of its release, the film's producers created a website full of fake police reports and newsreel-style interviews, while the relevant IMDb page listed the actors as "missing, presumed dead" for the first year after its release, making everyone unsure of whether this was a real-life documentary or a fiction film. There were even posters depicting the actors as missing persons. Consumers were not expected to just passively watch the film, as this promotion encouraged online activity—from visiting the website, to searching for the actors on IMDb—in order to have a full experience of the product that eventually became a brand. The promotion had a positive result, since it helped a very low-budget horror film ($60,000) to become one of the most profitable horror films of all time,[10] with a gross of $248,639,099 worldwide, according to Box Office Mojo.

After the success of *The Blair Witch Project* marketing, a lot of films and television series, such as *The Dark Knight* (2008), *Alien: Covenant* (2017), *Game of Thrones* (HBO, 2011–2019), and *Stranger Things* (Netflix, 2016–2025), replicated this formula by creating official viral content, such as videos, pictures, texts and news, in order to promote and expand the identity and image of the audiovisual work. This method has at its core two fundamental terms coined by Henry Jenkins: media convergence and participatory culture.[11]

Media convergence is the flow of content across multiple media platforms based on the increase of the migratory behavior of consumers, who will go "anywhere" in search of entertainment experiences. Participatory culture takes place when media producers and consumers do not occupy separate roles but become participants who interact with each other.[12]

As Susan Fournier and Lara Lee point out, from packaged goods to industrial equipment industries, marketers try to build communities around their products.[13] The two main requirements for the creation of an audiovisual brand community are the existence of a brand and mechanisms for fans/consumers to engage in that brand's public experience.[14] The audiovisual genre of horror can be interpreted as an umbrella brand with a plethora of dedicated consumers who constitute a potential brand community.

Members of a brand community share a common consciousness, traditions, and a sense of moral responsibility, while they play a vital role in the brand's history formation as well as potential legacy.[15] As Albert Muniz and H.J. Schau comment, members of a brand community may even determine the agenda and specific activities of the brand itself through interrelationships among its members.[16] As they trade online information, they form a kind of subculture, which can be used as a brand management tool.[17] In the social media era, every active consumer can contribute a small piece to the creation of a given brand image by forwarding and/or expanding information, sharing and exchanging ideas about the brand.[18] The way brand communities work brings us to Jenkins's concept of collective intelligence, described as follows:

> None of us can know everything; each of us knows something; and we can put the pieces together if we pool our resources and combine our skills. Collective intelligence can be seen as an alternative source of media power. We are learning how to use that power through our day-to-day interactions within convergence culture.[19]

Of course, not every member of a brand community has the same amount of commitment with the brand. As Won-Moo Hur, Kwang-Ho Ahn, and Minsung Kim point out, "the concept of commitment is used as a predictor of members' actual behaviors in an online community, such as participating in community activities, offering help to the community, and solving problems for others."[20] David Kalman speaks about four main categories of members that belong to a brand community: the prospect, the non-committal, the brand admirer, and the brand enthusiast.[21] Prospects are possible new consumers, non-committals choose the brand out of convenience or habit, brand admirers truly prefer the brand, and brand enthusiasts both prefer and promote it. The more commitment there is, the more interaction exists between the brand and the brand communities. Brand enthusiasts are the most committed members of a community and form the core of participatory culture, since they are not only faithful to a brand, but they try to promote and expand it.

Cinema aficionados who admire a genre and/or a creator are behaving like brand enthusiasts, with fan theories, fan fiction, fan edits, and memes being some of their most common tools in order to promote or even expand the brand image of the audiovisual narrative in question. This original content can even enrich a brand identity. An example of an audiovisual brand that enjoys unofficial viral content abundantly is *Game of Thrones*. The variety of this content is astonishing: from fan films, such as *The Wild Wolf* (2017), and viral videos, like the trailer of a modern-day fictitious TV series with the name *Westeros: The Series*,[22] to an 8-bit fan-made GOT game,[23] and an interactive map of Westeros and Essos with spoilers control,[24] *Game of Thrones* enjoys a range of forms of unofficial content.

The main conclusion regarding this categorization between official and unofficial content is that the unofficial content of an audiovisual brand has the same potential to become viral as the viral campaign of the original brand management, as it is uploaded in an instant and can be easily found by each prospect.

## Joint Brand Management and the Horror Genre

In my article "A Case for Joint Brand Management in Film and Television Promotion" (2020), I coined the term joint brand management in order to best describe the aforementioned framework in which both official and unofficial brand content develops and flows. Even if the stages of joint brand management are by definition abstract and are differentiating between the needs of every brand, we can identify three key phases[25]:

1. First, official content is distributed in order to create an interactive relationship with an already established brand community, like the horror fans. This content is created and controlled by the producing and/or managing team of the audiovisual brand.

2. Second, if the audiovisual work is prosperous enough to galvanize its community, brand enthusiasts create their own content and can succeed in making it viral through social media and online platforms.

3. Third, both official and unofficial content can be used for the promotion of the brand by attracting prospects and/or raising the level of commitment of the other members of the community. Most often, these two categories coexist peacefully without altering the official brand identity, although there are instances when these content types contradict each other.

The possible existence of two viral identities of an audiovisual brand could have implications in two different aspects—on its fictional world and/or its brand image. The fictional world of an audiovisual brand is the solid foundation of the narrative, loved by enthusiasts who try to be a small part of it by creating unofficial content, while on the other hand, the brand image of audiovisual texts is dependent on extratextual parameters, like the casting of the work and/or its lifespan.[26]

There are several audiovisual narratives that belong to the horror genre and have been influenced in both these categories. An example regarding a major influence by the brand community to the fictional world of a horror narrative is Netflix's *Stranger Things* (2016–2025). *Stranger Things* is a science fiction–horror television series created by the Duffer Brothers. The show is set in the fictional town of Hawkins, Indiana, in the 1980s, and its first season focuses on the disappearance of a boy, while supernatural events take place around the town.

After the killing of Barbara Holland (Shannon Purser), a secondary character of the first season, the fans created a viral campaign under the name "Justice for Barb," demanding justice for a character they believed died in vain. Not only did the campaign give more exposure to the brand, but it also even resulted in an Emmy nomination for the actress who portrayed Barb. It also affected the final closure of this storyline in the second season, as the creators decided to give justice by punishing the culprit and divulging the truth about her murder.[27]

Another example regarding a major influence by the brand community to the brand image of a horror film is *It: Chapter 2* (2019). One aspect of an audiovisual brand image is the casting decisions of the film. When a new installment is announced, enthusiasts start to speculate about the stars. If their preferences or even dislikes go viral, this could be a way of pressuring the production team to cast some fan-favorite actors.

*It* (2017) is a horror film directed by Andy Muschietti, based on the homonymous novel by Stephen King published in 1986. The story involves seven children in the small town of Derry in Maine who are terrorized by Pennywise, a demon clown, while facing their own personal fears. Because of the famous novel and its 1990 adaptation into a TV miniseries, a brand community was already established. After the promotion of the 2017 film and its phenomenal success, fans began revisiting older fan theories and creating unofficial viral content, usually in the form of memes. News of the 2019 sequel set the brand enthusiasts searching for actors to play the adult versions of each character from the first film, and some choices went viral. Brand enthusiasts supported Jessica Chastain for the adult version of Beverly by even creating fan-made posters of the sequel.[28] In February 2018, it was confirmed that Chastain had officially joined the cast.[29]

There are cases, however, when brand communities create backlash, especially when their members feel that a new episode or film does not truly represent the real essence of the brand as they perceive it. In these instances, brand enthusiasts can choose to rebel against official brand management to "save" what they believe is the "correct" brand image or the canon (official continuity of events, stories, and works within the fictional world).

The 2016 reboot of *Ghostbusters* is such a case. Months before its release, the brand community had a negative response, because they thought that the all-female reboot would destroy the brand image as they knew it. The immediate result of this backlash was that the trailer of the film became the most disliked trailer on YouTube of all time.[30] Their strong reactions seriously impacted the brand's financial revenue as the film lost more than $70 million, something that caused more than a loss, making a sequel of this film an unlikely possibility.[31] As a matter of fact, Sony

Pictures released *Ghostbusters: Afterlife* in 2021, continuing the story from the 1984 original film and its sequel while disregarding the 2016 female-led reboot.[32]

This exemplifies how every community of a popular audiovisual brand protects its canon (for example, refer to how the term "canon" is used on the *Star Wars* and *Lord of the Rings* Wikias). Just like the *Ghostbusters* case, even if the canon refers to the works that officially belong to the brand, the brand community can find themselves in conflict with it and try to alter it.

With the support of the aforementioned horror examples, it is clear that franchises and/or audiovisual genres, like horror, work as a unified brand with a strong brand community and faithful enthusiasts who are capable of supporting, promoting, or even influencing the fictional world and/or the brand image of each narrative. Every film is created and promoted in a manner that serves the official brand management, but since fans are unpredictable, the core and the essence of this narrative can drastically change.

## Babadook and the Creation of a Queer Icon

*The Babadook* is a 2014 Australian horror film. It is the directorial debut of Jennifer Kent, and it was based on her 2005 short film *Monster*. The film, which premiered at the 2014 Sundance Film Festival, was produced by Kristina Ceyton and Kristian Moliere. The film was welcomed with critical acclaim in both the United States and Europe. As Tomás Prower points out, "it was a critically acclaimed financial success, but it didn't rock world culture in any significant way."[33]

The film is centered around Amelia (Essie Davis) and her child, Samuel (Noah Wiseman), who fall into a deep well of terror when a peculiar children's book, titled *Mister Babadook,* appears in their home. Amelia's late husband, Oskar (Ben Winspear), was killed in a car crash as he drove Amelia to the hospital during labor. Amelia, as a single mother, faces difficulties while raising her son, because Sam begins displaying irregular behavior. He becomes an insomniac and is building weapons to fight an imaginary monster. One night, Sam asks his mother to read a storybook called *Mister Babadook*, which describes a monster that is a tall, pale-faced humanoid with a top hat and taloned fingers who plagues its victims after they become aware of its existence. Amelia is disturbed by the book and its mysterious appearance, while Sam becomes convinced that Babadook is real. Sam's persistence about Babadook leads Amelia to have sleepless nights herself while strange events start to occur. She thinks that the events are coming from Sam's behavior, but Sam blames Babadook.

Amelia starts to become isolated and more impatient, shouting at her son for constantly defying her, while she starts having frequent visions of Babadook, making her mental health fragile with disturbing hallucinations, where Amelia violently murders Sam. After a possession of Amelia by Babadook and the constant help of Sam, they ultimately confront Babadook, making him retreat into the basement. At the end, Amelia and Sam manage to recover, while Amelia comes to terms with the existence and cohabitation with Babadook.

From the above short synopsis, it is clear that there are no queer elements in the narrative of the film. As the fictional world of the film develops, the audience does not witness any LGBTQ representations and/or any thematic content that is closely connected to queer culture. Nevertheless, despite the intentions of the film's creators, ultimately *The Babadook* was established in pop culture as a queer icon. This did not happen by the official management of the audiovisual work, but by fans of the film who identified traits of Babadook that can be related to queer culture. The film is part of the horror genre, so it can work as an excellent example of analysis of the way joint brand management works.

*The Babadook* premiered in 2014, but it was not acknowledged or connected with queer culture until late 2016. One of the earliest comments regarding the queerness of Babadook that officially started the public discourse came on Tumblr. Tumblr is a well-known and established website that at the time was very popular among teenagers. This website allows people to exchange and reblog ideas, jokes, memes and other content that is part of the participatory culture of social media. As Elspeth Reeve explains:

> Sometimes those one-liners spread across continents, tweaked by thousands of other teens who add their own jokes as they reblog the original. The very best tweaks spread further, reblogged again and again, reappearing periodically in the feed, disconnected from time. Some posts get more than a million notes—imagine a joke whispered in biology class getting a laugh from a city the size of San Francisco.[34]

One of the most prominent uses of Tumblr is the concept referred to as "The Discourse," or, as Brian Feldman explains the term, the overarching conversation that the site's many fandom communities participate in to craft noncanonical (i.e., unofficial) theories about their favorite movies, TV shows, and YouTube series.[35] During one of these discourses, in October 2016, Tumblr user Instagram posted a thought complaint: "Whenever someone says the Babadook isn't openly gay it's like?? Did you even watch the movie???"

Instagram's post about the queerness of *Babadook* started to create some buzz around the film and received more than 100,000 likes and reblogs.[36] This threat was named Babadiscourse, by incorporating the term discourse and the name of the character in question. Among the followed reposts and replies, some users were opposed to Instagram's claim, stating that *The Babadook* "is just a movie," but others supported this claim and enriched the initial post. Tumblr user To-quote-hamlet-no stated that "the B in LGBT stands for Babadook. Everyone knows this," while the user Necromantics said, "I mean he created a pop-up book of himself for the drama of it all." After the initial buzz, Instagram returned to defend his reading, stating that "a movie about a gay man who just wants to live his life in a small Australian suburb? It may be 'just a movie' to you, but to the LGBT community, the Babadook is a symbol of our journey."[37]

A couple of months after the creation of the idea that *Babadook* is part of queer culture, Ryan Broderick, then an editor at BuzzFeed, tweeted on February 15, 2017, about Instagram's Tumblr post and gave an even bigger publicity boost to this claim. Afterwards, and almost two years after the initial premiere of the film, Babadook started an internet sensation with the creation of several posts in different online platforms that support his queer identity. Apart from one-liners and comments on Tumblr and Twitter, one of the most popular forms of content created to support this idea was memes.

According to Paul Gil, "a meme is a virally-transmitted cultural symbol or social idea,"[38] while Karen Schubert notes that a meme can take various forms, from captioned photographs and videos to verbal expressions, and often acts as mimicry or humorous depictions.[39] After the original post on Tumblr, brand enthusiasts created unofficial content of the film that support and expand the idea of Babadook being a queer icon. Pictures and videos of Babadook holding the rainbow flag, wearing queer accessories like extravagant flamingo glasses, attending the Stonewall protest, or participating in *RuPaul's Drag Race* made their appearance in different social media and strengthened the unofficial queer vibes of the film, making it part of the contemporary queer culture.

This online buzz led to an alleged error in the algorithm of Netflix. In December 2016 a screenshot of the platform emerged that listed *The Babadook* in the category of "LGBT interest" on Netflix America.[40] This had such an effect that in the summer of 2017 the *Los Angeles Times* wrote that "this year's LGBTQ Pride Month has found an unlikely mascot: The Babadook."[41] Even Netflix finally applauded this theory by promoting the film during the first week of 2017's Pride Month.[42] On June 10, 2017, the online platform acknowledged the spread of the gay Babadook meme by tweeting, "Be the Babadook you want to see in the world."[43] The viral sensation of Babadook as a queer icon during the Pride Month of 2017 was so enormous that even Massachusetts attorney general Maura Healey tweeted a picture of Babadook waving a rainbow flag with the caption, "We believe in equal rights for everyone, and we mean everyone. Happy #Pride2017."

A notion that was started by brand enthusiasts and had no logical claim according to the official brand management succeeded in influencing the brand image of the film and altering the core of its narrative's meaning. Initial interpretations theorized that Babadook is actually a symbol of Amelia's grief, as she goes through stages like denial, anger, bargaining, and depression before finally coming to acceptance, but two years after its premiere *The Babadook* had transformed into a queer film. In the minds of the members of the brand community, Babadook is no longer a metaphor for grief, but a queer icon, or, as Twitter user @kehhbean mentions, a "cinematic masterpiece AND gay icon. Not the ally we wanted but the ally we deserved."

Kent, the creator of the film, was silent about this situation for a long period of time. After a couple of years and a lot of persistence by journalists, Kent finally made a statement about Babadook as a queer icon. In her interview with the podcast *Bloody Disgusting* at Sundance Film Festival for her new film *The Nightingale* (Kent, 2018), Kent said: "That was mad, that was crazy. Of course, I love that story. I think it's crazy and just kept him alive. I thought ah, you bastard. He doesn't want to die so he's finding ways to become relevant."[44] So, even the director and writer of the film found the claims of the brand community regarding the queer identity of Babadook obscure, but the power of the brand enthusiasts prevailed over the official promotion of the film. As Renee Middlemost mentions:

> By poaching the Babadook to form paratexts meaningful to the LGBT community rather than a close reading of the implied narrative, the Babadook can exist independently as a gay icon, rather than merely a manifestation of, or metaphor for Amelia's grief.[45]

Even if the narrative did not intend to incorporate gay aspects in this particular metaphysical character, the viral buzz around a fan theory managed to change the public discourse around the film.

After the aforementioned details of how Babadook managed to become a queer icon, it is clear that this film has been highly affected by the consequences of joint brand management. As part of the horror genre, *The Babadook* had an already established brand community even before its premiere. The managing team of the film created an official brand image based on the fictional world that was established by the narrative. From the initial premiere in 2014 until 2016, the only managing plan was solely based on the needs and desires of the creators of the film. Then, brand enthusiasts started to create fan theories about the homonymous character of the film that led to an explosion of viral content that was not based on the official brand management. This new unofficial content forced an innovative reading of the fictional world of the film that consequently required the construction of a new brand image. *The Babadook* was no longer an allegorical horror film about grief and motherhood, but it transformed into a queer film about an oppressed entity.

## Conclusion

The promotion of audiovisual narratives is a complicated procedure that includes several aspects that can be characterized as unpredictable. Even if the promotion team of a film decides on every detail of the managing plan, fans around the world can influence the promotion. This is why the notion of a brand is very valuable in analyzing the mechanisms of promoting and interpreting an audiovisual narrative.

Each franchise, cluster of films or even audiovisual genre can be interpreted as a brand. Therefore, horror films are functioning as a unified audiovisual brand that has a faithful brand community, which is ready to interact on multiple levels with its products. Of course, some of the members of this community are extremely loyal to the essence of the brand and are willing to confront and attempt to alter its official image. Brand enthusiasts are communicating via online means by creating and promoting unofficial content that is interacting with the brand image and the fictional world of the narrative. This is the foundation of joint brand management, a theoretical approach of this dual interaction between the official production team of an audiovisual narrative and the loyal fans who belong to its brand community.

In this essay, I analyzed the case of *The Babadook*, a horror film that was highly influenced by this experience of contradictory promoting content. Even if the initial brand image of the film that was solely based on its fictional world was built around grief and acceptance, the brand community spurred a public discourse around a different theme.

A fan theory that Babadook is a queer character started to circulate around social media, and this led to a meme sensation that began to highly influence the brand image of the film. While the film began as an allegory, the second life of *The Babadook* within the LGBTQ community centers on the reading of Babadook as a character independent from Amelia and her grief. Although the narrative of the film could not easily support this argument, the persistence of brand enthusiasts managed to change both the promotion of the brand image and also the interpretation of its fictional world. Thanks to the brand community and their activeness, Babadook has taken its place in pop culture as a queer icon.

NOTES

1. Jerry McLaughlin, "What Is a Brand, Anyway?" *Forbes*, December 21, 2011, retrieved April 13, 2020.

2. Sotiris Petridis, "A Case for Joint Brand Management in Film and Television Promotion," *Ex-Centric Narratives: Journal of Anglophone Literature, Culture and Media* 4 (2020): 101.

3. Daragh O'Reilly and Finola Kerrigan, "A View to a Brand: Introducing the Film Brandscape," *European Journal of Marketing* 47, no. 5/6 (2013): 772.

4. Petridis, "A Case for Joint Brand Management," 101.

5. Ralph F. Wilson, "The Six Simple Principles of Viral Marketing," *Web Marketing Today* 70 (2000).

6. See Marshall McLuhan, *The Gutenberg Galaxy: The Making of Typographic Man* (Toronto: University of Toronto Press, 1962), and Marshall McLuhan, *Understanding Media: The Extensions of Man* (New York: McGraw-Hill, 1964).

7. The statistics are from the website *Internet Live Stats*.

8. Justin Kirby, "Viral Marketing," in *Connected Marketing: The Viral, Buzz and Word of Mouth Revolution*, edited by Justin Kirby and Paul Marsden (Oxford: Elsevier, 2006), 92.

9. Sam Webb, "Going Down? Terrifying Moment Lift Floor Drops into Shaft," *Daily Mail*, October 22, 2012, retrieved April 10, 2018.

10. Jason Notte, "25 Top-Grossing Horror Movies of All Time," *The Street*, October 25, 2017, retrieved April 13, 2020.

11. See Henry Jenkins, *Convergence Culture: Where Old and New Media Collide* (New York: New York University Press, 2006).

12. *Ibid.*, 3.

13. Susan Fournier and Lara Lee, "Getting Brand Communities Right," *Harvard Business Review*, April 2009, retrieved October 25, 2020.

14. David M. Kalman, "Brand Communities, Marketing, and Media," *Terrella Media* (2009): 1.

15. Albert M. Muniz and Thomas C. O'Guinn, "Brand Community," *Journal of Consumer Research* 27, no. 4 (2001): 412.

16. Albert M. Muniz and H.J. Schau, "Religiosity in the Abandoned Apple Newton Brand Community," *Journal of Consumer Research* 31, no. 4 (2005): 737–747.

17. J.W. Schouten and J.H. McAlexander, "Subcultures of Consumption: An Ethnography of the New Bikers," *The Journal of Consumer Research* 22, no. 1 (1995): 43–61.

18. Petridis, "A Case for Joint Brand Management," 103.

19. Jenkins, *Convergence Culture*, 4.

20. Hur Won-Moo, Kwang-Ho Ahn, and Minsung Kim, "Building Brand Loyalty Through Managing Brand Community Commitment," *Management Decision* 49, no. 7 (2011): 1197.

21. Kalman, "Brand Communities, Marketing, and Media," 1–5.

22. Alex Wong, "Fan-Made 'Game of Thrones' Spin-Off Gives the Show a Modern Update," *Inverse*, August 31, 2017, retrieved September 23, 2017.

23. Devon Maloney, "Go Play This 8-Bit Version of Game of Thrones Immediately," *Wired*, November 9, 2013, retrieved November 23, 2017.

24. Julia Alexander, "Interactive Game of Thrones Map Will Make You an Expert on Westeros," *Polygon*, July 4, 2016, retrieved November 21, 2017.

25. Petridis, "A Case for Joint Brand Management," 104.

26. *Ibid.*, 105.

27. Laura Bradley, "How Stranger Things Season 2 Brought Justice for Barb," *Vanity Fair*, October 27, 2017, retrieved September 23, 2020.

28. Ryan Scott, "IT 2 Fan-Made Posters Predict the Adult Losers' Club Cast," *MovieWeb*, October 24, 2017, retrieved March 12, 2018.

29. Zack Sharf, "'It: Chapter Two': Jessica Chastain in Talks to Star as Adult Beverly in Horror Sequel," *IndieWire*, February 20, 2018, retrieved April 23, 2020.

30. Michael Baggs, "Why Do Lots of Ghostbusters Fans Already Hate the New Movie?" *BBC*, May 27, 2016, retrieved September 10, 2017.

31. Pamela McClintock, "Ghostbusters Heading for $70M-Plus Loss, Sequel Unlikely," *The Hollywood Reporter*, August 8, 2016, retrieved October 13, 2017.

32. Trilby Beresford, "Leslie Jones Slams New 'Ghostbusters' Film: 'It's Like Something Trump Would Do,'" *The Hollywood Reporter*, January 19, 2019, retrieved January 27, 2019.

33. Tomás Prower, *Queer Magic: LGBT+ Spirituality and Culture from Around the World* (Woodbury, Minnesota: Llewellyn, 2018), 18.

34. Elspeth Reeve, "The Secret Lives of Tumblr Teens," *The New Republic*, February 17, 2016, retrieved November 23, 2020.

35. Brian Feldman, "The Secret Gay History of the Babadook," *Intelligencer*, June 9, 2017, retrieved November 30, 2020.

36. Elle Hunt, "The Babadook: How the Horror Movie Monster Became a Gay Icon," *The Guardian*, June 11, 2017, retrieved November 23, 2020.

37. Alex Abad-Santos, "How the Babadook Became the LGBTQ Icon We Didn't Know We Needed," *Vox*, June 25, 2017, retrieved November 23, 2020.

38. Paul Gil, "What Is a Meme? The More You Know About Memes, the Cooler You Are," *Lifewire*, November 2, 2017, retrieved November 15, 2020.

39. Karen Schubert, "Bazaar Goes Bizarre," *USA Today*, July 31, 2003, retrieved November 15, 2020.

40. Eren Orbey, "The Babadook Is a Frightening, Fabulous New Gay Icon," *The New Yorker*, June 17, 2017, retrieved December 10, 2020.

41. Jessica Roy, "The Babadook as an LGBT Icon Makes Sense. No, Really," *Los Angeles Times*, June 9, 2017, retrieved November 15, 2020.

42. Julie Miller, "The Babadook Creator Finally Acknowledges Her Character Becoming a Gay Icon," *Vanity Fair*, January 31, 2019, retrieved November 30, 2020.

43. Laura Bradley, "It's Official: The Gay Babadook Has Netflix Babashook," *Vanity Fair*, June 9, 2017, retrieved December 10, 2020.

44. In Fred Topel, "Director Jennifer Kent Comments on Those LGBTQ 'Babadook' Memes [Interview]," *Bloody-Disgusting*, January 30, 2019, retrieved November 30, 2020.

45. Renee Middlemost, "Babashook: The Babadook, Gay Iconography and Internet Cultures," *The Australasian Journal of Popular Culture* 8, no. 1 (2019): 6.

## Works Cited

Abad-Santos, Alex. "How the Babadook became the LGBTQ icon we didn't know we needed." *Vox*, June 25, 2017. Retrieved November 23, 2020. https://www.vox.com/explainers/2017/6/9/15757964/gay-babadook-lgbtq.

Alexander, Julia. "Interactive Game of Thrones map will make you an expert on Westeros." *Polygon*, July 4, 2016. Retrieved November 21, 2017. www.polygon.com/2016/7/4/12093570/game-of-thrones-map-westeros.

Baggs, Michael. "Why do lots of Ghostbusters fans already hate the new movie?" *BBC*, May 27, 2016. Retrieved September 10, 2017. www.bbc.co.uk/newsbeat/article/36360428/why-do-lots-of-ghostbusters-fans-already-hate-the-new-movie.

Beresford, Trilby. "Leslie Jones Slams New 'Ghostbusters' Film: 'It's Like Something Trump Would Do.'" *The Hollywood Reporter*, January 19, 2019. Retrieved January 27, 2019. www.hollywoodreporter.com/heat-vision/leslie-jones-slams-new-ghostbusters-film-like-something-trump-would-do-1177578.

Bradley, Laura. "How Stranger Things Season 2 Brought Justice for Barb." *Vanity Fair*, October 27, 2017. Retrieved September 23, 2020. https://www.vanityfair.com/hollywood/2017/10/stranger-things-season-2-barb-story-justice-for-barb-what-happened-to-barb.

Bradley, Laura. "It's Official: The Gay Babadook Has Netflix Babashook." *Vanity Fair*, June 9, 2017. Retrieved December 10, 2020. https://www.vanityfair.com/hollywood/2017/06/babadook-gay-icon-netflix-tweet.

Feldman, Brian. "The Secret Gay History of the Babadook." *Intelligencer*, June 9, 2017. Retrieved November 30, 2020. https://nymag.com/intelligencer/2017/06/the-secret-gay-history-of-the-babadook.html.

Fournier, Susan, and Lee Lara. "Getting Brand Communities Right." *Harvard Business Review*, April 2009. Retrieved October 25, 2020. hbr.org/2009/04/getting-brand-communities-right.

Gil, Paul. "What is a meme? The more you know about memes, the cooler you are." *Lifewire*, November 2, 2017. Retrieved November 15, 2020. www.lifewire.com/what-is-a-meme-2483702.

Hunt, Elle. "The Babadook: how the horror movie monster became a gay icon." *The Guardian*, June 11, 2017. Retrieved November 23, 2020. https://www.theguardian.com/film/2017/jun/11/the-babadook-how-horror-movie-monster-became-a-gay-icon.

Hur, Won-Moo, Kwang-Ho Ahn, and Minsung Kim. "Building brand loyalty through managing brand community commitment." *Management Decision* 49, no. 7 (2011): 1194–1213.

Jenkins, Henry. *Convergence Culture: Where Old and New Media Collide*. New York: New York University Press, 2006.

Kalman, David M. "Brand Communities, Marketing, and Media." *Terrella Media* (2009): 1–5.

Kirby, Justin. "Viral Marketing." In *Connected Marketing: The Viral, Buzz and Word of Mouth Revolution*, edited by Justin Kirby and Paul Marsden. Oxford: Elsevier, 2006.

Maloney, Devon. "Go Play This 8-bit Version of Game of Thrones Immediately." *Wired*, November 9, 2013. Retrieved November 23, 2017. www.wired.com/2013/09/8-bit-game-of-thrones/.

McClintock, Pamela. "Ghostbusters Heading for $70M-Plus Loss, Sequel Unlikely." *The Hollywood Reporter*, August 8, 2016. Retrieved October 13, 2017. www.hollywoodreporter.com/news/ghostbusters-box-office-loss-sequel-unlikely-918515.

McLaughlin, Jerry. "What is a Brand, Anyway?" *Forbes*, December 21, 2011. Retrieved April 13, 2020. www.forbes.com/sites/jerrymclaughlin/2011/12/21/what-is-a-brand-anyway/#4dc0a7122a1b.

McLuhan, Marshall. *The Gutenberg Galaxy: The Making of Typographic Man*. Toronto: University of Toronto Press, 1962.

McLuhan, Marshall. *Understanding Media: The Extensions of Man*. New York: McGraw-Hill, 1964.

Middlemost, Renee. "Babashook: The Babadook, gay iconography and Internet cultures." *The Australasian Journal of Popular Culture* 8, no. 1 (2019): 7–26.

Miller, Julie. "The Babadook Creator Finally Acknowledges Her Character Becoming a Gay Icon." *Vanity Fair*, January 31, 2019. Retrieved November 30, 2020. https://www.vanityfair.com/hollywood/2019/01/the-babadook-movie-gay-icon.

Muniz, Albert M., and H.J. Schau. "Religiosity in the abandoned Apple Newton brand community." *Journal of Consumer Research* 31, no. 4 (2005): 737–747.

Muniz, Albert M., and Thomas C. O'Guinn. "Brand Community." *Journal of Consumer Research* 27, no. 4 (2001): 412–432.

Notte, Jason. "25 Top-Grossing Horror Movies of All Time." *The Street*, October 25, 2017. Retrieved April 13, 2020. www.thestreet.com/slideshow/14351962/1/25-top-grossing-horror-movies.

Orbey, Eren. "The Babadook is a frightening, fabulous new gay icon." *The New Yorker*, June 17, June 17, 2017. Retrieved December 10, 2020. https://www.newyorker.com/culture/rabbit-holes/the-babadook-is-a-frightening-fabulous-new-gay-icon.

O'Reilly, Daragh, and Finola Kerrigan. "A view to a brand: introducing the film brandscape." *European Journal of Marketing* 47, no. 5/6 (2013): 769–789.

Petridis, Sotiris. "A Case for Joint Brand Management in Film and Television Promotion." *Ex-centric Narratives: Journal of Anglophone Literature, Culture and Media* 4 (2020): 100–112.

Prower, Tomás. *Queer Magic: LGBT+ Spirituality and Culture from Around the World*. Woodbury, Minnesota: Llewellyn Publications, 2018.

Reeve, Elspeth. "The Secret Lives of Tumblr Teens." *The New Republic*, February 17, 2016. Retrieved November 23, 2020. https://newrepublic.com/article/129002/secret-lives-tumblr-teens.

Roy, Jessica. "The Babadook as an LGBT icon makes sense. No, really." *Los Angeles Times*, June 9, 2017. Retrieved November 15, 2020. https://www.latimes.com/entertainment/movies/la-et-mn-babadook-gay-icon-lgbt-history-20170609-story.html.

Schouten, J.W., and J.H. McAlexander "Subcultures of consumption: an ethnography of the new bikers." *The Journal of Consumer Research* 22, no. 1 (1995): 43–61.

Schubert, Karen. "Bazaar goes bizarre." *USA Today*, July 31, 2003. Retrieved November 15, 2020. usatoday30.usatoday.com/tech/news/2003-07-28-ebay-weirdness_x.htm.

Scott, Ryan. "IT 2 Fan-Made Posters Predict the Adult Losers' Club Cast." *MovieWeb*, October 24, 2017. Retrieved March 12, 2018. movieweb.com/it-chapter-two-posters-fan-cast-adult-losers-club/.

Sharf, Zack. "'It: Chapter Two': Jessica Chastain in Talks to Star as Adult Beverly in Horror Sequel." *IndieWire*, February 20, 2018. Retrieved April 23, 2020. www.indiewire.com/2018/02/jessica-chastain-beverly-marsh-it-chapter-two-sequel-1201930635/.

Topel, Fred. "Director Jennifer Kent Comments on Those LGBTQ 'Babadook' Memes [Interview]." *Bloody-Disgusting*, January 30, 2019. Retrieved November 30, 2020. https://bloody-disgusting.com/interviews/3543658/sundance-2019-jennifer-kent-says-lgbtq-babadook-memes-kept-bastard-alive-exlcusive/.

Webb, Sam. "Going down? Terrifying moment lift floor drops into shaft." *Daily Mail*, October 22, 2012. Retrieved April 10, 2018. www.dailymail.co.uk/sciencetech/article-2221569/Terrifying-moment-lift-floor-drops-shaft-people-inside-dont-worry-just-stunt-advertise-TV-screens.

Wilson, Ralph F. "The six simple principles of viral marketing." *Web Marketing Today* 70 (2000).

Wong, Alex. "Fan-Made 'Game of Thrones' Spin-off Gives the Show a Modern Update." *Inverse*, August 31, 2017. Retrieved September 23, 2017. www.inverse.com/article/36056-game-of-thrones-modern-westeros-spinoff-youtube-trailer.

# Beyond the Boundaries of Jump Scare

## OTT Platforms and the Discourse of Elevated Horror

Sony Jalarajan Raj *and* Adith K. Suresh

## Introduction

The way horror films attract audiences from all over the world reflects a universality tethered to the genre's structural identity that depends on transgressive acts that produce fear. Horror fans are audiences whose existence is defined by this affinity to explore the realm of fear and the thrilling experience derived from it. But what really satisfies a horror fan? Is it the occasional viewing of narratives that offer repetitive "out of the blue" jump scares or the experiments that try to portray new formats of horror? In the present time, it is not only the structural changes but the medium of distribution that affects the viewing experience of horror.

In the 21st century, one can find horror films that do not follow the typical jump-scare methodology to evoke fear getting more attention than those that adhere to it. Changes in the media environment and global entertainment industry have led to such productions receiving more recognition and appreciation on an international level. An emerging context where perspectives and stories from non–Western worlds gain visibility has both challenged and redefined the attitude of horror in general. The most observable aspect of this is arguably the deconstruction of the emotion of fear. Questions related to what constitutes fear and what contributes to its construction are essential to a more critical definition of horror, and more crucially they add insights into the renegotiations that surround its redefinitions.Subgenres like techno-horror, ecohorror, and body horror have found new relevance in the changing social, cultural, and political scenarios, and their significance is more pronounced in terms of the psychological effect they produce. Real-life conflicts associated with technological expansion, ecological degradation, global disasters, and violence related to gender, race, and religion are traumatizing enough to nourish fear, and horror based on such fears affects the mental health of characters. Some critics define the 2010s as the decade of "grief horror,"[1] where the portrayal of psychological degradation through narratives that emphasize loss and grief contextualizes a new mode of elevated horror cinema that focuses on evaluating imminent threats of suffering that do not merely come from the external but, on the contrary, are part of the psyche of the subject who suffers.[2] Films like *The Babadook* (2014), *It Follows* (2014), *The Witch* (2015), *Mother!* (2017), *Hereditary* (2018), *Midsommar* (2019), and *The Lighthouse* (2019) are noted for their treatment of subjects different from the conventional Western notions of horror. Such films often experiment with the genre of psychological horror and can be cited as examples of the "revival of horror" with a new ideology of horror that goes deep into discussions about topics rather than just scaring the spectator with momentary cheap thrills.

The popularization of digital streaming has contributed to the reawakening of the horror genre through new possibilities. Digital spaces created by online streaming platforms have decentralized the meaning of the "popular," which is perceived today as not only a measure of quantity but also as a measure of quality. In an era where artistic and capitalistic dimensions of the audiovisual influence content creation, distribution, and reception, new strategies and approaches to horror narratives depend on the platforms in which they find new meanings after their exposure to a variety of audiences all around the world. This essay analyzes how the emergence of over-the-top (OTT) platforms has changed the mode of horror film/series reception by challenging the conventional methods of screening practices. Horror, unlike other genres, has always had a limited but selective fandom. Social, cultural and moral restrictions frequently dissuade people from watching horror films, and the way such films are censored and banned in many countries speaks volumes about why people could not get access to horror materials in the mainstream media. OTT platforms subvert this historical reality by streaming horror of all subgenres for all people from all places. Transgressing censorship rules and allowing consumers to access content in their private spaces are some of the revolutionary aspects of modern horror in the digital age. Discussing this transformation in detail, this essay examines the discourse of horror and explores how this new idea is celebrated and accepted through streaming platforms like Netflix, Amazon Prime, Hulu, Shudder, etc. It also investigates how this changed scenario gave birth to new experimental horror films and series that refer to the notion of "elevated horror," a category of horror that utilizes the artistic aspects of the horror genre to create a cinematic form that subverts the archetypal jump scare tropes of conventional horror.

## OTT Streaming: Uses and Gratifications

Digitalization of everyday life has become a recognizable phenomenon as technological developments and new media forms are exponentially transforming the social and cultural coordinates of populations all over the world. Entertainment platforms are expanding to integrate more heterogeneous, complex, and interdisciplinary elements to create more content. Studies show that global over-the-top (OTT) media services are highly competitive in limited regional markets and are affecting the technological, economic, and cultural effects of broadcasting and content production.[3] The popularization of OTT video streaming platforms exemplifies this specific phenomenon of concocting information, communication, and entertainment to engender a new cultural mode of interactivity that emerged to encapsulate the change in both universal and local structures of culture, society, and the individual.

The emergence of OTT platforms not only made possible a newly "connected user" who has 24/7 access across multiple devices and media contents but also initiated a behavioral shift of viewers from traditional cable television to OTT media through a process known as "video cord cutting."[4] Previous studies observed the digitalization culture as a significant effect of media use that indicates how new media interferes with existing cultural practices of society. Regarding the self-regulating nature of content creation and distribution, there is growing anxiety concerning the structure, content, and impact of OTT on existing fan cultures and the way they perceive new content. Combined with globalization and technological expansion, media delivery is marketized by external forces,[5] thus compromising the preexisting structural configurations of cultural modes.

The Uses and Gratification (U&G) Theory assumes the position of an active user in consuming media and therefore constantly challenges the longevity of existing media forms. For example, consumer priorities for real-time broadcasting have challenged traditional cable TV to adopt new strategies to cope with the market.[6] It has been found that OTT platforms are engendering new reasons for using them,[7] thereby gratifying new motivations. The mass media effect in a technologically expanding era demands the need to centralize the consumer in an active position where selectivity and convenience are of supreme importance. This conceptualization of the independent user is the driving force of the modern digital consumer culture where telecommunication service providers and OTT platforms fight for customer ownership.[8] Instead of treating the audience as passive consumers, the Uses and Gratifications Theory argues that people use media for their own needs and get satisfied when their needs are fulfilled, allowing them access to more possibilities to use media.

Theories that focus on consumption value/customer value have found that unique factors like fandom and social viewing are deciding online media viewing behavior.[9] Jang, Baek, and Kim also found that movies with fandom or part of a shared imaginary entertainment environment are more accepted in the video-on-demand market.[10] However, the cultural effect of such factors needs to be elaborated to understand the degree to which they become established as collective effects. Here, U&G models are useful in understanding the "mediated communication situations" by studying "psychological needs, motives, communication channels, communication content, and psychological gratifications within a cross-cultural context."[11] The media culture is therefore defined by different scales of motivations for using particular media platforms.

New advancements in U&G research deal with new media technologies in an evolving psychological, sociological, and cultural context to answer why people prefer one medium over the other to meet their needs.[12] New media often blends technology with culture to execute new styles of behavior, where new motives like interactivity are key to future research that predicts streaming television viewing.[13] A combination of different attributes of these platforms has integrated diverse business models for the user, and practices like "binge-watching" have emerged as a cultural behavior.[14] Since online streaming platforms are transforming the television landscape by the way users select, view, interpret and decode the content, U&G models can predict how OTT content is locally produced and are in tune with local popular interest to cope with exploding market challenges.

## New Market and Audiences' Preferences

The contemporary digital environment has given more visibility to horror fandom, and fans are given the freedom to experiment with source texts.[15] Horror films are noted for creating an excess in production, often expanding the source material to different franchises through which characters and concepts are celebrated. Such celebrations are rooted in the reproduction of materials in new ways that aim to satisfy a target audience. The sequels and reboots serve this function as they keep the audience active by using intertextual references in new films and promoting an updated version of the source text that would fit well with a newer audience. Discussing the fan-culture transgressions associated with the *Saw* franchise, Paul Booth observes that *Saw*, as a horror franchise and a fan-centric text, encouraged "textual renegotiation" through "digital production and circulation techniques."[16] The digital environment has allowed fans to create their own excess through the creation and dissemination of videos, trailers, and interpretations of their own through online modes.

The intertextual references make horror films formulaic by emphasizing the recycled nature of content.[17] The OTT-targeted production and distribution of horror also reflect this excessively refurbished content, and different streaming platforms present such content in different ways. For example, Netflix, Amazon Prime, and Hulu have original shows and films from different horror subgenres that are meant for a general audience. However, streaming platforms like Shudder approach more focused content creation and developed a strategy of niche horror programming to make experimental and low-budget productions for more committed audiences.[18] Working as a VOD service, Shudder, unlike large platforms like Netflix, focuses only on horror and, more specifically, on original productions, curated collections, cult classics, and international releases from other languages. It concentrates on horror as a broad genre and breaks it down into fragments and varieties for a centralized horror audience. Shudder made the impression that it is the best streaming service available as it caters to all types of dedicated horror fans.[19] The genre-focused structure of Shudder thus exploits the affective pleasures of cinephile subcultures surrounding horror.[20]

The convenience of OTT platforms as opposed to traditional methods of broadcasting, which lack a "user-friendly" approach, has given a sense of freedom and choice to people. OTT video streaming is focused on the consumer desire to ensure a more satisfactory experience, like ad-free viewing.[21] This centralization of the user as an active agent is a virtual displacement as OTT has replaced television, radio, and newspaper. This new "boundless" and "fluid" nature of OTT platforms is maximized by modes of "anonymity" and "free access." In addition to this, horror streaming through OTT platforms also creates a "community feeling," where people watch new films and series because they were recommended to them by friends or family. "Exploring new content," "familiarizing with famous shows," "updating with new trends," and "peer pressure" emerged as reasons that foster community inclusion. This involves users in conversations that explore new dimensions of modern horror.

Benefits such as easy access to quality content, time and effort saved, convenience of "pause and resume," and fewer distractions underscore the superiority of OTT platforms over cinema halls. Using OTTs has helped viewers to transgress the barriers of language and culture. This is partly because of a new environment created by OTTs where the inflow of overseas content takes over the production of domestic content. OTTs help users to turn on subtitles or switch between different audio versions to understand more foreign and local content.

As streaming services have proliferated in content production and expanded their space across regional contexts, new users are exposed to new content that often gives them the opportunity to explore more exotic content. Platforms like Netflix, Amazon Prime, and Hulu have massive content, which they "recommend" to users, and viewers always have an affinity to watch new releases. Kwon, Park, and Son argue that recommendation agent artifacts like thumbnail images and recommendation lists are related to search experience variables such as perceived diagnosticity and perceived serendipity.[22] Accidental as well as deliberate discovery of new content satisfies users and encourages continuous use. Horror films contain elements of sexual activity, violence, and vulgar comedy, which are subjects of curiosity. The advantage of OTT platforms over traditional public media is that the former supersedes cultural, moral, and political censorship.

## Changing Dimensions: The Rise of "Elevated Horror"

In conventional terms, the concept of horror is associated with a range of signifiers capable of evoking fear as a fundamental emotional outcome. It often conceptualizes the monstrous in a way that terrorizes the realm of imagination by violating certain boundaries of normalcy and rational discourse. In cinema, archetypal horror narratives that introduce a distorted version of reality are accompanied by monsters with nonhuman shape-shifting forms that are explicitly visible on screen as a source of disgust. As they are spectacles that aimed to startle the audience, techniques of jump scare, makeup, and other props are extensively used in a horror narrative. Fans of horror look for possibilities to get scared, and a good horror film has always been popularly identified and judged for its ability to scare its audience. However, the problem of overused narrative and thematic styles stale the genre's reputation when clichéd approaches keep on reproducing classic horror texts with less critical interventions. Remakes, reboots, and spin-offs drain the fountain of imagination as they create shallow hit-or-miss flicks that suffer from a lack of originality. For example, the subgenre of slasher has produced notable franchises including *Halloween*

(1978), *The Texas Chainsaw Massacre* (1974), *Friday the 13th* (1980), *Saw* (2004), etc., where a series of films are made by repeating the themes used in the critically acclaimed original. It is, therefore, crucial to look for experimental approaches, paradigm shifts, and alternative horror narratives to explore new possibilities for the development of the genre in contemporary times.

Outside the hegemony of the Western horror canon, the phenomenology of fear and grief consists of varying meanings depending on the unique sociocultural contexts. For instance, one of the distinguishing qualities of the Korean horror film is its "emotional tone, the sense of tragedy and sadness … revealing cultural specificity and playing to local sensibilities."[23] Similarly, films from Japan, Vietnam, Indonesia, Thailand, the Philippines, and Taiwan have captured the attention of the global audience. The Asian horror scene can be observed through an oriental lens where suffering and grief are incorporated with the cultural and ideological anxieties of the land. Andrew Hock Soon Ng observes that horror films in Southeast Asia use local myths in their narratives to address contemporary ideological issues.[24] Historical moments defined by violence and terror engender "ghosts of the past," making the horror genre more symbolic and interpretive. For example, the reception of Japanese and Indonesian horror films in the United States can be viewed in light of the shared past of these countries in the Second World War and the Vietnam War, respectively, and now the horror genre offers a new perspective dimension for interpretation.[25] When tragedies of the past haunt the present, they must be viewed as a resuscitation of the narrative of grief and the political and social connotations associated with it.

Since grief is a universal phenomenon closely related to the human experience, it can be understood as a varying category that affects individuals differently, and the expression of grief through different stages of life defines its very transformative semiotics. The linguistic and performative terrain of grief consists of a range of expressive states, such as sadness, unhappiness, trauma, depression, gloominess, and melancholy, to name a few. In all these emotional forms of grief, the psychological state of the subject is imagined as "abnormal" and the person is perceived as "unwell." The horror of grief, therefore, depends on the revelation of its causes or their concealment; two instances that result in extreme discomfort, especially when subjects lack the knowledge to resolve the problem of grief. The psychological approach to horror films reveals that they are cultural and social tales that provide a context to negotiate with anxieties, trauma, guilt, separation, identity, loss, and autonomy.[26] Here, the narratives of grief that focus on the loss of a loved one, a tragic accident, and traumatic experiences in the past become narratives of elevated horror.

In the discourse of elevated horror, the notion of grief is not just about its expression and performance; it has a narrative structure that "ties together and makes sense of the individual elements of emotional experience—thought, feeling, bodily change, expression, and so forth—as parts of a structured episode."[27] The narrative structure of grief can be aligned with distinct social, cultural, and mythical archetypes that control the way humans behave in a particular context. Screening grief through horror films draws attention to the way the emotional quotient of the characters is represented through their bodies, and their actions significantly contribute to the narrative mode of the film. Films like *Melancholia* (2011), *It Follows* (2014), *The Babadook* (2014), *Personal Shopper* (2016), *A Ghost Story* (2017), *Hereditary* (2018), and *Midsommar* (2019) are examples of narratives with female protagonists playing the role of a grieving subject who acts in transgressive ways such as irrational, provocative, exaggerated, and often calm and depressed. Take the example of *A Ghost Story* (2017), in which the scene where the protagonist frantically eats a pie can be interpreted as a sign of her grief expressed in full desperation.[28] *The Babadook* effectively demonstrates how the disruptive power of grief endangers one's normative sense of the world or rather intensifies the imbalance caused by grief and fear to emphasize the need to confront it.

Horror films frequently follow a narrative that ends in the destruction of the monster or the escape of the protagonist from its active influence. Slasher films generally have a "final girl" protagonist who heroically overcomes the villain. Films that belong to the category of elevated horror usually rely on the protagonists' state of mind and attempt to portray the aberrations that result in the evocation of horror. They subvert the common archetypes of horror in the sense that the total viewing experience of the horror film is changed. Filmmakers like Ari Aster, production houses like A24, and streaming services like Shudder have created new possibilities for elevated horror as a subgenre to flourish.

## Conclusion

Over-the-top (OTT) video streaming platforms are gradually replacing traditional television all over the world. With the aid of cheap mobile data, increased smartphone usage, and new technological advancements, the OTT market is enforcing a digitalization that integrates information, communication, and entertainment to engender a new mode of media discourse. This spontaneous digital change has reshaped the reception and consumption of horror media where user interactions and gratifications play a significant role in the process of adapting to a new streaming environment. Based on the Uses and Gratification (U&G) method, OTT platforms offer a set of motives for users to explore gratifications that collectively encourage them to accept textually reoriented horror narratives.

Streaming giants like Netflix and Amazon Prime use their platforms to cater to a wide range of audiences that prefer diversity in horror content. The emergence of Shudder as a VOD service that concentrates on the exclusive production and distribution of horror has established a new niche in the horror community. This facilitated low-budget and experimental explorations of the genre, allowing dedicated fans access to content that is not available on other platforms. The availability of curated cult classics on Shudder lets people revisit or find old movies. The popularity of "elevated horror" as a category shows that the clichés that defined horror and its jump scares are shifting the narrative toward explorations through psychological, metaphorical, and philosophical angles. Production houses like A24 have become the new face of art-based drama horror that challenge the conventional canon of jump scare–based narratives. The new discourse of elevated horror focuses on notions of grief, trauma, depression, and female psychology to portray films and shows in a way that brings deep discussions to the narrative fore.

## Notes

1. Ron Breton, "The Decade of Grief Horror: Reflecting on Shared Themes in the Horror Movies of the 2010s," *Bloody Disgusting*, July 30, 2021.

2. See Guy Lodge, "The Horror of Grief: How Loss Is the Ultimate Boogeyman in Hereditary," *The Guardian*, June 7, 2018; Eren Orbey, "Mourning Through Horror Movie," *The New Yorker*, November 22, 2016; Scout Tafoya, "The Pain Needs to Mean Something: On Horror and Grief," *RogerEbert.com*, August 26, 2019.

3. Chun-Mei Chen, "Evaluating the Efficiency Change and Productivity Progress of the Top Global Telecom Operators Since OTT's Prevalence," *Telecommunications Policy* 43 (2019): 1–24; Pirongrong Ramasoota and Abhibhu Kitikamdhorn, "'The Netflix effect' in Thailand: Industry and Regulatory Implications," *Telecommunications Policy* 45 (2021): 1–17.

4. Morana Fuduric, Edward C. Malthouse and Vijay Viswanathan, "Keep It, Shave It, Cut It: A Closer Look into Consumers' Video Viewing Behavior," *Business Horizons* 61 (2018): 85–91.

5. Jean K. Chalaby and Steve Plunkett, "Standing on the Shoulders of Tech Giants: Media Delivery, Streaming Television and the Rise of Global Suppliers," *New Media & Society*, 2020.

6. Jungwoo Shin, Yuri Park, and Daeho Lee, "Strategic Management of Over-the-Top Services: Focusing on Korean Consumer Adoption Behavior," *Technological Forecasting & Social Change* 112 (2016): 329–337.

7. Emil Steiner and Kun Xu, "Binge-Watching Motivates Change: Uses and Gratifications of Streaming Video Viewers Challenge Traditional TV Research," *Convergence: The International Journal of Research into New Media Technologies* 10 (2018): 1–20.

8. Adeolu Dairo and Krisztián Szűcs, "Battle for Digital Customer Ownership Between the Telcos and Over-the-Top (OTT) Players: Emerging Markets Perspective," *African*

*Journal of Science, Technology, Innovation and Development* (2021): 1–8; Bidit L. Dey, Dorothy Yen, and Lalnunpuia Samuel, "Digital Consumer Culture and Digital Acculturation," *International Journal of Information Management* 51 (2021).

9. Sang-Hyeak Yoon, Hee-Woong Kim, Atreyi Kankanhalli, "What Makes People Watch Online TV Clips? An Empirical Investigation of Survey Data and Viewing Logs," *International Journal of Information Management* 59 (2021).

10. Moonkyoung Jang, Hyunmi Baek, and Seongcheol Kim, "Movie Characteristics as Determinants of Download-to-Own Performance in the Korean Video-on-Demand Market," *Telecommunications Policy* (2021).

11. Carolyn A. Lin, "Looking Back: The Contribution of Blumler and Katz's Uses of Mass Communication to Communication Research," *Journal of Broadcasting & Electronic Media* 40 (1996): 574.

12. Thomas E Ruggiero, "Uses and Gratifications Theory in the 21st Century," *Mass Communication & Society* 1 (2000): 3–37.

13. Alec Charles Tefertiller and Kim Bartel Sheehan, "Innovativeness, Interactivity, and the Adoption of Streaming Television," *Southwestern Mass Communication Journal* 35, no. 2 (2020): 17–27.

14. Eun-A Park, "Prevalence of Business Models in Global OTT Video Services: A Cluster Analysis," *International Journal on Media Management* 21, no. 3–4 (2019): 177–192; Emil Steiner and Kun Xu, "Binge-Watching Motivates Change: Uses and Gratifications of Streaming Video Viewers Challenge Traditional TV Research," *Convergence: The International Journal of Research into New Media Technologies* 20, no. 10 (2018): 1–20.

15. Karen Hellekson and Kristina Busse, eds., *Fan Fiction and Fan Communities in the Age of the Internet* (Jefferson, NC: McFarland, 2006).

16. Paul Booth, "*Saw* Fandom and the Transgression of Fan Excess," in *Transgression 2.0: Media, Culture, and Politics of a Digital Age,* eds. Ted Gournelos and David J. Gunkel (Maiden Lane, NY: Continuum International Publishing Group, 2012), 79.

17. Brian Ott and Cameron Walter, "Intertextuality: Interpretive Practice and Textual Strategy," *Critical Studies in Media Communication* 17, no. 4 (December 2000): 429–446.

18. Stella Marie Gaynor, "Shudder and the Specific Niche," in *Rethinking Horror in the New Economies of Television,* ed. Stella Marie Gaynor (Cham: Palgrave Macmillan, 2022), 129–155.

19. Brad Miska, "Shudder: Horror streaming service launches," *Bloody Disgusting,* July 15, 2015; Brian Tallerico, "The 30 Best Horror Movies on Shudder," *Vulture,* December 21, 2022.

20. Jessica Balanzategui and Andrew Lynch, "'Shudder' and the Aesthetics and Platform Logics of Genre-Specific SVOD Services," *Television & New Media* 24, no. 2 (2022).

21. Minjung Shon, Jungwoo Shin, Junseok Hwang, and Daeho Lee, "Free Contents vs. Inconvenience Costs: Two Faces of Online Video Advertising," *Telematics and Informatics* 56 (2021): 1–12.

22. Yeeun Kwon, Jaecheol Park, and Jai-Yeol Son, "Accurately or Accidentally? Recommendation Agent and Search Experience in Over-the-Top (OTT) Services," *Internet Research* 31, no. 2 (2021): 562–586.

23. Daniel Martin, "South Korean Horror Cinema," *in A Companion to the Horror Film,* ed. Harry M. Benshoff (West Sussex: John Wiley and Sons, 2014), 426.

24. Andrew Hock Soon Ng, "Sisterhood of Terror: The Monstrous Feminine of Southeast Asian Horror Cinema," *A Companion to the Horror Film,* ed. Benshoff.

25. Lan Duong, "Diasporic Returns and the Making of Vietnamese American Ghost Films in Vietnam," *MELUS* 41, no. 3 (2016): 153–70, http://www.jstor.org/stable/44155266; Jay McRoy, "Recent Trends in Japanese Horror Cinema," in *A Companion to the Horror Film,* ed. Benshoff.

26. Bruce Ballon and Molyn Leszcz, "Horror Films: Tales to Master Terror or Shapers of Trauma?" *American Journal of Psychotherapy,* 2007.

27. Peter Goldie, *The Emotions: A Philosophical Exploration* (Oxford: Oxford University Press, 2002), 4–5.

28. Totaro Donato, "A Ghost Story (2017, David Lowery): Grief, Sorrow and Meloncholia," *Offscreen* 22, no. 6 (June 2018): 1–17.

## Works Cited

Balanzategui, Jessica, and Andrew Lynch. "'Shudder' and the Aesthetics and Platform Logics of Genre-Specific SVOD services." *Television & New Media* 24, no. 2 (2022).

Ballon, Bruce, and Molyn Leszcz. "Horror Films: Tales to Master Terror or Shapers of Trauma?" *American Journal of Psychotherapy* 61, no. 2 (2007): 211–230.

Booth, Paul. "*Saw* Fandom and the Transgression of Fan Excess." In *Transgression 2.0: Media, Culture, and Politics of a Digital Age*, edited by Ted Gournelos and David J. Gunkel. Maiden Lane, NY: Continuum International, 2012.

Breton, Ron. "The Decade of Grief Horror: Reflecting on Shared Themes in the Horror Movies of the 2010s." *Bloody Disgusting*, July 30, 2021. https://bloody-disgusting.com/editorials/3675480/decade-grief-horror-reflecting-shared-themes-horror-movies-2010s/ (accessed December 12, 2022).

Chalaby, Jean K., and Steve Plunkett. "Standing on the shoulders of tech giants: Media delivery, streaming television and the rise of global suppliers." *New Media & Society*, 2020.

Chen, Chun-Mei. "Evaluating the efficiency change and productivity progress of the top global telecom operators since OTT's prevalence." *Telecommunications Policy* 43 (2019): 1–24.

Dairo, Adeolu, and Krisztián Szűcs. "Battle for digital customer ownership between the Telcos and Over-the-Top (OTT) players: Emerging markets perspective." *African Journal of Science, Technology, Innovation and Development (2021)*: 1–8.

Dey, Bidit L., Dorothy Yen, and Lalnunpuia Samuel. "Digital consumer culture and digital acculturation." *International Journal of Information Management* 51 (2020).

Duong, Lan. "Diasporic Returns and the Making of Vietnamese American Ghost Films in Vietnam." *MELUS* 41, no. 3 (2016): 153–170. https://www.jstor.org/stable/44155266.

Fuduric, Morana, Edward C. Malthouse, and Vijay Viswanathan. "Keep it, shave it, cut it: A closer look into consumers' video viewing behavior." *Business Horizons* 61 (2018): 85–91.

Gaynor, Stella Marie. "Shudder and the Specific Niche." In *Rethinking Horror in the New Economies of Television*. Manchester: Palgrave, 2022.

Goldie, Peter. *The Emotions: A Philosophical Exploration*. Oxford University Press, 2002.

Hellekson, Karen, and Kristina Busse, eds. *Fan Fiction and Fan Communities in the Age of the Internet*. Jefferson, NC: McFarland, 2006.

Hock Soon Ng, Andrew. "Sisterhood of Terror: The Monstrous Feminine of Southeast Asian Horror Cinema." *In A Companion to the Horror Film*, edited by Harry M. Benshoff. West Sussex: John Wiley and Sons, 2014.

Jang, Moonkyoung, Hyunmi Baek, and Seongcheol Kim. "Movie characteristics as determinants of download-to-own performance in the Korean video-on-demand market." *Telecommunications Policy*, 2021.

Kwon, Yeeun, Jaecheol Park, and Jai-Yeol Son. "Accurately or accidentally? Recommendation agent and search experience in over-the-top (OTT) services." *Internet Research* 31, no. 2 (2021): 562–586.

Lin, Carolyn A. "Looking back: The contribution of Blumler and Katz's uses of mass communication to communication research." *Journal of Broadcasting & Electronic Media* 40 (1996): 574–581.

Lodge, Guy. "The horror of grief: how loss is the ultimate boogeyman in Hereditary." *The Guardian*, June 7, 2018. https://www.theguardian.com/film/2018/jun/07/hereditary-toni-collette-horror-grief (accessed December 15, 2022).

Martin, Daniel. "South Korean Horror Cinema." *A Companion to the Horror Film*, edited by Harry M. Benshoff. West Sussex: John Wiley and Sons, 2014.

McRoy, Jay. "Recent Trends in Japanese Horror Cinema." *In A Companion to the Horror Film*, edited by Harry M. Benshoff. West Sussex: John Wiley and Sons, 2014.

Miska, Brad. "Shudder: Horror streaming service launches." *Bloody Disgusting*, July 15, 2015. https://bloody-disgusting.com/news/3353277/shudder-horror-streaming-service-launches/ (accessed December 23, 2022).

Orbey, Eren. "Mourning through horror movie." *The New Yorker,* November 22, 2016. https://www.newyorker.com/books/page-turner/mourning-through-horror-movies (accessed December 15, 2022).

Ott, Brian, and Cameron Walter. "Intertextuality: Interpretive Practice and Textual Strategy." *Critical Studies in Media Communication* 17, no. 4 (December 2000): 429–446.

Park, Eun-A. "Prevalence of Business Models in Global OTT Video Services: A Cluster Analysis." *International Journal on Media Management* 21, vol. 3–4 (2019): 177–192.

Ramasoota, Pirongrong, and Abhibhu Kitikamdhorn. "'The Netflix effect' in Thailand: Industry and regulatory implications." *Telecommunications Policy* 45 (2021): 1–17.

Ruggiero, Thomas E. "Uses and gratifications theory in the 21st century." *Mass Communication & Society* 3, no. 1 (2000): 3–37. https://doi.org/10.1207/S15327825MCS0301_02.

Shin, Jungwoo, Yuri Park, and Daeho Lee. "Strategic management of over-the-top services: Focusing on Korean consumer adoption behavior." *Technological Forecasting & Social Change* 112 (2016): 329–337.

Shon, Minjung, Jungwoo Shin, Junseok Hwang, and Daeho Lee. "Free contents vs. inconvenience costs: Two faces of online video advertising." *Telematics and Informatics* 56 (2021): 1–12.

Steiner, Emil, and Kun Xu. "Binge-watching motivates change: Uses and gratifications of streaming video viewers challenge traditional TV research." *Convergence: The International Journal of Research into New Media Technologies* 20, no. 10 (2018): 1–20.

Tafoya, Scout. "The Pain Needs to Mean Something: On Horror and Grief." *RogerEbert.com*, August 26, 2019. https://www.rogerebert.com/features/the-pain-needs-to-mean-something-on-horror-and-grief (accessed 15 December 15, 2022).

Tallerico, Brian. "The 30 best horror movies on Shudder." *Vulture*, December 21, 2022. https://www.vulture.com/article/best-horror-movies-on-shudder-streaming.html (accessed December 23, 2022).

Tefertiller, Alec Charles, and Kim Bartel Sheehan. "Innovativeness, Interactivity, and the Adoption of Streaming Television." *Southwestern Mass Communication Journal* 35, no. 2 (2020): 17–27.

Totaro, Donato. "A Ghost Story (2017, David Lowery): Grief, Sorrow and Meloncholia." *Offscreen* 22, no. 6 (June 2018): 1–17.

Yoon, Sang-Hyeak, Hee-Woong Kim, and Atreyi Kankanhalli. "What makes people watch online TV clips? An empirical investigation of survey data and viewing logs." *International Journal of Information Management* 59 (2021).

# Monstrous Morality

*Making Unreal Villains Within Reality TV*

NEELIMA MUNDAYUR

The Boulet Brothers' *Dragula* (2016) is a reality television competition show centered on drag monsters who use gender play alongside horror, filth and glamour as a form of art. It premiered in 2016 on the YouTube channel *Hey Qween* and was quickly mainstreamed, first picked up by OutTV for its second season, and Amazon Prime for its third before finding a home in AMC's niche horror platform, Shudder. The series is primarily based on pageants held by the Boulets, nightlife personalities, and often pays homage to iconic moments in horror, reality TV and drag, including *RuPaul's Drag Race* (2009). The two series are often compared, and the Boulets consider *Dragula* a radical alternative to the sanitized and commercialized *Drag Race*.[1] While noting the importance of visibility, the Boulets have criticized *Drag Race* for "cleaning up"[2] the rebellion, punk attitude, and rudeness of drag. Their ethos is that in celebrating queer monstrosity rather than seeking out assimilation, the series also attacks heteronormative culture and centers those who are most excluded and vulnerable within the same.

In his seminal work on horror films, Robin Wood[3] explored queer subtext within the genre, arguing that monsters present as "Others" who disrupt heterosexual normality. But instead of positing that the horror genre would reinforce a heteronormative ideal alone, Benshoff examined the queer legacy of horror, including explicit as well as implicit depictions of undoing gender convention, especially through drag, as well as of homosexuality; the ritualistic overturning of normality could be exhilarating for queer spectators.[4] While monstrosity is not chosen but imposed by heteropatriarchal society, in reappropriating these representations through affective reception, queer audiences created an acceptable form of expressing transgressive desire. As Lynskey writes:

That which is grotesque, what causes repugnance and the destabilization of borders, is transgressive because of this breaking of boundaries, but also affective through its negative response of disgust and abhorrence.... Resistance through queer monstrosity in these actions of the grotesque and transgression is not to rid queerness of oppression, but instead to rearticulate and resist the oppressive voice through different forms of representation. Many times, these forms of representation are often taken on or engaged with by the queer monster in a reversed way when already imposed upon them by the oppressor. For instance, when queerness is depicted as grotesque, the queer monster will often embrace the grotesque in order to reclaim its meaning or context. Essentially, the queer person being mocked or disparaged reverses this and becomes the one mocking the oppressor.[5]

In the context of reality television, however, the queer monster is stripped of their control over their own image. Furthermore, while queer cult cinema has embraced monstrosity by rejecting frameworks of morality, as well as assuming a sense of being unnatural and unreal, reality television does the opposite: selling an "authenticity of the ordinary"[6] as a way of reaffirming social morals. With its editing for storylines and melodrama, expectations of "polish" (a term that is often criticized in drag for upholding classist notions of "high art") and rules and regulations, reality TV acts as a disciplinary tool.[7] Media scholarship on reality TV has extensively explored how melodramatic aesthetics are utilized to reaffirm normative social ethics, and the "immoral villains of reality television" serve to provoke the audience's sentiment.[8] This sense of holding contestants morally accountable becomes even more pronounced in the case of queer reality television, as audiences are acutely aware of the impact of media representation on social progress for LGBTQ+ communities.[9]

This may especially be the case for fans of *Dragula*, who often migrate to the show with a sense of moral righteousness. As expressed by one contestant, Maxi Glamour, on Twitter: "Let's be real [season 3] was the breakout season of Dragula" (@MaxiGlamour, October 26, 2022). Queer media heralded the inclusion of two well-established AFAB contestants—drag king Landon Cider[10] and post-binary drag artist Hollow Eve.[11] The year prior, RuPaul was repeatedly criticized for lack of inclusivity and discrimination; firstly, several drag artists and fans lambasted RuPaul for a *Guardian* interview, where he stated that the show would likely not include trans women who have undergone top surgery.[12] The Vixen,[13] a Black contestant who was on the contemporaneous season (10), further brought attention to the "villain edit"[14] on the show and racial bias.[15] Former contestants such as Peppermint also highlighted the precarity that was created because of *Drag Race*'s hegemony.[16] These issues were brought to the forefront once again in 2020, especially following the Black Lives Matter protests and the racial attacks by the *RuPaul's Drag Race* fandom towards season 12 contestant Brita during the same time.[17] In this context, fans often create a dichotomy, presenting *Dragula* and the Boulets as morally pure in comparison to the morally tainted *RuPaul's Drag Race*:

> If you're still watching RuPaul's drag race you've obviously never watched Dragula bc its superior and extremely inclusive. They actually let the artists be themselves and embrace the weird and unconventional.[18]

Consumers of drag reality TV have also become increasingly attuned to *Drag Race*'s specific production practices and affect, and many embrace deconstructing storylines, editing tropes and audience reactions as a source of play.[19] This comes with varying levels of disappointment, cynicism or even disgust towards RuPaul and the show, as the way the contestants are portrayed on the series has a critical impact on their livelihoods; queens who are portrayed negatively on the show, or are received negatively by the fan base, not only receive hateful aggression, including hate-speech, from audiences, but can even lose out on bookings. Furthermore, both audiences and the production teams' gaze towards the queens are informed by their own biases, and as a result queens of color, plus-sized queens, queens who seem older (either because of their age, or style of drag), and those who may be considered gendered others[20] are easily villainized. Because of this awareness of the show and its audience, queens often express the need to censor themselves, and contestants from marginalized backgrounds in particular tiptoe to portray their communities perfectly. YouTuber @kaysays expresses a sentiment shared by many fans of drag reality television: "it has become very sterilized to me in the sense that with a lot of these competition-based shows, drag race included, you can almost feel contestants censoring themselves in real time for fear of how they'll be perceived by online fan bases."[21]

One of the appeals of *Dragula* over *RuPaul's Drag Race* for many fans is the idea that the drama on the show is neither "overproduced" nor sanitized and instead "real." As expressed by one YouTuber and drag queen, Chloe Curiosity, "It's just real-life drama, not just made-up for the camera."[22] Though they have put out messages against hate received by the contestants, the Boulets also play into the narrative of the show as "real"[23] and not "overproduced"[24] in their marketing. As a result, contestants who are edited as villains are subject to violent hate by fans who believe it is their moral obligation to hold them accountable, as suggested by this response to season 4 "villain" Merrie Cherry on Twitter:

> I don't agree with death threats or racial slurs, but I fully support those calling you the fuck out for your behavior. If sig was so bad then why did the boulets not show it. They're not shady with editing like Whopaul. And it straight up lied on camera about your own behavior.[25]

While *Dragula* received mainstream attention with season 3, the show's fandom grew massively in season 4. This is perhaps because of the surprising inclusion of a former *RuPaul's Drag Race* contestant, Jade Jolie, who was most famous until then for being a Taylor Swift impersonator and appearing in her 2019 music video, "You Need to Calm Down."[26] As the season was airing, the *Dragula* subreddit itself grew from 28,000 to 34,000, the highest leap in the show's run. The season especially received attention because of the perceived misogyny from several contestants towards Sigourney Beaver, a cisgender white woman and drag queen. Virtually all the contestants who received backlash were also from marginalized backgrounds and received transphobic and racialized hate: Merrie Cherry, a plus-sized Black man; La Zavaleta, nonbinary Latine person; Hoso Terra Toma, a Korean transfemme person; and Bitter Betty, a transsexual woman. Fans, contestants and the Boulets themselves attributed such harassment to "fans of the other show" finding *Dragula*,[27] though contestants such as Hollow Eve had similarly expressed receiving harassment from the fanbase in the past.[28]

Nevertheless, as with most reality TV, melodrama has allowed for the show to expand its viewership, as the Boulets have expressed:

> Some of [the contestants] are being attacked right now, and ultimately, they're making an unforgettable season and it's all going to come out and everyone's going to love them.... I feel like the results with the people that are watching, the response from AMC and Shudder, everything is fireworks across the board, so it's just a win for everybody.[29]

While commending the show's inclusivity as well as underscoring its significance in challenging RuPaul's increasing hegemony over drag globally, I ask, what does it mean to "sell" punk and monstrous drag as a brand, especially within the confines of a televised, reality competition? This essay will examine the same by closely studying (i) character arcs of villains in *Dragula* and production tools used in constructing them and (ii) affective responses shared online, on discussion platforms such as Reddit and Twitter or video-edits on YouTube. This essay is divided into six sections; I begin with an introduction and literature review, which discusses queer monstrosity, reality TV and the role of morality, and drag reality TV. In the subsequent sections I discuss the structure of the show and provide a brief history, and then discuss the methodology used for this study. This is followed by the findings and discussions section, where I put forth an analysis of how "villains" are constructed by both the show and the fandom. This is temporally organized, with the first subsection, "Respectable Femininity and Dangerous Monstrosity," focusing on season 4, and the second, "In the Dragula Graveyard: Saint," focusing on *Dragula:*

*Titans.* In the conclusion, I discuss how neoliberal, reality TV and online fandom resignifies the queer monstrous Other within a normative, moral economy.

## Structure of the Show

Since 2016, the Dragula franchise has produced four regular seasons; one Covid-19 special, "Resurrection," during which previous contestants competed from their hometowns for the chance to be returned for season 4; and one *Titans* season constituting a whole cast of returning contestants. In seasons 1 to 4, each episode begins with a skit by the Boulets, often an ode to iconic queer and horror cinema. The contestants then have discussions amongst themselves regarding the previous episodes' events, after which the Boulets introduce the new challenge to them. There may be a segment where the contestants rehearse, sew their costumes, and express their ideas for the challenge. Typically, this is followed by a floorshow and the judges' critiques, following which the winner and the contestants who are up for elimination are announced. Season 1 of the show does not include any confessionals, as there was less focus on individual storylines of the monsters. Instead, the season is driven by the idea of what it means to be an alternative drag performer. There are minor conflicts between the contestants, but the editing style this season is closer to a documentary form than reality television; conflicts between characters/contestants are not as exaggerated as in future seasons. From season 2 onwards, they adopt aesthetics more familiar within the reality TV genre, producing clear character-driven storylines. The season is very melodramatic and conflict-heavy and is often considered to be "lightning in a bottle" by the most active fans, and the Boulets have themselves expressed that they were surprised by the conflict this season.

The way fans engage with the monsters changed significantly from season 3 onwards, as they began showing the contestants out-of-drag extensively; in seasons 1 and 2, they are mostly shown in drag or half-drag for the majority of the season and are mostly shown out-of-drag towards the end of the season, when traveling to off-set locations. According to the Boulets, the purpose of this was to protect the privacy of the contestants, and to give greater focus to their drag character rather than their "real" self. From season 3 onwards, the monsters introduce themselves out-of-drag in their confessionals. While the "boudoir" is primarily a makeup room in seasons 1 and 2, from season 3 onwards the contestants begin spending significant portions of the episode in it, out-of-drag, discussing conflicts. These are likely based on prompts by story producers. In

seasons 1 to 3, the contestants who are up for elimination are also immediately announced. Sometimes, they show backstage moments following
the announcement, especially if they are melodramatic and emotional. In
season 4 and *Dragula: Titans*, these backstage moments are solidified as
part of the structure of the episode; the contestants are taken into a room
known as the "cauldron," where they discuss their emotions, often leading to sensational and melodramatic fights. Following this, the monsters
who did the worst take part in elimination challenges known as "exterminations" that determine who is sent home, or, within the lore of the show,
"gets killed." These range from jumping out of a plane to being buried alive
to taking a lie detector test. This is followed by a skit where the contestant is "killed off." Since *Dragula: Titans* showcased past contestants who
were killed off in previous seasons, they did not have exterminations or
kill scenes. According to the winner of *Resurrection*, Saint,[30] who was on
seasons 3 and 4, contestants in these seasons were also asked to study reality shows such a *Bad Girls Club* and encouraged to engage in controversy
and conflict.

## Method

This study used a two-pronged approach to examining the series and
its fandom. Firstly, I conducted a critical analysis of melodrama within
the series, with a focus on the storylines of "villains" in season 4 of *Dragula*. With regards to editing techniques, particular attention was given
to the use of confessionals in the series, to understand whose narratives
are privileged. As Grobe explains, "reality TV is defined by how it inter-
cuts fly-on-the-wall footage with direct-to-camera monologues by the
cast or confessionals."[31] Confessionals offer two purposes: to frame scenes
and to show the "real" or "true self" of the character presented. Since the
contestants also wear the same clothes in all confessionals, sentences can
easily be manipulated and stitched together with the right cuts and used
in different contexts as per the story that is being told. Typically, a story
producer would ask the contestant questions depending on the storyline
being told, asking them to reframe sentences as necessary, as a camera
is uncomfortably placed directly in front of them. The ability to perform
authenticity well within this setting is highly beneficial to the competitor,
as confessionals present a sense of intimacy with the viewers.[32] Comments
made by the production team and contestants/former contestants on various platforms were also considered to make sense of these storylines.

I also conducted an ethnographic study of the digital fandom using
a passive approach, without revealing my research activity or engaging in

online participation to ensure that participant interaction was uninhibited. The study focused on Reddit, Twitter, and YouTube, as they are often referred to by contestants as the spaces where most dedicated fans reside. The three platforms also offer different modes of interaction; most contestants have an active social media presence on Twitter, and so fans often actively interact with the contestants there. On the other hand, the subreddit is considered a forum to freely discuss the show as a fan-community, away from the contestants. For Reddit, data collection consisted of collating posts shared to the *Dragula* subreddit (https://www.reddit.com/r/Dragula/) as bookmarks on a weekly basis. For Twitter, keyword searches were used to identify active participants and to follow the conversations that they were partaking in. Interactions with the contestants directly were also studied. YouTube acts as a platform both for fans to showcase their reactions to the show and for the show to reach new audiences. For YouTube, keyword searches were used to find and study video edits, reaction videos and their comments. Besides this, posts relating to *Dragula* on other popular subreddits, as well as cross-posts from platforms such as Instagram were also considered. Though the study was focused on active discussions and ongoing conversations, keyword searches on both platforms were also used to study older, archived posts to get a sense of the conversations. The study began in November 2021, as season 4 of *Dragula* was airing. Initially, it was supposed to end in November 2022, but it was extended for another month following new insights regarding the treatment of Black contestants. Names of participants who are not celebrities or public figures have been removed to preserve anonymity.

## *Findings and Discussions*

### Respectable Femininity and Dangerous Monstrosity

Since the very first episode, even before any conflict takes place, the series sets up Sigourney as being victimized through confessionals despite being an excellent competitor. In the first scene, the monsters enter an unspecified location through a haunted house. In a confessional, Betty describes being intimidated by a "couple of people," and then, Sigourney enters the house. When Merrie compliments her and says hello, Sigourney runs to a fellow Chicago queen, Bitter Betty, and Merrie, laughing, says, "Fuck you too." They cut to a confessional of Sigourney saying she only knew Betty and shrugging. Merrie then introduces herself to Sigourney and makes a comment about her not coming too close, and the show cuts to a confessional of Sigourney saying, "I think she doesn't like me." Similarly, in the first two episodes, when La Zavaleta "throws shade" or "reads" someone,[33] they are interspersed with confessionals where they're called "bitchy" or "mean." However, they do not do the same with Sigourney.

The Boulets themselves consider these fights a consequence of cultural clashes, and differences in what is considered "authentic" behavior in different regions and drag scenes: "Sigourney is almost like Elvira in way, she has this almost put on personality … is she performing right now?"[34] Besides, the desire to identify "real" or authentic emotions as a way of developing trust has been seen time and again in reality TV, and is expressed by both contestants and audiences. In *Dragula: Titans* itself Koco Caine, Melissa BeFierce and Kendra Onixx often suggest that the other contestants are "fake," and that they can only trust each other. However, the fans perceive these two situations differently because in season 4, the confessionals privilege Sigourney, who comments that Merrie is threatened by her, whereas in *Titans*, Koco acts as the "narrator" of the season.

Furthermore, very similar clashes are framed differently based on the person. For instance, in episode 2, both Merrie and Sigourney's partners, Koco and Astrud, express feeling forced to compromise their drag to suit the other person. In this, they barely show the discussions which led to these feelings. However, in Merrie and Koco's case, they immediately cut to a confessional where Koco expresses that Merrie was trying to tell her how to do her drag. In Astrud's case, however, this is revealed as she is having a panic attack and an angry meltdown in the cauldron before her extermination. During this scene, multiple contestants call Astrud out for being unprofessional and rude, framing her feeling of being "controlled" by Sigourney as an excuse, but Koco's feeling as legitimate. The critiques from the judges towards the monsters also encourage feelings of insecurity towards their partners, as they repeatedly emphasize how they let their partners shine instead.

Fan reaction towards Merrie's style of drag also worsened as time went on. In the first episode, some fans perceived her as funny and campy, but by the third, she appeared to be universally hated. This is in part because of the perceived favoritism towards Merrie, and what is often described as the "delusional edit."[35] Episode after episode, the judges pointed towards her flaws in their private critiques but declared her as "safe" and placed other contestants for extermination instead of her. In episode 2, they specifically point out that seasoned and legendary performers such as Merrie often become complacent and get away with poor performances. They also point towards her having a "mean look" during the performance, painting a negative impression for fans. While the judges declare her as safe because of the "comedic charm" of her performance—which does not translate to the audience because of the way floorshows are edited—they also cut to other performers being shocked. Repeatedly, contestants critique Merrie for being "delusional" or "messy" with her looks. The discrepancy between what the audience is shown regarding perceptions of her performance on the one hand and the contestants' own knowledge on the other allows the narrative to present her as "delusional." Because of this, fans feel frustrated and even become angry towards the contestant.

The conflict between Merrie and Sigourney comes to an explosive close in episode 4, during the "Monsters of Rock" challenge. The Boulets openly state that they're dividing the teams to create drama, and they place Jade, Betty, Merrie, and Sigourney in one group and Zavaleta, Dahli, Hoso, and Saint in another. In their announcement, Dahli and Sigourney are described as the lead singers, but not the leaders, but by convention the lead singer is also the leader and usually wins the challenge if their group is at the top. This leads to conflict between Merrie and Sigourney, as Merrie believes that Sigourney is the lead singer and not the leader. At the same time, Jade also repeatedly attacks Betty without any explanation. Though Jade was perceived by the audience as a cisgender man and Betty as a trans woman, Jade attacking Betty unprovoked was not perceived as misogyny by the audience.[36] This conflict escalates in the second half of the episode, where Merrie seems angry with Sigourney for not finishing sewing an outfit for Merrie to wear. Their show is a disaster, and when asked who should be exterminated in the challenge, everyone in both groups names Merrie. Merrie, in the confessional, expresses that she believes Sigourney fed the other group "lies." In the cauldron, both Betty and Merrie state that Sigourney would not ask them what they want to do and instead took everything upon herself even when they asked. Before the scene cuts to a confessional where Sigourney describes Merrie as utterly incompetent, Sigourney asks, "What would you have offered, though?" As Betty and Merrie explain their frustration, Jade accuses them of bullying Sigourney and in a confessional says that Betty has become a pot-stirrer who helps Merrie "bully" and "attack" Sigourney and that she (Jade) feels terrible that she felt close to them before. However, this is completely overturned in the reunion. Sigourney explains that footage of them working together was not shown. Merrie, Jade, and Betty also explain that while Sigourney was with the other team buying fabric, the three of them were together working and rehearsing, with no knowledge of where she was. Swanthula Boulet expresses that the viewers only had a keyhole view of the work Merrie put in as a result.

Another notable piece of footage that is played in the reunion has been wholly ignored by the fandom. In episode 5, after Merrie is elimi-nated, the monsters discuss Merrie's performance in episode 4, but Betty complains that Sigourney should not return as she got a chance that few women do in the drag industry and "flopped at it." Sigourney returns, the group criticizes Merrie's drag, but Betty praises Merrie's success in the drag industry and her personality. Betty and Jade get into a huge fight after Jade repeatedly makes sly comments towards her about her person-ality and how "real" Betty and Merrie are. In the original scene, they cut between footage of Betty calling Jade fake and rude, Jade stating that Betty talks behind everyone's backs and confessional clips of Sigourney affirm-ing this, Betty accusing Jade of switching from "Jekyll to Hyde" and Jade accusing Betty and Merrie of "plotting against Sigourney." This is followed by a confessional of Betty claiming it's "time to bring out Petty Betty," Jade making an offhand comment about Betty being a "boozehound" as Betty tells her to "let Hyde out," and a confessional of Jade stating that not engaging in immediate aggression does not make her "less real."

In the reunion, they show additional footage of Jade shocking Betty repeatedly, stating that she shocked her as Betty "shared some shady infor-mation." This is followed by a confessional of Merrie explaining to a story producer that Jade told him and Betty off-camera that Sigourney was "playing the victim" and that Jade would lie if they brought it up. Multiple ghouls, including Zavaleta and Sigourney, look shocked, as if this is new information to them. This is followed by a scene in the boudoir where Jade states that she advised Merrie and Betty that Sigourney comes off as vic-timized, while, before the clip is abruptly cut off, Betty insists, "You said she was trying to play the victim." The clip from the boudoir is wedged in between short, previously seen clips as the drama between the two esca-lates. Betty goes on to state that Jade behaved erratically with her, and Merrie explains that Jade told them multiple stories that led to a sense of distrust, culminating in explosive drama in episodes 4 and 5. Jade goes on to explain that they misunderstood, and she backtracked. Jade tearfully apologizes to Merrie and Betty and describes her struggles with bipolar disorder, the pain she has caused friends because of her inability to control herself, and the shame that comes with it. The others comfort her, and the tension with Jade is laid to rest.

Because of the confusing way this is edited, very often people ignore the scene regarding victimhood altogether and instead praise Jade for opening up about her mental health struggles and for her performance on the show in spite of them. In contrast, when Zavaleta spoke about being a "bitch" because of their trauma in the first episode, they were criticized by the fandom. As Bell suggests, audiences identify sentimentality that is "worthy of the feeling," and the difference in treatment suggests that this identification may further be affected byethnolinguistic and racial barriers as well. A second set of people suggest that Jade realized that Merrie and Betty were victimizing Sigourney, tried to warn them about how they would come off in the edit (as a former *Drag Race* contestant), and, based on their responses, began supporting Sigourney instead. Others suggest that Jade may have caused a misunderstanding between Betty and Sigourney but consider Merrie's treatment of Sigourney in the first three episodes to be rooted in misogyny. Many also praise Jade for apologizing despite having done no wrong in the audience's eyes. As the clip was released at the very end of the competition, almost an entire month after episodes 4 and 5, many fans don't see why Sigourney presenting herself as a victim may be controversial, as expressed in a YouTube comment by ThanatosOnPluto:

> Honestly even if Sig was going to play the victim and Jade had told Merrie that verbatim, so? Who cares? She would be fully in her right to play the victim in that situation and how is that seen as not genuine when Merrie acting like a toddler on speed for the cameras isn't? Also I was surprised no one said that besides the whole perceiving Merrie as doing nothing she looked a hot ass mess and her performance was bad so she should have gone home regardless?

The scene in the boudoir raises further questions regarding the reactions of the other competitors, as well as their perception towards Sigourney, Betty, and Jade during episode 5, the "Ghostship Glamour" challenge. The episode is framed by Jade, who also drives the episode; Betty is portrayed as the antagonist. Jade finds a key that allows her to either save herself or put someone else in the bottom. After repeated comments from Betty about Jade being too worried about her image, Jade puts Betty in the bottom, and the Boulets make it a point to state that the "ranks have shifted" (they did this in season 3 as well), naturally creating resentment from Betty towards Jade. All the ghouls besides Dahli and Sigourney receive negative critiques, and Sigourney is ultimately declared the winner. This leads to one of the most chaotic and sensationalized cauldron moments as several of the contestants argue with each other. Though the monsters lambast Jade for "stirring the pot" and Sigourney for repeatedly only showcasing glamour, comments on Twitter, Reddit and YouTube admonish them for being misogynistic.

Clips from the cauldron were widely shared online, and the cauldron as a whole was uploaded to YouTube by several users. With more than 340,000 views, the full scene of this cauldron shared by houseofdragula @ houseofdragula7289 is the most popular clip related to the show,[37] besides trailers or full episodes. Comments range from praise for the show being "reality TV gold," praise for Sigourney and Jade, and criticisms of the cast for being misogynistic. Very often, people comment on the video asking for details regarding the show, suggesting that this scene has become an entry point for people into the show. While the engagement of fans on Reddit shot up with episode 4 and the confrontation between Merrie and Sigourney, barring the finale, the engagement was the highest with this episode. Since then, many YouTube channels that solely present "iconic moments" and "tea"—that is, moments of melodrama—from the show have risen in popularity. This is in stark contrast to the landscape of videos when I embarked on this ethnography, the majority of which focused on the artistry of the monsters. The circulation of melodramatic moments also reduces many monsters to their "villainous" moments, negatively impacting image, especially since the show is not easily accessible. For instance, though Zavaleta received a positive edit during the second half of the season, performing extremely well and growing to be fan favorite, the most popular videos of them on YouTube are related to their conflicts with Sigourney.

Because of the way the show repeatedly edited Merrie, a plus-sized Black man, as an aggressor towards Sigourney, leaving out the extent of work that she had done as well as the cause for misunderstanding, they play into the stereotype of the "angry Black man." Though many fans criticize the use of racial slurs, comments citing the role of white victimhood are typically downvoted or receive backlash for "using the race card." In interviews,[38] Merrie discussed receiving racial slur and death threats, emails describing her as a "dried up monkey," along with accusations of misogyny. She further explains mourning her grandmother and not being able to check on her costumes, many of which weren't dropped off at the location given by the show and ultimately sent back. She also discusses being in a depression for months after returning from filming, being unable to move, and losing work after the show began airing. Nevertheless, many comments reacting to these podcasts reduce it to her complaining about Sigourney.[39] Moreover, whenever Merrie discusses her time on the show, she's labeled as "crazy" or "obsessed," rather than as someone struggling because of long-term racial harassment. Thus, as a racialized monster, she is stripped of her humanity.

Though all the contestants who argued with Sigourney received backlash and even racial and/or transphobic hate, Hoso Terra Toma, who is trans femme and Korean, stands out. Hoso was a fan favorite and consistently excelled in most challenges. However, she got into a few arguments with Sigourney and was attacked by the fan base as a result. With the "Ghostship Glamour" challenge, Hoso attempts to destabilize what it means to be glamorous, creating a filthy *yokai*, who remains glamorous despite the oceanic pollution. When she is put up for extermination for not showing glamour, Hoso gets upset and joins in on the arguments. Notably, some clips where she is criticizing Jade's outfit—based on both the description and angle—are edited to seem as if she is speaking to Sigourney. A conflict in episode 8 between the two regarding who should be a finalist is also framed by the show from Sigourney's perspective alone through confessionals. This is further exacerbated in fan edits; for instance, though Saint explicitly stated that she believes Sigourney should be in the finale over Hoso, the most popular video regarding this conflict is titled "They still don't think Sigourney Deserves to be on Dragula,"[40] and the comments criticize the cast as a whole for being "chauvinistic." After these two conflicts, Hoso received racial harassment and was repeatedly misgendered by audiences, with many describing her as a "jealous man." She shared one personal message, where a viewer called her a "Chinc"; described her, Betty, Merrie, and Zavaleta as "disgusting"; and accused them of hating Sigourney as she is "actually pretty" and "actually a woman."[41]

While fans attempt to make a distinction between racial or transphobic harassment and calls for accountability, Hoso pointed out that criticisms towards her, both as a person as well as a drag artist, are heightened when her drag is explicitly Asian and does not meet the American/Western gaze.[42] In both her original season and *Dragula: Titans*, Hoso was also repeatedly criticized by fans and the judges for not meeting American cultural expectations of East Asian art; when she wears a Korean hanbok for her glamour performance or eats a dog in a filth-based performance critiquing anti–Asian racism, her drag receives praise as it meets an American gaze. However, when they attempt cultural mimesis and challenge boundaries, their drag becomes untranslatable to Western audiences and is thus criticized or even reproached. As Cohen explains, "refusal to participate in the 'classificatory' order of things is true of monsters generally: they are disturbing hybrids whose externally incoherent bodies resist attempts to include them in any systematic structuration." Thus, being a racialized monster, who is incoherent or untranslatable, is punished by invoking morality.

Season 3 contestant Maxi Glamour also commented on double standards in fandom discussions around misogyny: "While everyone is talking about misogyny on season 4 of that one show let's not forget how much misogyny played a role in season 3 as well as every single local drag scene."[43] Hollow Eve, a plus-sized, nonbinary AFAB contestant, was treated as the "villain" in season 3. Unlike season 4, Hollow's confrontations were explicitly related to misogyny and transphobia in drag space. In episode 1, they confront another performer for the use of the term misogynistic and transphobic term "fishy."[44] The scene is edited together in a way to create a tense atmosphere, using music and multiple, short cuts. In episode 5, the "Trash Queen" challenge, Hollow creates a costume entirely out of panty liners and tampons based on the manifesto *Cunt*. Hollow eventually has a meltdown, which is presented as their inability to listen to critique. Significantly, Hollow had originally planned to use their own costume, but this idea was nixed by producers as it was considered inappropriate for TV as it made use of menstrual blood. Notably, the show often has contestants drinking pig blood, eating live spiders, consuming their own bodily fluids, etc., and celebrates "filth" as a core tenant. However, this context is removed, and Hollow's meltdown regarding "cis white gay" spaces is presented as their inability to take critique, rather than frustration with being censored on a platform meant to celebrate filth and punk queer expression. In relation to the same, Prins writes[45]:

> Even on a show where filth is celebrated, menstrual refuse is considered too disgusting to be tolerated by AMAB queens or a mainstream television audience.... Hollow's monstrosity is magnified in relation to Landon's taciturn appearance on the show (although this, again, may be a result of editing). Landon is quiet, polished, and focused; his monsters are beautifully painted and sculpted, even when they are vile or terrifying.

Similarly, Sigourney is quiet, polished, and focused, even described as a perfectionist by her fellow competitors. As with Prins's critique of Landon, Sigourney's success in the show and the eyes of the audience is because her drag is "inscribed in the commercial, femme, and highly performative."[46] Though she fails at bringing the horror, filth and gore expected of *Dragula*, she retains the glamour expected of queens in the mainstream. Thus, her drag remains nonthreatening and consumable for audiences. Further, presentation of trans and non-white contestants as aggressors towards cisgender white women, who must then be protected by cisgender white men, reaffirms the notion of "respectable" femininity, which exists as a tool of capitalist and colonial domination.[47] This is not to say that Sigourney could not have faced misogyny during her time as a contestant—on the contrary, regardless of intent, she would have likely felt gendered isolation as the only cisgender woman in the cast. However, the reaction of the fan base is also evidently charged by racial and transphobic bias. As Phipps writes, the "damsel in distress evokes a protective response: and simultaneously, colonial archetypes of people of color as aggressive and frightening come into play. This is the pretext on which white men, enraged, *tear the place apart.*"[48]

## In the Dragula Graveyard: Saint

While *Dragula: Titans* was airing, many fans in the subreddit as well as Twitter frequently complained that the show had "too much drama" and was less focused on the artistry of the competitors. This was somewhat surprising, considering that very often, the most celebrated moments from seasons 2 and 3 are conflicts. This could be, perhaps, because of the time spent on the conflict; previous seasons opened with a skit and ended with an extermination challenge. However, in *Titans,* the exterminations are removed, and instead competitors are swiftly dropped down a trapdoor by the Boulets. Because of this, the conflict in the boudoir at the beginning of the episode and the conflict in the cauldron in the final quarter together bookend each episode.

A second reason could be the aesthetic of the conflict, which lacked melodramatic emotional expressions. The primary conflict this season came from a love triangle between season 2 "villain" and fan favorite Abhora, Hoso and Astrud. Hoso and Astrud were in a relationship since season 4, and Abhora expressed having been in love with Hoso for many years. Hoso, however, looked up to and loved Abhora as a mentor and guide. While Abhora was showcased as the villain in the first couple of episodes, attacking contestants whenever she feels upset, in the third episode she apologized. Moreover, outside of the show, Hoso clarified that they were in a polyamorous relationship with Astrud and another person, and that Abhora had been aware of their boundaries. Hoso and Astrud received harassment from fans, but many others felt uncomfortable with the heteronormative moral gaze with which this queer relationship was presented on the show. Astrud especially received backlash because of the show's repeated villainization of her autistic traits, as well as the moral objection from many fans towards her dressing up as a furry.[49] During this season, many contestants also labeled the Reddit community as "toxic," as harassment that they received increased when their social media posts were cross posted onto Reddit. But, as returning contestants, they also seem much more aware of the way any on-camera meltdown on their end would be perceived.[50] Thus, though the season had conflict, they were largely only presented through confessionals, and lacked moments of melodrama to justify them. Notably, the episode that was most popular and discussed at large by the fan base was episode 7, where a contestant from season 1 of the show, Melissa, had a breakdown because of the perceived inauthenticity of other contestants and ultimately quit. As Biressi and Nunn explain,[51] "emotional excess is one of the marked characteristics of reality television." In keeping conflict without the emotional excess that is expected of reality television, the affect created for many fans is discomfort, rather than the moral righteousness that makes reality television feel "real."

While *Dragula: Titans* was airing in November and December 2020, season 4 contestants Saint and Sigourney hosted live viewing parties at the famous Roscoe's Tavern in Chicago, which films and uploads reactions to their YouTube channel. In the first few episodes, Saint (who initially appeared in season 3 and won the 2020 special *Dragula: Resurrection,* which allowed them to return in season 4) made drunken comments inciting conflict with many past contestants. The subreddit had already been criticizing Saint, when Meatball (season 1), one of the earliest Black contestants to be on the show, outed Saint for sending group conversations where Black contestants were expressing their experience of anti–Blackness to the production team.[52] Season 3 contestant Maxi Glamour elaborated upon this further, suggesting that Saint was rewarded for this during *Resurrection* and her run during season 4. Meatball further recounted an experience when the Boulets stated that she shouldn't consider herself Black or criticize white people as she was adopted by white parents. A few commenters pointed towards Meatball's previous complaints against production practices and her criticism towards the show for lacking people of color in the crew. In the past, Merrie Cherry also levied criticism against them for her treatment on season 4,[53] and Hollow Eve[54] and Maxi Glamour[55] in season 3 spoke of their negative experiences as nonbinary contestants. Koco Caine, who was on season 4 and *Titans*, spoke in support of the Boulets, saying that they had grown and citing the support and care she received.[56] While some fans, especially on Twitter, critiqued the show and raised concerns regarding the mistreatment of Black contestants, the majority were quick to villainize Saint as the primary antagonist, considering the situation to be "drama" rather than discrimination. During this time, Koco Caine (@theekococaine) pointed towards this hypocrisy within the fandom, tweeting: "I need y'all to engage in important productive conversations as much as you engage in Drama. But y'all don't like drama … right." The conflict between Saint and other former contestants seemed to eclipse all other conversations, with many commenting that they're finally getting the "real drama" that the show was lacking. During this time, engagement regarding *Dragula* from other subreddits, such as rpdrdrama and rpdrcringe, also increased.

In the month following these tweets, this was used to discredit Saint's competence altogether, his win on *Resurrection*, and abilities as a drag performer, and many campaigned for him to lose his platform in Roscoe's as well as his podcast with Sigourney. On Reddit, Saint regularly receives criticism from fans, and posts in support of him are downvoted. While the critique of structural issues within the show spiked again after the finale of *Titans*—which was largely considered underwhelming and lacking filth—the show was soon rehabilitated to the older status as an ideal for diversity. In the past, the Boulet Brothers have opposed "political correctness," pointing out that many contestants who are given this platform come from extremely vulnerable backgrounds, without the privilege of knowing what is considered the "right language" at the time. After Saint apologized, former contestants responded with a range of emotions, with some continuing to throw shade towards her while others forgave her. Notably the latter resolution was not shared on Reddit immediately, though this is typical with regards to conflict between drag artists, especially those who are Black. Nevertheless, for the fandom itself, this allowance for growth remains confined to those with relative power, and as one Reddit user suggested, Saint remains buried deep in the "Dragula Graveyard."[57] Thus, the reality TV mentality of needing to identify a (often racialized) monster or villain pervades critical discussions within this space. The popularity of this in comparison to the drama showcased on *Titans* itself further emphasizes the role of morality in engendering fan engagement with the show.

## Conclusion

When the season finale of *Dragula: Titans* aired, the most popular sentiment amongst the fan base was frustration regarding the lack of filth in the season. This was surprising for many, as some of the most noted filth performances were by monsters who returned for *Titans*; in season 1 Melissa, dressed as a nun, tore apart a Bible and pulled out a bloodied crucifix from her anus. While the extent to which each element was showcased throughout the season slowly diminished over the years, typically each monster in the finale would showcase "horror," "glamour" and "filth" in their final floorshows. In the *Titans* finale, however, they were asked to present one look combining all three. Yet, though *Dragula* is often reduced by media outlets to "spooky drag,"[58] the element that truly sets it apart from other shows is filth:

> Douglas proposes the notion of filth or dirt as a rejected element, one that does not belong in the given order. Transgression of order entails danger to the categories and structures of thought that entire cultural frameworks are woven around; to flirt with that hazard is taboo. It is that uncategorizable inbetweenness which the ghouls in *Dragula* exploit.[59]

In season 1, contestants such as Meatball and Frankie Doom presented a campy, filthy, and unpolished form of drag, reminiscent of the work of John Waters and Divine. In fact, Frankie Doom explicitly stated that she doesn't want to seek out "polish," thus rejecting bourgeois aesthetic sensibilities. During this season, the Boulets often also used "punk" and "filth" interchangeably. Vander Von Odd and Meatball also expressed that this form of drag is rooted in counterculture and not necessarily in line with stereotypical images of "horror drag." Their art was in stark contrast to the camp brought forth in *RuPaul's Drag Race*, that is glamorous, ostentatious, and chic. However, over the course of the seasons, such forms of drag have been dismissed as "messy" by the audience, who have moved towards understanding filth as moments created for shock value—which have ultimately also been censored for TV.

Moreover, while the show has repeatedly emphasized that the drama that they present on-screen is simply a reflection of the "messiness" of drag scenes in real life, and not meant to villainize its monsters, it is noteworthy that every winner of the show was edited to seem quiet and focused on their drag despite the circumstances that surround them. The season 4 winner, Dahli, even expresses "embarrassment" following the fights in the season, considering how their community would be viewed by others. Minimizing their "messiness" to suit the normative gaze of the audience is beneficial for the shows' contestants. As suggested by the Boulets in the finale of season 1, they're also picking contestants who can represent their own brand, as well as the brand of the show, to the world. Moreover, contestants who have breakdowns or panic attacks, and those who stand up against such practices, are repeatedly told that they are "unprofessional,"[60] though the show places them in situations that force sensory overload and would not be acceptable within a different workplace setting. Even while the labor of the villains of the series has been necessary for the show to succeed, it comes at the detriment of any contestant's own "brand." Thus, as with *RuPaul's Drag Race*, it exploits their artistic labor services with the promise of exposure, while reiterating neoliberal notions of the ideal laborer as one who is always able to provide service with a fanged smile.[61]

## NOTES

1. Catherine Earp, "Dragula's the Boulet Brothers Reveal How They Feel About the Show Being Compared to RuPaul's Drag Race," *Digital Spy*, last modified September 5, 2018, https://www.digitalspy.com/tv/ustv/a865528/the-boulet-brothers-dragula-rupauls-drag-race-comparisons-season-amazon-netflix/.

2. *Ibid.*

3. Robin Wood, *Robin Wood on the Horror Film: Collected Essays and Reviews* (Detroit: Wayne State University Press, 2018), PDF e-book, 73–81.

4. Harry M. Benshoff, *Monsters in the Closet: Homosexuality and the Horror Film* (Manchester: Manchester University Press, 1997), PDF e-book, 1–31.

5. John Lynskey, "Late Night Double Feature: Queer Monstrosity and Cult Cinema," PhD diss., University of Edinburgh, 2021, https://era.ed.ac.uk/bitstream/handle/1842/38265/Lynskey2021.pdf?sequence=1&isAllowed=y, 57–58.

6. Minna Aslama and Mervi Pantti, "Labourers of the Real: Authenticity Work in Reality Television," in *Media in the Swirl*, ed. Ravi K. Dhar and Pooja Rana (Delhi: Pentagon Books, 2012).

7. Kai Prins, "Monsters Outside of the Closet: Reading the Queer Art of Winning in The Boulet Brothers' Dragula," *QED: A Journal in GLBTQ Worldmaking* 8, no. 2 (Summer 2021): 53, https://muse.jhu.edu/article/851613.

8. Hsuan-Chih Kuo, "'I Feel Very Attacked!': RuPaul's Drag Race Fans' Perception on Fandom Toxicity," master's thesis, Erasmus University Rotterdam, 2021, 5.

9. Michael Lovelock, *Reality TV and Queer Identities: Sexuality, Authenticity, Celebrity* (Cham: Springer, 2019).

10. It is noteworthy that the show had wanted to cast Landon Cider since season 1, but could not do so because of his contract, though it is also odd that the show has not found another Drag King in five years.

11. Daniel Reynolds, "'Dragula' Is First U.S. Reality TV Competition with a Drag King," *Gay, Lesbian, Bisexual, Transgender, Queer News & Politics*, last modified August 7, 2019, https://www.advocate.com/television/2019/8/07/amazons-dragula-first-us-reality-competition-drag-king.

12. Caroline Framke, "How RuPaul's Comments on Trans Women Led to a Drag Race Revolt—and a Rare Apology," *Vox*, last modified March 7, 2018, https://www.vox.com/culture/2018/3/6/17085244/rupaul-trans-women-drag-queens-interview-controversy.

13. World of Wonder, "Tap That App," *RuPaul's Drag Race Untucked*, directed by World of Wonder, Los Angeles: VH1, April 5, 2018.

14. In reality television, a "villain edit" refers to the way a character's storyline is pieced together to make them seem disagreeable or hateful, often to serve the storyline of a "hero." It is often employed against Black and plus-sized contestants.

15. Matthew Rodriguez, "A 'Drag Race' Editor Says the Villain Edit Doesn't Exist. Fans of Color Know Better," *Them*, last modified September 9, 2020, https://www.them.us/story/rupauls-drag-race-villain-edit.

16. Billboard, "Spillin' the Tea: RPDR vs. Local Drag with Guests Marti Gould Cummings & Tina Burner," YouTube, December 13, 2018, https://www.youtube.com/watch?v=4qVL9Zd5h9E&t=1050s.

17. For instance, see Rajdeep Singh, "Drag Race Star Brita Filter 'Tried to Hurt Herself' After Toxic, Racist Bullying from So-Called Fans Became 'Too Much to Bear,'" *PinkNews | Latest Lesbian, Gay, Bi and Trans News | LGBTQ+ News*, last modified October 22, 2020, https://www.thepinknews.com/2020/10/22/brita-filter-drag-race-bullying-overdose-racist-toxic/; Tim Murray, "RuPaul's Drag Race: What Brita's Villain Edit Did Not Show," *ScreenRant*, last modified April 14, 2020, https://screenrant.com/rupauls-drag-race-brita-filter-villain-edit-not-show/; Bob the Drag Queen, "We finally discuss racism in the fandom—Only Child," YouTube, May 12, 2020, https://www.youtube.com/watch?v=0Gy_nlsDcAw&t=2314s.

18. If you're still watching RuPaul's drag race you've obviously never watched Dragula bc its superior and extremely inclusive. They actually let the artists be themselves and embrace the weird and unconventional," Twitter post, February 12, 2021, https://x.com/greenxbby/status/1360252621110575113.

19. An examination of popular drag race YouTube channels—excluding reaction channels—shows a shift from channels dedicated to chronicling the interpersonal relationships of rugirls, such as Jakeyonce or Hey Qween, to those deconstructing production practices, legacy of "problematic" queens and fandom behavior, such as Bussy Queen, JackFed, Uckey Lee, Green Gay, etc.

20. The aesthetics of the show assumes the average contestant to be a cisgender, gay man. As a result, even while excluding transgender persons, nonbinary AMAB contestants have historically had access to the show, but at the cost of being misgendered. In recent seasons, the show has attempted to shift away from this (for instance, rewriting the phrase "gentlemen, start your engines and may the best woman win"), but this assumption remains in terms of storylines, marketing, and audience perception. As a result, transgender men and women, cisgender women as well as nonbinary persons who openly discuss their identity on the show receive hypervisibility and are othered.

21. @kaylasays, "The Dynamic Drama of Dragula Season 4," YouTube, October 5, 2022, https://www.youtube.com/watch?v=xyE-ntNqmGY.

22. Mera Mangle, "Dragula Titans Rumored Cast List | Boulet Brothers' All Stars + Drag Race Philippines Host!" YouTube, July 18, 2022, https://www.youtube.com/watch?v=jlu81xcBQeA&t=7s.

23. Boulet Brothers, "The Boulet Brothers' Dragula S4 Recap Special (Part 1)," podcast audio, November 2021, https://open.spotify.com/episode/3dD4MKqR9EtEx0J9R0bNnR?si=GT-t4b58Rii7j91_UjgHxA.

24. Angel Melanson, "The DRAGULA Universe Is Expanding: The Boulet Brothers Dish on (Some of) the Details," *Fangoria,* October 24, 2022, https://www.fangoria.com/original/the-dragula-universe-is-expanding-the-boulet-brothers-dish-on-some-of-the-details/.

25. I don't agree with death threats or racial slurs, but I fully support those calling you the fuck out for your behavior. If sig was so bad then why did the boulets not show it. They're not shady with editing like Whopaul. And it straight up lied on camera about your own behavior," Twitter post, November 12, 2021, https://x.com/LucasPoocus/status/1458895318276206594.

26. Taylor Swift, "Taylor Swift—You Need to Calm Down," YouTube, June 17, 2019. https://www.youtube.com/watch?v=Dkk9gvTmCXY.

27. Brothers, "Season 4 Recap: Part 1."

28. Bizarre Buffet, "All About Hollow Eve," podcast audio, August 31, 2020, https://omny.fm/shows/bizarre-buffet/all-about-hollow-eve#description.

29. Brothers, "Season 4 Recap: Part 1."

30. Roscoestavern, "Roscoe's The Boulet Brother's Dragula Titans Viewing Party with Lúc Ami, Sigourney Beaver & Saint," YouTube, November 17, 2022. https://www.youtube.com/watch?v=RGfPSQu9ixc&t=1294s

31. Christopher Grobe, "Broadcast Yourself: The Confessional Performance of Reality TV," in *The Art of Confession: The Performance of Self from Robert Lowell to Reality TV* (New York: NYU Press, 2017), 286–287.

32. *Ibid.*

33. Entering drag vocabulary from Ballroom culture, "throwing shade" and "reading" are ways of subtly insulting another person and is often considered an art in itself, and a means of remaining sharp and witty, especially in the context of discriminatory attacks from heteronormative culture.

34. Brothers, "Season 4 Recap: Part 1."

35. An editing style often employed in reality TV to portray a contestant as overly confident in comparison to what they're presenting for comedic effect or to villainize them. As with the villain edit, it is often used against Black and plus-sized contestants.

36. While Jade Jolie presented as a cisgender drag queen during her time on the show, she came out as a trans woman in October 2023. This chapter was written in January 2023 regarding events that took place between 2021 and 2022, and audience perceptions. Nevertheless, the author does not wish to misgender Jolie.

37. House of Dragula, "Dragula Season 4—Episode 5 Full Cauldron Drama," YouTube, November 18, 2021, https://www.youtube.com/watch?v=CWPomxnEGBg&t=8s.

38. Good Judy, "Merrie Cherry," podcast audio, November 2021, https://open.spotify.com/episode/5yE5ByDfygUCccrybmJLAQ?si=sia-fNN1T1K-bzTjOeGexg; Hello Uglies, "Merrie Cherry Interview," podcast audio, December 2021, https://open.spotify.com/episode/6olHtUrodNa3eZvfosyGTU?si=melgKIHpSkyycDKII-EXow, Sloppy Seconds.

39. "Merrie Cherry Interview with some backstage tea," Reddit post, December 20, 2021, https://www.reddit.com/r/Dragula/comments/rkedni/merrie_cherry_interview_with_some_backstage_teas/.

40. Hiro Evangelista, "They still don't think Sigourney Deserves to be on Dragula," Youtube, December 8, 2021, https://www.youtube.com/watch?v=m-nO4b0-Ddo.

41. Hoso Terratoma (@hosoterratoma), "ChinC w two Cs cuz I come with EXTRA rice," Twitter post, November 17, 2021, https://x.com/hosoterratoma/status/1461006570834169862.

42. Hoso Terratoma (@hosoterratoma), "I was VISIBLY and RECOGNIZABLY asian in drag for the first time in this competition and if yall think that has nothing to do w the racially charged hate i am getting, you are willfully ignorant," Twitter post, November 18, 2021, https://twitter.com/hosoterratoma/status/1461151444770250756.

43. "While everyone is talking about misogyny on season 4 of that one show let's not forget how much misogyny played a role in season 3 as well as every single gle local drag scene," Twitter post, November 12, 2021, https://x.com/MaxiGlamour/status/1458884867706417171.

44. In drag culture, "fishy" is a term used to describe someone who is able "pass" as a

cisgender woman and is derived from the notion that vaginas smell like fish. Many progressive drag artists consider the term to be exclusionary, and Hollow's discussion brought attention to the same. It is now slowly fading from mainstream use, and in 2022 even RuPaul changed a lyric from her song "Call Me Mother" from "fishy" to "flashy." Hollow's discussion of the term "fishy" resurfaced recently, after the term was critiqued by Victoria Scone, a cisgender woman from multiple *Drag Race* franchises.

45. Prins, "Winning Dragula," 58.

46. *Ibid.*, 57.

47. Alison Phipps, "White Tears, White Rage: Victimhood and (as) Violence in Mainstream Feminism," *European Journal of Cultural Studies* 24, no. 1 (2021), doi:10.1177/1367549420985852.

48. *Ibid.*

49. A subculture where people show interest in anthropomorphic animals, often (though not necessarily) as a kink. It is not the same as Zoophilia, though is often misconstrued as such.

50. Astrud Aurelia repeatedly expressed disappointment and confusion in the way their autistic traits were presented, and awareness regarding produced meltdown. For instance, see (@astrudqueen), "Maybe somebody wanted another nosterstu beach party moment 🤷 🤷 🤷," Twitter post, December 14, 2022, https://twitter.com/astrudqueen/status/1603100739223494656.

51. H. Nunn and A. Biressi, "'Walking in Another's Shoes': Sentimentality and Philanthropy on Reality Television," in *A Companion to Reality Television*, ed. Laurie Ouellette (Hoboken: John Wiley & Sons, 2013), PDF e-book, 478.

52. Meatball (@fatdragmeatball), "Imagine screenshotting a conversation between all the queens of color talking about their experiences on the show and sending it to the Boulets," Twitter post, November 27, 2022.

53. "More Merrie Meltdowns," Reddit post, November 6, 2022. https://www.reddit.com/r/Dragula/comments/yncz3a/more_merrie_meltdowns/.

54. Buffet, "Hollow Eve."

55. Maxi Glamour (u/MaxiGlamour), "My biggest competition was white supremacy and people placating to a binary drag system. Do with that what you will. All-Losers Hell-Stars or whatever you like I'd question doing it. It was a lot of emotional energy and I'm still combatting the PTSD of what we went through it would be a lot of soul searching if I want to do that again..." Reddit comment, November 19, 2019, https://www.reddit.com/r/Dragula/comments/dy01k3/comment/f7zlmt6/?utm_source=share&utm_medium=web2x&context=3.

56. "Koco Weighs in on Conversations of Racism Regarding the Boulets," Reddit post, December 2, 2022, https://www.reddit.com/r/Dragula/comments/zafez6/koco_weighs_in_on_conversations_of_racism/.

57. "Saint, Monikkie Shame, Merrie Cherry, Loris: All Girls That Are Now in the Dragula Graveyard," Reddit post, January 2, 2023, https://www.reddit.com/r/Dragula/comments/101le3y/saint_monikkie_shame_merrie_cherry_loris_all/.

58. Desirée Guerrero, "The Boulet Brothers on Their History of Spooky Drag," *Advocate*, last modified July 20, 2022, https://www.advocate.com/exclusives/2022/7/20/boulet-brothers-their-history-spooky-drag.

59. Valeria Lindvall, "You Look Vile. You Look Disgusting. You Look Perfect: The Redeeming Indeterminacy of Dragula's Zombie Queens," *Grim*, June 2019, 25–32.

60. Most recently, on *Dragula: Titans*, episode 4, Evah Destruction was called "unprofessional" by the judges and contestants for having a panic attack after filming their required scenes in extremely hot weather.

61. Lovelock, *Reality TV,* 159.

## Works Cited

Aslama, Minna, and Mervi Pantti. "Labourers of the Real: Authenticity Work in Reality

Television." In *Media in the Swirl*, edited by Ravi K. Dhar and Pooja Rana. Delhi: Pentagon Books, 2012.

Benshoff, Harry M. *Monsters in Closet: Homosexuality and the Horror Film*. Manchester: Manchester University Press, 1997. PDF e-book.

Billboard. "Spillin' the Tea: RPDR vs. Local Drag with Guests Marti Gould Cummings & Tina Burner." YouTube. December 13, 2018. https://www.youtube.com/watch?v=4qV L9Zd5h9E&t=1050s.

Bob the Drag Queen. "We finally discuss racism in the fandom—Only Child." YouTube. May 12, 2020. https://www.youtube.com/watch?v=0Gy_nlsDcAw&t=2314s.

Brothers, Boulet. "The Boulet Brothers' Dragula S4 Recap Special (Part 1)." Podcast audio. November 2021. https://open.spotify.com/episode/3dD4MKqR9EtEx0J9R0bNnR ?si=GT-t4b58Rii7j91_UjgHxA.

Buffet, Bizarre. "All About Hollow Eve." Podcast audio. August 31, 2020. https://omny.fm/ shows/bizarre-buffet/all-about-hollow-eve#description.

Earp, Catherine. "Dragula's the Boulet Brothers Reveal How They Feel About the Show Being Compared to RuPaul's Drag Race." *Digital Spy*. Last modified September 5, 2018. https://www.digitalspy.com/tv/ustv/a865528/the-boulet-brothers-dragula-rupauls-drag-race-comparisons-season-amazon-netflix/.

"Exclusive: The Boulet Brothers on Dragula Season 4 and How 'Queerness and Horror Go Hand in Hand.'" *Gay Times*. Last modified October 25, 2021. https://www.gaytimes. co.uk/drag/exclusive-the-boulet-brothers-on-dragula-season-4-and-how-queerness-and-horror-go-hand-in-hand/.

Framke, Caroline. "How RuPaul's Comments on Trans Women Led to a Drag Race Revolt—and a Rare Apology." *Vox*. Last modified March 7, 2018. https://www.vox.com/ culture/2018/3/6/17085244/rupaul-trans-women-drag-queens-interview-controversy.

Good, Judy. "Merrie Cherry." Podcast audio. November 2021. https://open.spotify.com/epi sode/5yE5ByDfygUCccrybmJLAQ?si=sia-fNN1T1K-bzTjOeGexg.

Grobe, Christopher. "Broadcast Yourself: The Confessional Performance of Reality TV." In *The Art of Confession: The Performance of Self from Robert Lowell to Reality TV*, 283–339. New York: NYU Press, 2017.

Guerrero, Desirée. "The Boulet Brothers on Their History of Spooky Drag." *Gay, Lesbian, Bisexual, Transgender, Queer News & Politics*. Last modified July 20, 2022. https://www. advocate.com/exclusives/2022/7/20/boulet-brothers-their-history-spooky-drag.

Hello Uglies. "Merrie Cherry Interview." Podcast audio. December 2021. https://open. spotify.com/episode/6olHtUrodNa3eZvfosyGTU?si=melgKIHpSkyycDKII-EXow.

House of Dragula. "Dragula Season 4—Episode 5 Full Cauldron Drama." YouTube. November 18, 2021. https://www.youtube.com/watch?v=CWPomxnEGBg&t=8s.

Kayla says. "The Dynamic Drama of Dragula Season 4." YouTube. October 5, 2022. https:// www.youtube.com/watch?v=xyE-ntNqmGY.

King, John. "Boulet Brothers crown drag king winner of 'Dragula' season 3." *Washington Blade*, November 6, 2019. https://www.washingtonblade.com/2019/11/06/ boulet-brothers-crown-drag-king-winner-of-dragula-season-3/.

Kuo, Hsuan-Chih. "'I Feel Very Attacked!': RuPaul's Drag Race Fans' Perception on Fandom Toxicity." Master's thesis, Erasmus University, Rotterdam, 2021.

Lindvall, Valeria. "You Look Vile. You Look Disgusting. You Look Perfect: The Redeeming Indeterminacy of Dragula's Zombie Queens." *Grim*, June 2019. https://www.academia. edu/39531067/_You_look_vile._You_look_disgusting._You_look_PERFECT._The_ redeeming_indeterminacy_of_Dragula_s_zombie_drag_queens.

Lovelock, Michael. *Reality TV and Queer Identities: Sexuality, Authenticity, Celebrity*. Cham: Springer, 2019.

Lynskey, John. "Late Night Double Feature: Queer Monstrosity and Cult Cinema." PhD diss., University of Edinburgh, 2021. https://era.ed.ac.uk/bitstream/handle/1842/38265/ Lynskey2021.pdf?sequence=1&isAllowed=y.

Mangle, Mera. "Dragula Titans Rumored Cast List | Boulet Brothers' All Stars + Drag Race Philippines Host!" YouTube, July 18, 2022. https://www.youtube.com/watch?v= jlu81xcBQeA&t=7s.

Melanson, Angel. "The DRAGULA Universe Is Expanding: The Boulet Brothers Dish On (Some Of) The Details." *Fangoria*, October, 24, 2022. https://www.fangoria.com/original/the-dragula-universe-is-expanding-the-boulet-brothers-dish-on-some-of-the-details/.

Murray, Tim. "RuPaul's Drag Race: What Brita's Villain Edit Did Not Show." *ScreenRant*. Last modified April 14, 2020. https://screenrant.com/rupauls-drag-race-brita-filter-villain-edit-not-show/.

Nunn, H., and A. Biressi. ""Walking in Another's Shoes" Sentimentality and Philanthropy on Reality Television." In *A Companion to Reality Television*, edited by Laurie Ouellette, 478–497. Hoboken: John Wiley & Sons, 2013. PDF e-book.

Phipps, Alison. "White tears, white rage: Victimhood and (as) violence in mainstream feminism." *European Journal of Cultural Studies* 24, no. 1 (2021): 81–93. doi:10.1177/1367549420985852.

Prins, Kai. "Monsters Outside of the Closet: Reading the Queer Art of Winning in the Boulet Brothers' Dragula." *QED: A Journal in GLBTQ Worldmaking* 8, no. 2 (Summer 2021), 43–67. https://muse.jhu.edu/article/851613.

Reynolds, Daniel. "'Dragula' Is First U.S. Reality TV Competition with a Drag King." *Gay, Lesbian, Bisexual, Transgender, Queer News & Politics*. Last modified August 7, 2019. https://www.advocate.com/television/2019/8/07/amazons-dragula-first-us-reality-competition-drag-king.

Rodriguez, Matthew. "A 'Drag Race' Editor Says the Villain Edit Doesn't Exist. Fans of Color Know Better." *Them*. Last modified September 9, 2020. https://www.them.us/story/rupauls-drag-race-villain-edit.

Sargent, Chloe. "'Dragula' Has an Openness to Gender Diversity That RuPaul's Drag Race Severely Lacks." *SBS*. Last modified September 1, 2020. https://www.sbs.com.au/guide/article/2020/08/27/dragula-has-openness-gender-diversity-rupauls-drag-race-severely-lacks.

Singh, Rajdeep. "Drag Race Star Brita Filter 'tried to Hurt Herself' After Toxic, Racist Bullying from So-called Fans Became 'too Much to Bear.'" *PinkNews | Latest Lesbian, Gay, Bi and Trans News | LGBTQ+ News*. Last modified October 22, 2020. https://www.thepinknews.com/2020/10/22/brita-filter-drag-race-bullying-overdose-racist-toxic/.

Swift, Taylor. "Taylor Swift—You Need To Calm Down." *YouTube*. June 17, 2019. https://www.youtube.com/watch?v=Dkk9gvTmCXY.

"Tap That App." *RuPaul's Drag Race Untucked*. Directed by World of wonder. Los Angeles: VH1, April 5, 2018.

Wood, Robin. *Robin Wood on the Horror Film: Collected Essays and Reviews*. Detroit: Wayne State University Press, 2018. PDF e-book.

# From Page to Screen

## Junji Itō Collection *and Affect*

### Ivan Jaramillo

## *Itō Junji's Doll from Hell*

Itō Junji is considered by many as one of the masters of horror manga today, both in Japan and overseas. His popularity has transcended national boundaries. Today, largely due to the advent of internet, social media, and streaming services, his oeuvre is well-known among horror enthusiasts. In 2018, some of his works were adapted into an animated anthology called *Junji Itō Collection,* which fans received with mixed reviews. Through a rather simple yet visually arresting style, his work covers a myriad of themes. Previous studies have focused on recurrent themes in his work such as body horror,[1] medium-related readings of the horror in his stories,[2] gender-based readings of violence depicted in *Tomie,*[3] H.P. Lovecraft's influence on Itō's work[4] and on ecological horror in *Uzumaki.*[5] Furthermore, very few studies have focused on the adaptations into different media of his works.[6] However, many of his lesser-known pieces are underanalyzed or altogether ignored. The work selected for this essay, "Hell Doll Funeral" (1998), makes use of the horrific doll trope, a figure that has resonance with diverse theories as it is a common element in genres like the Gothic and the affective responses provoked by this figure are body-bound. Its corresponding anime adaptation, in theabovementioned horror anime anthology series, can be interpreted from different perspectives related to media, horror and the uncanny. This story encapsulates two elements of interest for this chapter: firstly, its horror stems from the common fear of the inability to move or the loss of agency while our body transforms, leaving its human form behind; secondly, Itō subverts the trope of the doll many audiences of the Gothic are familiar with.

In this essay, I discuss how narrative and stylistic techniques that

61

originated in cinema are present in this sample of Itō's work and how these are used in the anime adaptation. My larger aim is to suggest that, on the one hand, Itō's ability to provoke affective responses from readers does not translate properly to the screen as it is through the printed medium that these intensities are enhanced and, on the other hand, this anime reveals certain qualities of Itō's work that are resistant to adaptation.

## Itō Junji and Gekiga

As a child, Itō Junji had an initial encounter with horror through Umezu Kazuo's (b. 1936) work. In multiple interviews, when being asked who his biggest manga influence is, Itō always remarks that Umezu left an indelible inspiration on him.[7] This influence can be seen in the way Itō transitions from panel to panel and the focus he gives to his characters through the use of medium shots, medium close-up shots, close-ups and extreme close-ups, cinematic techniques that are commonly used in modern *seinen* manga (young men's manga). *Seinen* manga developed from the earlier genre of *gekiga* ("dramatic pictures") as most of its defining characteristics—mature storylines, graphic depictions of sex, violence or nudity, as well as realistic style and stark black and white contrasts—are still prominent. But what is *gekiga?*[8]

During the 1960s, manga artist Umezu Kazuo was part of this movement which originated in Japan in tandem with counterculture of the time, when the country witnessed student uprisings, civic and intellectual participation in politics, and radical artistic experimentalism.[9] As a response to Tezuka-style *shōnen* manga, in terms of style and content, the *gekiga* genre was developed by a loosely organized group of teenagers who were looking to publish serious stories told in a dramatic visual style borrowed from film noir.[10] However, when discussing the use of cinematic style in manga, the name that usually pops up is Tezuka Osamu (1928–1989), the so-called "father of manga," whose early works evidenced the use of a higher number of frames as an attempt to imitate the "moving image" of cinema, but, as Deborah Shamoon explains, "cinematism (*eiga-teki shuho*) was a key part of *gekiga* from its beginning."[11] There was a particular focus on British and American film noir as well as French New Wave films: low-key lighting that accentuated the high contrast of light and darkness, as well as the use of distorted camera angles and jarring montage in order to convey the characters' anxiety, fear and/or tension in a scene are among the elements adopted by *gekiga* creators whose concern was the (often gloomy) ambience of setting or scene.[12] In *gekiga*, there was a departure from cute, round, anthropomorphic animal characters to down-to-earth humans who inhabited heavily contrasted worlds inspired by real-life scenarios and whose stories revolved around themes of social anxiety and alienation brought about by postwar struggles.

Itō's work evinces stylistic affinities with the *gekiga* school. His characters are drawn in bold, clean lines against an elaborate realistic background. Objects and surroundings in each panel are given many details; by using a lot of lines and contrasting shading, he thoroughly creates surfaces and textures that feel almost palpable. His cinematism is present in his use of chiaroscuro reminiscent of film noir not only to provide his pages with a gloomy atmosphere and to highlight specific traits in his creations—particularly the face—but also as a defining stylistic choice taken from his inspirational figure, Umezu. Itō's panel composition is mostly uniform; except for the frames in which he deliberately leads the reader's gaze to a moment of horror in full display, most panels remain at a consistent size. Additionally, his skill in conjuring tension that leads into unavoidable horror is achieved through a well-balanced combination of the transitions that Scott McCloud calls moment-to-moment (changes in panels take a few seconds, giving off a sense of slow motion), action-to-action (a sequence to show a complete action from the beginning to end) and, especially, aspect-to-aspect transitions (this transition bypasses time and sets a wandering eye on different aspects of a place, idea or mood).[13] This last technique, a defining characteristic brought forth by the *gekiga* movement, functions to enhance the rhythm and mood of the page.[14]

Discussing some of the drawing styles adopted from manga artist Tezuka Osamu, Roman Rosenbaum points out one important feature implemented by *gekiga* artists that is still ubiquitous today: the depiction of psychological landscapes through close-ups.[15] A distinctive trait in Itō's style is the use of close-ups to convey the state of fear, horror or stress of the characters and, at the same time, facilitate affective responses in his readers. In this regard, Yi-Shan Tsai explains that, similar to what movie directors do, "manga artists employ close-ups extensively to preview, review or break down emotional moments in a story, so as to slow down the narrative and encourage readers to reflect on the inner emotional drama of a character."[16] On the one hand, close-up framing helps readers connect with manga characters at an emotional level, as there is an unconscious automatic empathic response when we encounter a display of emotion in the form of a zoomed-in face. On the other hand, since close-ups do not happen as frequently in our everyday life as in movies or other media like comic and manga—it is very rare for us to see a person so closely in real life—close-ups are the tools used to help the viewer/reader get clues of the mental or psychological state of the characters. Furthermore, close-ups guide the audience to see beyond the scope of the screen, when the character's gaze points us, the viewers, into something that is not showcased within the limits of what the camera can show us. This happens similarly within the limits of the panel in a manga, a technique that Itō uses rather frequently to elevate the sense of tension before an unfolding horror by usually placing them in the last panel right before the turn of a page.

## Itō, Dolls and the Uncanny

The previous section was an attempt to characterize Itō's work and style, and to identify from a technical perspective those aspects that may set him apart from other manga artists but at the same time can situate him within a specific subgenre. Thematically speaking, it is quite challenging to define Itō's prolific work, as it includes a myriad of horror tropes that range from body to cosmic horror, from people being cursed by unnamed and unseen forces to people showing some kind of crazed mob behavior when terrorizing one particular individual, from people being addicted or obsessed with something or someone to phobias taking literal physical manifestations, among many others. Perhaps the most predominant theme in his work can be narrowed down to situations when the mundane blends with the horror.

In Itō's work, the doll elicits feelings of dread through her liminal status as humanlike, yet inanimate, object. This image has traditionally been linked to the Gothic genre and more recently in horror. It is a pervasive figure in Gothic texts such as E.T.A. Hoffmann's *The Sandman* (1816), M.R. James's *The Haunted Dolls' House* (1923), and Daphne du Maurier's *The Doll* (1937),[17] in horror movies like Roman Polanski's *The Lamp* (1959) and Otto Preminger's *Bunny Lake Is Missing* (1965) and more recently in popular horror franchises like *Annabelle* (2014) and its corresponding prequel, *Annabelle: Creation* (2017) and sequel *Annabelle Comes Home* (2019), just to name a few. In all these instances, dolls are inanimate objects whose possible ability to move provokes fear, while in Itō's piece discussed in this chapter, we witness a "reversed" process.

The popularity of dolls in horror media owes in part to the powerful affective responses they produce in audiences. There have been numerous attempts at understanding why dolls provoke that kind of unsettling feelings, particularly when used as a central motif in Gothic and horror. To begin with, dolls do not actually pose a real menace, but they are rather a representation of a potentiality hidden underneath their rigid surface. As explained by Susan Yi Sencindiver:

> The question regarding the distinct quality of the strange unease and related affects the uncanny doll excites is intriguing when considering that the

menacing threat it poses does not primarily pertain to a fear of physical harm, or in the case of Gothic fantastic fiction, the reader is arguably less agitated by a vicarious concern for the plight of characters than by the apprehension aroused by the suspicion of a doll's furtive inner life.[18]

Thus, what we fear is what may lurk within the doll, a force that may provide it with the ability to move of its own volition. In the Gothic, the anxiety we experience is brought forth by the potential vivification of this humanlike object, since when confronted with this possibility, we realize that qualities we once thought exclusive to human beings, such as agency and likeness, no longer serve or suffice to describe us accurately.[19] The boundaries between what makes us human and differentiates us from inanimate nonhuman objects are blurred when in the presence of a humanlike figure that makes us wonder what the extent of their potential agency is; though this agency may not be entirely intrinsic as "it is often implied that the uncanny animation of dolls, puppets, and ventriloquist's dummies depends on a mysterious external manipulation or demonic possession."[20] So, when fearing a doll that is thought to be possessed, there is a certain level of "animistic" beliefs to this uncanny affect, which, in Freudian terms, should not affect individuals who have overcome that primitive kind of mindset.

Psychoanalyst Sigmund Freud popularized the concept of the uncanny, as it is widely used and understood nowadays, in his 1919 essay "The Uncanny." Freud drew upon the work of earlier German theorists such as Ernst Jentsch, who first attempted to define the uncanny in his well-known 1906 essay as being a product of intellectual uncertainty since "intellectual certainty provides psychical shelter in the struggle for existence."[21] By exploring the etymology of the German word *unheimlich*, which roughly translated to "unhomely," Freud sees the uncanny as something that is unfamiliar, quite the opposite of the comforts of home; he defines the uncanny as that class of the terrifying that leads back to the sense of the unfamiliar, the strange, or the disquietingly (but not quite) familiar.[22] However, he claimed that the uncanny experience occurs either when repressed infantile complexes (like the fear of castration) have been revived by some impression or, as mentioned above, when primitive beliefs (animism) we think we long ago put behind us suddenly seem to be confirmed.[23] Although Freud's notion of the familiar becoming unfamiliar can work for the current analysis in the many instances in which that familiarity within the story is progressively broken, the deeper implications he poses—which seem to seek to confirm the principles of his oedipal scheme—do not correspond to the affective reading intended for the current chapter.[24]

In order to get a fuller understanding of the concept of the uncanny so that I can apply it in the analysis further ahead, I will now turn my attention to the work of Mori Masahiro, who, in 1970, published a paper in the field of robotics in which he coined the term "The Uncanny Valley." In this paper he hypothesized that our response to humanlike entities, like robots and dolls, would drastically shift from empathy to revulsion as it approached, but failed to attain, a lifelike appearance. He explained this through a graph that described the relationship of familiarity and similarity in human likenesses and the positive or negative feelings that they produced.[25] Mori explained that the more similar to humans robots and other simulacra are, the more positively we are respond, but only to the point in which we start noticing the details that make the entity artificial, thus provoking in us an eerie sensation that makes us lose our affinity and makes the object in question uncanny.[26] He also highlights that a stronger sense of both familiarity and eeriness intensifies as a result of an entity's movement, as movement is considered "generally a sign of life" and concludes that this sense of eeriness is probably a form of instinct that protects us from proximal, rather than distal, sources of danger.[27]

To conclude, the notion of the uncanny for the sake of the argument of this chapter thus combines the uncertainty caused by the interruption of the familiar proposed by Freud—leaving out possible repressed complexes or beliefs—with Mori's decrease of affinity or familiarity when presented with humanlike entities. In other words, I am interested in understanding the uncanny firstly as our response to everyday occurrences being altered and secondly as the uncertainty caused by entities that resemble or own humanity.

## "Hell Doll Funeral"

Released in Japan by *Comic Gon!* in 1998, "Hell Doll Funeral"[28] is a brief one-shot manga by Itō Junji later reissued in the tenth volume of *Itō Junji's Masterpieces Collection* published by Asahi Comics in 2013. Its English version was released by VIZ Media in the United States in October 2018. Before that, in January of the same year, this story was part of the animated anthology series *Junji Itō Collection*. It tells the story of a young girl named Marie who, just like around thirty percent of the world's children, is dollifying. Her parents find solace in the idea that she will remain like a beautiful doll and, though unable to move or speak of her own volition, will accompany them forever. They cannot begin to fathom how the parents of other children with the same condition have decided to get rid of them. However, when Marie continues to mutate into a more and more grotesque creature, they are forced to finally lay her to rest.

The "Hell Doll Funeral" manga starts in a first page dissected into four frames, an editorial decision that speaks to Itō's use of panel construction to pull readers into his story. In the upper part we have panel one[29]; in this frame, which takes about one third of the page, the eponymous title of the story is written in Japanese in a curved heading, and just below it, two large doll-like eyes stare at the reader. Their contour, as well as the rest of the frame, is filled with a vertical texture reminiscent of a wooden surface, a composition that foretells what the story is going to be about. Underneath it, on the right, and taking vertically half of the remaining space on the page, the second frame shows in a low-angle shot the upper section of a mansion while a crashing lightning takes up most of the space accompanied by the Japanese onomatopoeia *"pikaa,"* which is typically used in manga to describe a short-lived glow (*crackle* in the English version).[30] Then, the next two panels progressively show a close-up of the unnamed main character and father of Marie. In the upper panel on the left that shows rain lashing on the window, accompanied by onomatopoeia for rain and thunder, he is shown for the first time. He is holding his head with both hands, a clear sign, along with the shocked look in his eyes, of worry and despair. The last panel of the page, lower left side, zooms in on his tensed face and his eyes looking back at something behind him.

The combination of these three panels works as an establishing shot for this story. By progressively diminishing the size of the panels, from the open vertical frame on the right to the close-up on the lower left, we are pulled into the psychological landscape of the father. This progression is subtly accentuated in two ways. Firstly, with a diagonal line separating the two smaller frames on the left from the larger one on the right; the diagonality of this line functions as a kind of funnel that directs and centers our eyes on the concerned face of the father. Secondly, the very narrow space in the gutter (empty space in between panels), conveys an immediacy of time. There is little closure—the way we connect the moments conveyed in each panel and mentally construct a continuous, unified reality—as this is a moment-to-moment transition.[31] As explained by Natsume Fusanosuke, there is a sense of compression (*asshuku*), which compels us psychologically to enter into the mind of the protagonist.[32] By doing this, Itō provokes an affective intensity in the reader and reinforces it by simply darkening the character's eyes through the use of heavy line work; for a millisecond we quiver at what his face transmits.

In the animated version, there are many additional elements that are not present in the manga and are a surplus in this medium. From the very first sequence, we are immediately submerged in a sequence that can easily be part of any classic Western gothic film. The establishing shot starts with the camera panning from right to left, then we are told straight away of the weather conditions by means of the sound of heavy rain, the howling wind and the ominous crash of thunder. Everything is dark, and we can barely make out the shapes of what is being shown in front of us, provoking a brief sense of disorientation. A grove of trees appears up front on the screen, and the branches and leaves move slowly, a display that deploys limited animation to help accentuate the enveloping gloomy atmosphere while increasing our sense of expectation. This is a stylistic choice that, while making the passing of time feel unnatural and somehow incongruent, adds to the eerie initial buildup. We hardly get to see a mansion in the background with its upper floor slightly illuminated when, all of a sudden, the horizontality of this slow shot is followed by a swift vertical shot with lightning that, for a second, strikes and illuminates the façade of the upper floor of the building, accompanied by a somber high-pitched vocalization that highlights the mystery of the whole scene. When watching this short opening sequence, which is an expansion of the original one-panel rainy scene of the Victorian mansion described before, the limited animation deployed serves an affective purpose. Paradoxically, perhaps this sequence works well in setting the dreadful mood for this animation because it was not an attempt to echo Itō's style as the rest of the episode seems to be.

Let us now return to the manga. The final panel on the first opening page of the story is compressed, which means that we, the readers, feel that our vision is closing in and we have no other choice but to focus on Marie's father's distressed face, provoking an affective intensity in us; for a few seconds we are full of expectation. And then, upon the turn of the page, we are slightly pulled away from the father. In the first panel on the top right corner, which occupies about one fourth of the width of the page, via a medium full shot, the father appears leaning on a windowsill, looking backwards at a dark silhouette. In the second panel on the left, which takes the rest of the width of the page, an encounter with the uncanny is revealed. A child-size doll is sitting on a sofa while holding a book; by juxtaposing this image against a scene of everyday familiarity, a living room, the familiar becomes unfamiliar. Her body seems to be completely immobile. There are lines on her neck and arms, and she has ball-joint elbows that confirm for us that she now is a toy. Were it not for her capability to speak, we would think she is just a toy. She asks her father if there is something wrong since he seems to be frightened. These two panels work in tandem as a release for the last panel in the previous page, in both narrative and composition terms. First, Itō liberates the spatial tension created in the close-up to the father's concerned face; we are led from an almost claustrophobic shot to a slightly more open scene, albeit still a closed one. Second, there is a kind of narrative relief as the cause of the man's concern is revealed and we get a glimpse of what is happening, albeit instead of reaching an actual resolution we are thrown into an additional enigma.

In the following three panels, Marie's condition is depicted with more detail. In the first one on the right, an extreme close-up shot shows one of her arms and parts of her torso; the details of the dress she's wearing and the texture of her hardened skin are thoroughly drawn. The middle panel zooms in on her eerie face; a subtle dotted boundary line from the corner of her mouth to her jaw and her seemingly unblinking unfocused eye indicate she's now more doll than human. The uncanny is maximized in this image as she is still able to speak; she asks her father if he is fine. The last image is again a close-up of the father's face: we see his face from the side as he tells his daughter that there is nothing to worry about, though this time he seems to be more nervous and uncomfortable than worried.

The arrangement of this page through aspect-to-aspect transition increases the tension in the story. Although the story itself does not move forward, we are provided with details of the girl's dollifying process. Here the uncanny becomes an issue in terms of the liminal condition Marie is in. She resembles a porcelain doll, but she has not fully turned into one as she still shows cognitive functions: not only can she utter words but she is also aware of her progenitor's nervousness. The detailed visual elements are reinforced with the father's voice as he explains, through several text bubbles juxtaposed to the close-up images of torso and face, that his daughter's body has changed. Then, the close shot in the last panel works in two ways. First, by looking at his nervous face, highlighted with some drops of sweat and an awkward smile, the tension he feels can be perceived. Secondly, by making the character look back, the author is placing us into the story and, at the same time, is reminding us that the father's source of despair is still behind him and affects him, no matter how hard he tries to conceal it. The page starts with a release that showed most of the girl's transformation into a doll and ends once again on a constrained image that visually foregrounds the man's mental state.

In the anime version, this sequence is emulated almost frame by frame. However, the tension that Itō manages to create at the turn of the page, the succinct intrigue felt after glimpsing the man's distress, is not as effective in the moving medium. Even though there is a close-up of sorts, it neither lasts long enough nor is sufficiently enclosed to recreate the strain generated in the original material. Hearing Marie's voice and seeing her mouth move as she speaks, however, adds the uncanny to the scene, the image of the doll slowly descending into the uncanny valley as the affinity we could have felt for the cute doll rapidly turns to shock as we hear her speak. Nonetheless, the uncanniness of this sequence is not enough to provoke an affective response as in the manga, this due to a lack of proper tension buildup. This short scene is so fast-paced in the animated version that we do not even have the time to properly process and react accordingly.

Be it printed or animated, thematically speaking, the horror in this first depiction unfolds in two ways. On the one hand, the sense of the uncanny is brought upon by the figure of the doll; the uncanny, as explained before, is that eerie sensation we experience when our sense of affinity toward a humanlike figure decreases.[33] When looking at dolls, as in this case, we recognize in them a certain human likeness, but their glassy stares and immobile bodies provoke negative familiarity or affinity.[34] Marie's fixed stare and motionless body provoke an affective intensity which is doubled, firstly, by the focus given to her father's concerned face previously shown— it is through him that we realize that the sense of familiarity has been broken beyond repair—and, secondly, by the fact that she seems unfazed by what is happening to her as she keeps on asking her father if there is something wrong. On the other hand, the trope of the doll is used here differently than in instances in which this image is common, namely the Gothic. In this case, and as discussed before, the horror stems from the notion that the motionless can become mobile, which means accepting the existence of a residual degree of inexplicable agency in lifeless matter.[35] In Itō's work, the source of horror is not an inanimate object gaining mobility; what terrifies us is a force that works in the opposite direction, a human being becoming a motionless doll, a living being losing the agency over her own body.

The process of "dollifying" involves "ascribing more or less psychic qualities to an object, and treating it as if it were an animate and sentient thing,"[36] namely, what children do when playing with their doll toys. When used in the Gothic, this process reveals underlying psychological issues that affect adult characters.[37] In Gothic tradition, dollifying is deemed as a metaphorical, or rather symbolic, practice, while in the case of "Hell Doll Funeral" this process happens literally. Marie's father is not ascribing doll attributes to her; she has physically become one and now seems to be trapped in a hard-skinned body.

Marie's mother is then shown in both media crying and holding her daughter desperately as she tells her husband that they will never see their cute girl smile again. A portrait of what Marie looked like before her transformation is also shown, an image that reinforces the feeling of hopelessness and irreversibility, a proof that the familiar has become unfamiliar. The father comes to terms with this situation by telling his wife to see the bright side of things, that even when she cannot respond, her daughter will remain as beautiful as she is forever (in the manga this is said by her mother). He cannot comprehend how some parents whose children have also been affected by this condition give up so easily on them and decide to cremate them, so they decide to keep her as she is.

However, Marie's metamorphosis does not end there. On the page, Itō manages to show this progression through a very few panels and by means of a very skillful use of a scene-to-scene kind of transition (in which we are required to be deductive as we are transported across significant distances of time and space from panel to panel).[38] The first panel shows the upper floor of the Victorian mansion accompanied by some curly clouds that give off a feeling of movement and passing of time; within this same panel, the father says that eventually they came to understand the feeling of the parents who lay their doll-children to rest. In the following frame, Marie resembles a very old porcelain doll whose paint is about to flake; detailed line work attests to the author's care for visual thoroughness and emphasis on the changes the doll is going through. The lines from the corners of her mouth to her jaw are much more pronounced, making her look now more marionette-like. Her unfocused eyes seem glassier and somehow more open. Then, the middle panel shows her mother leaning close to her as her afflicted father—in the foreground—wonders why her body transformation continues to progress. Marie's mouth is now hanging open and her posture is stiffer than before; her ball-joint elbows are slightly bent and her hands are open; she no longer seems to be sitting but is simply propped up against the sofa. Then, the next frame offers a close shot to an even more horrific state of the girl: her mouth hangs open more widely, and the downward openings on either side of it are now lined with pointy teeth giving her the appearance of some deep-sea fish. Her hair is wavier and her eyes now seem painted wooden balls that stare wide open. Her skin is even flakier than before, and her arms are no longer resting by her side. They are now positioned in an unnatural ninety-degree angle. In the last panel, right before the turn of the page, Itō once again uses a close-up to amplify the reader's anxiety and sense of expectation, a sideways close shot at both parents looking at something "off-panel." The father's mouth is slightly open, his bulging eyes and sweaty face revealing what he is going through as he tells his wife, who seems to be more resigned than shocked, that they should lay their daughter to rest.

This whole one-page sequence is a great example of Itō's cinematic style applied to convey anxiety and build up tension. The scene-to-scene transition focuses on only three stages of Marie's horrific transformation, but they are enough to give a sense of the passing of time without being too disruptive. We are not sure whether it has been hours, days or weeks, but we are certain that time has passed. Even if the size of the panels is not the same, they are consistent enough for Itō to create a compression that carries us along this progression. Frame by frame the reader is pulled into the parents' desperate psyche, and with that final affective display, we are prepared to learn what is in store for us on the following page.

As for the anime adaptation of this scene, this metamorphosis is very similar to the printed iteration, although with different results. The doll-girl's skin progressively gets more and more cracked and her teeth become pointier and more animal-like; limited animation, akin to slow motion, shows this progression through three clearly defined stages—as in the manga—each more grotesque than the previous one. The position of her arms changes similarly as well. They also end up pointing outwards, although although this last change is accompanied by an angry look in her eyes. Her eyebrows seem to start frowning, which, instead of providing the image with a scary or eerie appearance, makes the doll look like a child who is about to throw a tantrum. After becoming an immobile toy, Marie is given motion once again, yet this does not happen of her own volition but as a result of her unnatural transformation. However, instead of heightening the sense of expectation in the viewer, as in the establishing shot at the beginning, or contributing to the strangeness of this mutation, the limited animation here does not cause any affective reaction. By trying to stay too close to the original material, this five-second sequence, which should be one of the highlights in the whole episode, is rushed, and there is no time to appreciate in detail the further changes this girl is going through. Furthermore, the details in the character's design are not as thorough as in the source material. Viewers should have been given some chance to build up expectation for a new transformation stage by stage and to be full of anticipation for the last horrendous moment to unfold. Finally, this iteration ends similarly as the parents make the decision to finally put their daughter to rest; the difficulty of this decision is slightly exacerbated by the enclosure of their desperate faces in a close-up shot.

On the last page of the manga, there is a full-page illustration of the final stage of Marie's grotesque transformation. The body horror for which Itō is known is in full display in fastidious line work: Marie's hair has grown and turned curlier with a root-like texture, and her mouth has turned into a gaping maw with long, sharp teeth and several tentacles coming out of it. Her face, torso and arms have a very warty and scaly texture; her forehead still shows some of the flakes portrayed in previous stages of her metamorphosis. Her eyes are beyond human appearance; they are more bulbous and display an unfocused wooden texture and are lined with unnaturally long eyelashes. Her long and segmented neck is bent in a very insect-like fashion, and from it, pointy insectile legs sprout, similar to those of a huge centipede. Her fingers have turned into long elongated twig-like sticks. Her girly dress is the only thing that hints she was once a human. The chiaroscuro style for which Itō is known helps give depth and texture to the whole horrific scene, and the details on the material and pattern of the sofa act as a reminder that this used to be a slice of this family's everyday life. On the upper side there is a bubble text that reads, "We can't let anyone see her like this…" and is continued by another text on the lower left side that says, "…Our poor Marie!" This dialogue line, absent in the anime adaptation, adds an extra layer of horror if we interpret this utterance as a reflection of the social shame these parents may feel should the girl's ghastly transformation becomes public.

The first thing we are shown in the anime, on the other hand, is one of Marie's eyes. It is a round and cracked bulging ball, with a permanent stare with no eyelids but long twisted eyelashes and a couple of eerie concentric circles in a bluish iris that encircle a pointy pattern—akin to a set of sharp teeth—where the pupil ought to be. Through a combination of limited animation and CGI, a close-up shot to the eye reveals all of these details while showing some texture of her wooden cracked skin; the eye movement is accompanied by a sharp, animalesque sound that increases the uncanniness of this horrific scene. Then, in a very brief horizontal panel of the camera, her crooked centipede-like neck palpitates at the same time as the insectile legs move, while a sound similar to that of rustling leaves is heard. Then most of girl's body is shown as the camera slowly zooms out. Similar to the manga, there are tentacles sprouting out of an open, sharp-teethed mouth. Her hair is not as detailed, its brown color and the different position of the head and body turning it almost into an afterthought. Her whole body also displays a warty/scaly texture, albeit with fewer details. This scene becomes even more poignant with the ominous soundtrack that can be heard in the animated version.

In both media, this last picture works as the ultimate display of horror for which we had been prepared all throughout the story. Through a balanced used of compression and release, achieved through a combination of different transitions between panels, Itō manages to create a lot of tension, which culminates in this detailed black-and-white manifestation of horror. He manages to first intensify the levels of tension and expectation with a close-up of the mortified parents who are looking at something beyond the limits of the page, in a cinematic manner, in the ultimate panel which is then rewarded with the release of the panel in a full page. In the anime equivalent of this scene, however, there is not a sense of urgency; in spite of the additional affordances in the sound and movement that are effective but momentarily, the uncanniness is somehow lost. A last point to make here is the use of color. All throughout this succinct two-minute episode, characters are shown with an ashen tone to their skin. Shades are exaggeratedly highlighted with big sections of black that, instead of being faithful to Itō's particular use of chiaroscuro, make the aesthetics of the animation somehow amateurish. This is particularly evident with Marie's final monstrous transformation. The entire composition is so dark, that many details of her body are lost in the opaqueness, and were it not for the purple color of the sofa and the light blue of her dress, she would just blend in with the background. In both instances, however, the final depiction of this creature sends Marie to the bottom of the valley of the uncanny. Although the human likeness is almost completely lost, we still can see some traces of what Marie used to be, yet our sense of affinity towards her has entirely decreased and what is left is an entire sense of revulsion.

## Conclusions

Itō's use of cinematic techniques—cinematism—helps him conjure stress, anxiety and anticipation in his readers. He can easily situate uncanny disruptions of his characters' routine lives through the transitions he makes from panel to panel (which we, as readers, unify through closure),the emphasis he gives to facial expressions as a way to connect affectively with the readers, and through his skill to create tensions and subsequent resolutions through the modulation of the size of the frames he creates. All of these aspects are evidence of his particular style that hailed from *gekiga*. Throughout the analysis done, I proved that when these devices are emulated frame by frame and too closely, without considering further implications as to why these are effective in the first place, the animated result may not be as effective as a horror piece. The anxiety and expectation are not built up properly in the animation, and the transitions that lead the reader through the pages do not translate equally onto the screen. Although a wider sample of works should be further considered to confirm this assertion, considering the mixed reviews that the anthology series *Junji Itō Collection* received, this may be the case.

Furthermore, in "The Hell Doll Funeral," Itō taps into devices that are commonly found in the Gothic genre: a family whose daily life is afflicted by an unknown force; a big, albeit claustrophobic mansion in which the uncanny unfolds; and a doll who becomes the center of this narrative. However, he combines these elements in ways that distance him from the Gothic. Firstly, the Gothic is related to the perception of fear and its experience in the mind rather than to vicious and visual attacks to bodily integrity.[39] The fear in the analyzed work is caused by something that happens in front of the parents of the victim and not some kind of insinuation that would make us doubt their mental health. Secondly, although both in the Gothic and in Marie's case delicateness metamorphoses into subtle evilness, and the doll becomes too lifelike, too realistic,[40] in the latter there is no room for subtlety as the girl transcends her doll stage by morphing into an indescribably bizarre monster. Lastly, the dollifying process occurs in a literal way but it is taken further beyond into the realm of horror as she goes through an ever more horrific bodily metamorphosis. In sum, we could argue that in this piece of Itō Junji's work, the Gothic metamorphoses into horror.

## NOTES

1. See Robert Shail, "Anxiety and Mutation in Charles Burns' Black Hole and Junji Ito's Uzumaki," in *Gender and Contemporary Horror in Comics, Games and Transmedia* (Emerald Publishing Limited, 2019); Shweta Khilnani, "Embodying Horror: Corporeal and Affective Dread in Junji Ito's Tomie," *Horror Fiction in the Global South: Cultures, Narratives and Representations*, 2021, 28–41.

2. See Isabel Luis Machado Cardodo Ricardo, "Taking Something Normal and Looking at It Backwards: A Comparative Analysis of Horror in Eastern and Western Cultures" (PhD Thesis, Instituto Politecnico do Porto [Portugal], 2019); Michael A. Lombardi, "Medium-Bound Horror in the Manga of Itō Junji" (Bachelor of Arts Thesis, Maine, Bates College, 2021).

3. See Juan A. García Pacheco and Francisco Javier López Rodríguez, "La Representación Icónica y Narrativa de La Mujer En El Cómic Japonés Masculino: El Shounen Manga y El Horror Manga," *Cuestiones de género: de la igualdad y la diferencia*, no. 7 (2012).

4. Álvaro Pina Arrabal, "El Influjo de HP Lovecraft En La Obra de Junji Ito," *Brumal: Revista de Investigación Sobre Lo Fantástico* 7, no. 1 (2019): 135–63, https://doi.org/10.5565/rev/brumal.578.

5. See Christy Tidwell, "Junji Ito's Uzumaki and the Scope of Ecohorror," *Fear and Nature: Ecohorror Studies in the Anthropocene* 8 (2021): 42.

6. See David Kalat, *J-Horror: The Definitive Guide to the Ring, the Grudge and Beyond* (Vertical, 2007); Jay McRoy, *Nightmare Japan: Contemporary Japanese Horror Cinema* (Brill, 2008); Lombardi, "Medium-Bound Horror in the Manga of Itō Junji."

7. Itō Junji, "An Interview with Master of Horror Manga Junji Ito (Full Length Version)," Online, June 10, 2019, https://grapee.jp/en/116016.

8. *Gekiga* (劇画) is a combination of two Japanese words: *geki* (劇) or drama, and *ga* (画) or picture. The word can literally be interpreted as "dramatic picture."

9. Shige CJ Suzuki, "Gekiga, or Japanese Alternative Comics: The Mediascape of Japanese Counterculture," *Introducing Japanese Popular Culture* (Routledge, 2018), 263.

10. Deborah Shamoon, "Films on Paper: Cinematic Narrative in Gekiga," *Mangatopia: Essays on Manga and Anime in the Modern World: Essays on Manga and Anime in the Modern World*, 2011, 27.

11. Shamoon, "Films on Paper," 28.

12. Suzuki, "Gekiga, or Japanese Alternative Comics," 266.

13. Scott McCloud, *Understanding Comics: The Invisible Art*, 70–72.

14. Shamoon, "Films on Paper: Cinematic Narrative in Gekiga," 29.

15. Roman Rosenbaum, "Gekiga as a Site of Intercultural Exchange: Tatsumi Yoshihiro's A Drifting Life," *Intercultural Crossover, Transcultural Flows*, 2010, 6.

16. Yi-Shan Tsai, "Close-Ups: An Emotive Language in Manga," *Journal of Graphic Novels and Comics* 9, no. 5 (2018): 487.

17. Joana Rita Ramalho, "The Uncanny Afterlife of Dolls: Reconfiguring Personhood through Object Vivification in Gothic Film," *Studies in Gothic Fiction* 6, no. 2 (2020): 28.

18. Susan Yi Sencindiver, "The Doll's Uncanny Soul," in *The Gothic and the Everyday* (Springer, 2014), 104.

19. Ramalho, "The Uncanny Afterlife of Dolls," 29.

20. Sencindiver, "The Doll's Uncanny Soul," 118.

21. Ernst Jentsch, "On the Psychology of the Uncanny (1906)," *Angelaki: Journal of the Theoretical Humanities* 2, no. 1 (1997): 15.

22. Scott G. Eberle, "Exploring the Uncanny Valley to Find the Edge of Play," *American Journal of Play* 2, no. 2 (2009): 168.

23. Eberle, 172.

24. Sencindiver, "The Doll's Uncanny Soul," 107.

25. Eberle, "Exploring the Uncanny Valley to Find the Edge of Play," 175.

26. Masahiro Mori, Karl F. MacDorman, and Norri Kageki, "The Uncanny Valley [from the Field]," *IEEE Robotics & Automation Magazine* 19, no. 2 (2012): 99.

27. Mori, MacDorman, and Kageki, 100.

28. There are several alternative translations for the title 地獄の人形葬 (*Jigoku no Ningyou Sou*) such as *The Hell of The Doll Funeral*, in the 2018 edition by VIZ Media, *Hell Doll Funeral* used in the anime adaptation by Studio Deen, as well as *A Doll's Hellish Burial* and *Hell'o Dollies* proposed by online unofficial translators in "scanlation" sites.

29. The narration in manga is encased within frames or panels called *koma*. When reading a page of manga, we start with the *koma* on the top right corner and we end with the *koma* on the bottom left corner.

30. Beyond phonetic onomatopoeia, Japanese language counts with *gitaigo* (擬態語) words that describe in terms of sound things that do not actually have sounds. So you can be slacking off and walking home in a *bura-bura* way or, when something flashes, for example when lightning strikes (as in the manga being discussed), it makes a visual burst in a *pika-pika* way. Jon Holt and Teppei Fukuda, "'The Power of Onomatopoeia in Manga,' an Essay by Natsume Fusanosuke with Translators' Introduction," *Japanese Language and Literature* 56, no. 1 (2022): 168.

31. McCloud, *Understanding Comics*, 67–70.

32. Jon Holt and Teppei Fukuda, "The Functions of Panels (Koma) in Manga: An Essay by Natsume Fusanosuke," *Electronic Journal of Contemporary Japanese Studies*, 2021.

33. Mori, MacDorman, and Kageki, "The Uncanny Valley [from the Field]," 99.

34. Ramalho, "The Uncanny Afterlife of Dolls," 32.

35. Ramalho, 32.

36. A. Caswell Ellis and G. Stanley Hall, "A Study of Dolls," *The Pedagogical Seminary* 4, no. 2 (1896): 132. Quoted in Ramalho, "The Uncanny Afterlife of Dolls," 35.

37. Ramalho, "The Uncanny Afterlife of Dolls," 35.

38. McCloud, *Understanding Comics*, 71.

39. Ramalho, "The Uncanny Afterlife of Dolls," 33.

40. Ramalho, 31.

## Works Cited

Eberle, Scott G. "Exploring the Uncanny Valley to Find the Edge of Play." *American Journal of Play* 2, no. 2 (2009): 167–94.

Ellis, A. Caswell, and G. Stanley Hall. "A Study of Dolls." *The Pedagogical Seminary* 4, no. 2 (1896): 129–75.

García Pacheco, Juan A., and Francisco Javier López Rodríguez. "La Representación Icónica y Narrativa de La Mujer En El Cómic Japonés Masculino: El Shounen Manga y El Horror Manga." *Cuestiones de género: de la igualdad y la diferencia*, no. 7 (2012).

Holt, Jon, and Teppei Fukuda. "The Functions of Panels (Koma) in Manga: An Essay by Natsume Fusanosuke." *Electronic Journal of Contemporary Japanese Studies*, 2021.

_____. "'The Power of Onomatopoeia in Manga,' an Essay by Natsume Fusanosuke with Translators' Introduction." *Japanese Language and Literature* 56, no. 1 (2022): 157–84.

Itō, Junji. "An Interview With Master of Horror Manga Junji Ito (Full Length Version)." Online, June 10, 2019. https://grapee.jp/en/116016.

Jentsch, Ernst. "On the Psychology of the Uncanny (1906)." *Angelaki: Journal of the Theoretical Humanities* 2, no. 1 (1997): 7–16.

Kalat, David. *J-Horror: The Definitive Guide to the Ring, the Grudge and Beyond*. Vertical Inc, 2007.

Khilnani, Shweta. "Embodying Horror: Corporeal and Affective Dread in Junji Ito's Tomie." *Horror Fiction in the Global South: Cultures, Narratives and Representations*, 2021, 28–41.

Lombardi, Michael A. "Medium-Bound Horror in the Manga of Itō Junji." Bachelor of Arts Thesis, Bates College, 2021.

McCloud, Scott. *Understanding Comics: The Invisible Art*. Kitchen Sink Press , 1993.

McRoy, Jay. *Nightmare Japan: Contemporary Japanese Horror Cinema*. Brill, 2008.

Mori, Masahiro, Karl F. MacDorman, and Norri Kageki. "The Uncanny Valley [from the Field]." *IEEE Robotics & Automation Magazine* 19, no. 2 (2012): 98–100.

Pina Arrabal, Álvaro. "El Influjo de HP Lovecraft En La Obra de Junji Ito." *Brumal: Revista de Investigación Sobre Lo Fantástico* 7, no. 1 (2019): 135–63. https://doi.org/10.5565/rev/brumal.578.

Ramalho, Joana Rita. "The Uncanny Afterlife of Dolls: Reconfiguring Personhood through Object Vivification in Gothic Film." *Studies in Gothic Fiction* 6, no. 2 (2020): 27–38.

Ricardo, Isabel Luis Machado Cardodo. "Taking Something Normal and Looking at It Backwards: A Comparative Analysis of Horror in Eastern and Western Cultures." PhD Thesis, Instituto Politecnico do Porto (Portugal), 2019.

Rosenbaum, Roman. "Gekiga as a Site of Intercultural Exchange: Tatsumi Yoshihiro's A Drifting Life." *Intercultural Crossover, Transcultural Flows*, 2010, 1–20.

Sencindiver, Susan Yi. "The Doll's Uncanny Soul." In *The Gothic and the Everyday*, 103–30. Springer, 2014.

Shail, Robert. "Anxiety and Mutation in Charles Burns' Black Hole and Junji Ito's Uzumaki." In *Gender and Contemporary Horror in Comics, Games and Transmedia*. Emerald Publishing Limited, 2019.

Shamoon, Deborah. "Films on Paper: Cinematic Narrative in Gekiga." *Mangatopia: Essays on Manga and Anime in the Modern World: Essays on Manga and Anime in the Modern World*, 2011.

Suzuki, Shige CJ. "Gekiga, or Japanese Alternative Comics: The Mediascape of Japanese Counterculture." In *Introducing Japanese Popular Culture*, 263–76. Routledge, 2018.

Tidwell, Christy. "Junji Ito's Uzumaki and the Scope of Ecohorror." *Fear and Nature: Ecohorror Studies in the Anthropocene* 8 (2021): 42.

Tsai, Yi-Shan. "Close-Ups: An Emotive Language in Manga." *Journal of Graphic Novels and Comics* 9, no. 5 (2018): 473–89.

# PART 2

# Forms of Narration
# and Narrative Representations

# Containing the Uncanny

## A Babysitter's Guide to Monster Hunting

### Christina Adamou

*A Babysitter's Guide to Monster Hunting* (2020) was branded by Netflix as a horror movie for children aged 7+. The film evokes the uncanny feeling in various ways, yet at the same time contains it in various ways. After briefly examining whether the genre of horror might be suitable or even desirable for children, we will analyze the film's relation to Freud's notion of the uncanny, how it evokes the feeling of uncanny as well as how it contains it, via the hybridity of genres and a series of creative aesthetic choices.

A horror movie for children may initially seem like a paradox, since most horror movies are deemed suitable only for 16+ or 18+. Yet, many popular children's narratives could arouse feelings of fear. The protagonists are often placed in mortal danger, in children's narratives ranging from classical fairy tales to contemporary films. A very popular and obvious example are Disney princesses. Whether based on classical fairy tales or featuring in original stories, they all face mortal danger before the happy ending.

The usefulness of terror or fear as well as destructive tendencies have been pointed out by distinguished child-psychoanalysts. According to the esteemed child psychologist Bruno Bettelheim, fairy tales enable children to explore themes and fears of growing up. Children are often unable to express their existential anxieties and dilemmas in words or can only do so indirectly. "The fairy tale ... addresses itself directly to them: the need to be loved and the fear that one is thought worthless; the love of life and the fear of death. Further, the fairy tale offers solutions that the child can grasp on his level of understanding."[1]

Melanie Klein also values terror in classical fairy tales as a valuable tool for identifying mental health issues and working through children's fears. She writes:

I have particularly selected listening to Grimm's tales without anxiety manifestations as an indication of the mental health of children because of all the various children known to me there are only very few who do so. Probably partly from a desire to avoid this discharge of anxiety a number of modified versions of these tales have appeared and in modern education other less terrifying tales, ones that do not touch so much—pleasurably and painfully—upon repressed complexes are preferred. I am of the opinion, however, that with the assistance of analysis there is no need to avoid these tales but that they can be used directly as a standard and an expedient.[2]

It is noteworthy that Klein prefers the more terrifying versions, which address repressed complexes. However, the tendency to offer both written and audiovisual narratives that do not cause fear to children has grown in the decades following her article, as there has been a growing concern not to scare children. As Buckingham notes, the main concern that parents voice with regard to their children watching violent media and films is not that they will imitate violence but rather that they will be frightened.[3]

However, the aims and functions of scary narratives are not limited to causing fear. Donald Winnicott points to yet another function of scary stories: working through destructive and aggressive ideas. He proposes that those "ideas must be there, and when they gradually appear in play or in dreams she [the mother] is not surprised, and she even provides stories or story-books which carry on the themes that arise spontaneously in the child's mind."[4] Children could therefore benefit both from identifying, empathizing or sympathizing with the main protagonist of fairy tales who strives for good and has to overcome obstacles and dangers representing repressed complexes, as well as identifying, empathizing or sympathizing with the evil characters, representing destructive tendencies.

In many Western cultures, children get the chance to dress up as evil characters, scare others and get scared at Halloween. Halloween points to contradictions in our myths and ideas of childhood. Children are often seen as vulnerable as well as innocent and inherently good, hence the mellowing down of many popular narratives for children and avoidance of violence. Developmental psychology and psychoanalysis, though, see childhood as a struggle with repressed complexes and aggressive tendencies. Halloween along with some written or audiovisual narratives provide a "safe space" for dramatizing repressed fears or destructive tendencies, as they are clearly separated from everyday life and reality. Not surprisingly, there is a huge market of Halloween products, venues and services aimed at children and teenagers that had already been well established by the early '90s.[5]

Halloween also offers adults the chance to get scared, through the film industry. As Rogers notes, there is a link between horror films and

Halloween. Although there is no precise moment in time that could be pinpointed as establishing that link, in the '70s a lot of horror movies had opening nights close to Halloween and horror films became the dominant genre around Halloween.[6] Quite tellingly, *Halloween* is widely considered to be prototypical of slasher films,[7] a subgenre of horror films characterized by graphic violence.

It seems that a Halloween horror movie for children was the logical next step. More recently, the need to let children explore their fears by engaging with horror films has been voiced in public discourse.[8] Yet, how do you avoid frightening children who are mentally healthy? It goes without saying that graphic violence does not feature in this horror film for children, but other methods are also used to reduce the feeling of horror.

A key factor in reducing horror is that the film is a genre hybrid: a horror film, a children's film and a teen movie that also alludes to action-adventure and fantasy films. The main protagonist is the babysitter, who is a young teenager. A central theme of the film is also in accordance with teen movies' conventions: the negotiation of the norms of adulthood, as she overcomes her own childhood fears and assumes responsibilities that focus on keeping a child safe, thus conforming to an adult role. As teen movies' protagonists try to assimilate ideals of adulthood that are normative, class, gender and race also play a part. The African American protagonist was not an obvious choice, as both teen movies and action-adventure films have neglected people of color.[9] It is in keeping, however, with a new trend in both action-adventure films and television programs and children's films to have non-white protagonists, a trend evident in Disney films and some Marvel films and television series.

The protagonist's gender, though, is stereotypical for a babysitter. The norms of adulthood that she will conform to are not stereotypical of a homemaker, though. As the narrative progresses and conventions of multiple genres are used, the protagonist can also be read as a female action heroine as well as the Final Girl.[10] Scholars have pointed out the link that exists between the Final Girl and the action heroine battling a monster. It has also been noted that the link becomes stronger where young heroines are concerned. The main difference between the Final Girl and the adult action heroine seems to be that the latter is (over)sexualized. Young heroines in both horror film and action-adventure are clever and brave and they react quickly, therefore strengthening the inter-genre link.[11] In this case, the protagonist evolves from a shy underdog to a brave monster-hunter. As we watch her diving into action and facing monsters successfully, we develop the expectation that she will use her newly acquired action skills to survive.

These expectations are strengthened by the narrative structure. The film's narrative format is complex in that it employs conventions from different genres, but it is rather straightforward in its use of the conventional three-act structure. Petridis explains:

> The function of the first act is to present all necessary information about the fictional world and the main characters as well as the main conflict of the plot, the second act develops the story and complicates the conflict with more antagonistic forces and obstacles, while the third act is maintained to solve the main conflict.[12]

It should be noted here that despite the film's hybridity and allusions to other media analyzed below, it does not display a high degree of "self-consciousness" or a complex timeline and therefore cannot be considered to adopt the mode of postclassical narration.[13] The classical three-act structure and employment of other genres can be reassuring for the audience. Teen movies, children's films and action-adventure films do not feature any deaths of good characters or main protagonists in the second or third act, and, more often than not, they have happy endings. As I will argue, the film uses these shared conventions and cultivates the expectation that all will be well in the end.

We will also be looking at aesthetics and creative choices used to contain the uncanny. The main difference between audiovisual texts—whether cinematic or on streaming platforms—and written texts is the plethora of sensory stimulation. It is perhaps significant that psychoanalysts and developmental psychologists refer to written texts, which are meant to arouse the imagination yet rely on the interpretation and perhaps filtering of words. Audiovisual texts address multiple senses simultaneously and could cause terror or a feeling of the uncanny with more immediacy. As Freeland notes with regard to a maître of horror: "The dark or uncanny feeling of the film [*The Birds*] is created by the medium as a whole. Hitchcock used music, sound, setting, acting, and visual effects to create and sustain an atmosphere of intense dread."[14]

I will argue that *A Babysitter's Guide to Monster Hunting* aims to arouse feelings of uncanniness, yet uses audiovisual means to reduce the dread. In order to discuss evoking and containing the uncanny, we need to define the concept. "The uncanny is not simply an experience of strangeness or alienation. More specifically, it is a peculiar commingling of the familiar and the unfamiliar."[15] The concept of uncanny has been redefined and used in literary criticism, philosophy and social studies by various important scholars. Its detailed definition, alterations in meaning and various uses are beyond the scope of this essay but have been analyzed in depth by Royle and Μπουσκα among others.[16]

The uncanny does not always cause dread. It is connected, though, with a return of the repressed and a blurring of Thus, the uncanny is often linked to fears and/or images of dismemberment that could potentially allude to the fear of castration. It is also linked to the return of the dead or being buried alive, fears that blur the boundaries of life and death. The uncanny is also related to dolls or mechanical movement, as they blur the boundaries between animate and inanimate.[17] Freud links the uncanny to a repressed desire for eternal life that can therefore be experienced through zombies, the undead or monsters that cannot be killed.[18]

The film's spooky elements are based on rendering familiar objects unfamiliar, blurring the lines between the known and the unknown, the inanimate and the animate—a technique that has often been used in the horror genre in addition to threats of death and dismemberment. At the same time, the uncanniness and horror are contained by preparing the audience for scary scenes, timing that does not prolong suspense, costumes and acting that stress performativity, genre hybridity and the consequent implicit promise of a happy ending.

The opening scene is indicative of the film's relation to the uncanny, as it uses elements that recur throughout the film. It opens on a stormy night with shots of the sky. It is a rather stereotypical opening for a horror film that remains ambiguous: it could be an opening for a film with a supernatural theme or it could be a realistic stormy night as a setting for realistic dangers. This ambiguity as to the nature of the fictional world hints to the uncanny. Seulin notes that Freud refers to literature and aesthetics with regard to art creating ambiguity in relation to the world where the story unfolds:

> The author can make his reader believe that he locates the action of his work in the ordinary physical reality, which is a frustrating solution for the reader, who finds himself caught in spite of himself. Elsewhere, more subtly, the author may leave aside the assessment judgment on the nature of the world in which he or she evolves his or her action, leaving the reader to imagine that this is a mundane reality, in order to surprise him or her even more.[19]

This kind of ambiguity is somewhat inherent in film, as it is photorealistic, constantly alluding to an ordinary physical reality, yet often creates fantasy worlds. Many of the shots that follow in this opening sequence are also uncanny: a teddy bear blinking, a door closing, mechanical devices switching on, a toy dinosaur appearing in a different place and roaring and a wardrobe door opening are all images that blur the boundaries between the animate and the inanimate. The objects used are familiar yet rendered unfamiliar through creating uncertainty as to whether they are indeed inanimate. The uncanny is intertwined with terror in this sequence, as we watch a scared little girl. The film repeatedly evokes the uncanny by blurring the boundaries between the animate and the inanimate.

This ambiguity between animate and inanimate is further linked to the supernatural. The wardrobe door opens, smoke comes out and a monstrous figure with fingers that can lengthen appears. The supernatural will also feature throughout the film, both through the central themes of nightmares becoming real and monsters appearing as well as through allusions to witches and potions.

What is crucial in the first sequence is that although no shots are from the point of view of the little girl, we share her view of the world, where inanimate or mechanical objects might have a life of their own. Seulin notes that, "[d]epending on the identification with the character, the uncanny may or may not arise."[20] Through avoiding a series of point-of-view shots, the film does not strengthen identification, thus possibly reducing the dread for the audience. On the other hand, this choice reinforces ambiguity, as we do not know whether the girl imagines these things or if they are really happening.

The film then moves forward in time, focusing on Kelly, the scared little girl in the first sequence, who is now a teenager having the nightmare described above or reliving the scene from her past. The shift in time is simultaneously a shift in genre, as the film now becomes a conventional teen or school movie, focusing on the nerdy teenager who gets picked on at school yet is a genius. Kelly in known at school as the "Monster Girl," because she claimed to have been attacked by a monster when she was a child.

Quite typically, she has a crush on a popular boy with little hope of getting noticed by him. Based on the genre conventions of teen films and school movies, there are implicit expectations that Kelly will use her special gift in mathematics to turn from underdog to heroine and that she will get the boy in the end.

The third theme is introduced in the following scene, as we learn that it is Halloween. Halloween films belong to various genres—horror movies, teen films and children's films—that employ terror to a greater or lesser extent. Halloween, however, is not just linked to terror and death, it is also a day for dressing up and assuming different roles. The film will employ dressing up to make intertextual and intermedia allusions to mythology, fairy tales, children's popular culture, the music industry and theater and to foreground its own constructiveness.

The last scene of the first act sets up the unfolding of the plot, as Kelly unwillingly agrees to babysit for her mother's boss, nicknamed the "Ice Queen" by Kelly and her mother and described as calculating and possibly vengeful. When Kelly goes to her house, her mother's boss appears actually dressed up as the Ice Queen—an ironic choice, briefly commented upon by Kelly, who asks, "The Ice Queen?" (8:33). The allusion to the fairy tale is thus stressed, and it is carried further as Kelly walks into a house with a lot of glass with stickers depicting ice, where she later discovers the little boy she will be babysitting, Jacob, hiding away in his tent, frightened (9:30). The mother then stresses that she will be back at midnight, sharp. This will later provide a deadline and contribute to a sense of urgency and suspense when Jacob gets abducted but can also be read as an allusion to Cinderella, expanding intermedia links to fairy tales.

Foregrounding dressing up and allusions to different texts, media and cultural industries can provide a safety net, because they can all be read as "not real." These allusions are consistently made throughout the text with regard to main characters and contain the uncanny. The main evil character is the Stealer of Dreams, more often referred to as the Grand Guignol, a theatrical name for "a dramatic entertainment of a sensational or horrific nature, originally a sequence of short pieces as performed at the Grand Guignol theatre in Paris."[21] The allusion to the Grand Guignol may also hint at the influence that works produced there at the end of the 19th century have had on slasher films.[22] Even if the allusion is read as a wink to the adult audience, there are other elements linking him to the entertainment industry. His sleek and performative movements, purple long coat, heavy makeup and rings on every finger allude to rock or heavy metal stars. The film does not glorify him, though, as he is extremely filthy, thus creating a grotesque figure. The allusions to the entertainment industry, music and theater foreground the fact that he is a constructed character and thus contain the sense of uncanny, created by his impossibly long fingers and tail that leaves burn marks.

Similarly, the second evil character, the Cat Lady, is introduced as a former silent movie star. Her long white robe, glittery heavy makeup and smooth long movements act as constant reminders of her being an actress. They are reminiscent of an era when exaggerated or stylized movements made up for the lack of sound and stress the performativity and constructed nature of her role. Though the entrance to her place looks like an abandoned bar or cinema theater, with a long, sheltered entrance and pink neon lights, it is very dark. The Cat Lady is also based on stereotypical images of witches as older women with cats. The sense of performativity and dressing up is also used here to contain the uncanny. We initially see the Cat Lady sitting on a black sofa. Liz and Kelly wonder where the cats are, as Liz is having an allergic reaction to them. The allergic reaction and the dialogue prepare the audience for the appearance of the cats and the uncanny scene that follows. The sofa is later revealed to be made out of living black cats (1:04:15) that chase Kelly when the Cat Lady orders them to eat her alive. The horror of the inanimate sofa turning to cats that are willing to dismember the protagonist is framed by dressing-up and performative elements.

The film invests again on blurring boundaries between animate and inanimate to evoke feelings of uncanniness but also proceeds to the threats of dismemberment and being eaten alive. Fears of death and dismemberment are at the heart of Freud's notion of the uncanny. The threat, however, is never actualized and there are no images of the cats attacking Kelly. On the contrary, the cats running toward her are soon turned into playful pets, as Kelly uses laser lights to distract them.

The rest of the evil characters and monsters, the Toadies, are short, rather cute, colorful and naïve, as they trade anything or anyone for sparkly things. The Toadies act as servants or helpers of the Grand Guignol. Although the Toadies are helpers/servants, they are rather important to the film, as they feature in many scenes. Indicative of the importance of the cute, unrealistic monsters and the comic relief they occasionally provide is that the title sequence at the end is made up almost entirely of images of Toadies. They could be placed in a category of cute monsters, along with the Minions from *Despicable Me* (2010) or Mike from *Monsters, Inc.* (2001).

Through allusions to dressing up, popular culture, theater and film and most evidently through presenting the Toadies a toylike monsters, the film moves away from Freud's uncanny as well as the "Uncanny Valley." As Hutchings notes, the Japanese roboticist Masahiro Mori termed a common unease we have towards virtual protagonists the "uncanny valley." "This is true of animated cartoons as well. The more stylized they are, the more comfortable we feel with the portrayal, but if a drawing is almost human, an avatar, it is deeply unsettling."[23] Animated children's films like *The Polar Express* (2004) and science-fiction animated films like *Final Fantasy: The Spirits Within* (2001) "have so far fallen into the uncanny valley" because of the photo-realistic animation.[24] The Toadies are the closest to animation and computer-generated effects that the film gets, but the characters are obviously not real, too toylike to evoke the uncanny in Freud's or Mori's sense.

Their only link to the uncanny is carrying over the theme of water monsters. As their name implies, the Toadies are amphibious, therefore thematically related to the fish tank in Jacob's room and the dismembered tentacle of an octopus that emerges from the tank and is part of Jacob's nightmares coming to life. The sea monsters theme is a motif in the film. Kelly and Liz, the protagonists, end up in a sea- and shark-themed play area with a ball pit (23:29–27–58). It is a familiar setting turned unfamiliar and uncanny by the presence of the Toadies, who try to kidnap the baby that Liz is babysitting. However, when a Toadie chases Kelly through a pool of soft balls, barely emerging, the scene is like a parody of *Jaws*. It provides comic relief, undermining any sense of suspense that had been built up.

Keeping scary scenes short and supplying comic relief are used to contain the uncanny. It should be noted here that no scary or suspenseful scene is more than a minute in length. Breaking the horror-movie convention of creating suspense by prolonging danger, e.g., by the evil character approaching unbeknownst to potential victims, the protagonists are never in danger for long, limiting the sense of suspense for the audience. The film also breaks a relevant convention of showing the audience where the evil character is while the protagonists do not realize they are in danger. In this case, there are no nasty surprises. Scenes that could become especially uncanny and scary, such as the flesh-eating cats, are also introduced through dialogue. Perhaps more importantly, the film uses a narrative convention from action films to structure its plot. Instead of the protagonists being hunted down, as is often the case in horror films, the babysitters hunt down the bad guys or—in this case—monsters. This convention places the protagonists in a position of knowledge and power.

The protagonists are empowered not only via their role as hunters in the narrative, but also through their traits and special powers. Kelly starts off as a nerd who gets bullied at school but also as a math genius. Liz, who appears when Jacob gets kidnapped and becomes Kelly's companion in their adventure, starts off as an action chick. She is blond, drives a big motorcycle, wears a leather jacket and carries a baby on her back. Her coolness extends to the baby, who is wearing an old-fashioned helmet (19: 20). Liz belongs to the Order of the Babysitters, a group that backs up Kelly and Liz in their adventure, providing gadgets, weapons and potions. The members of the Order of the Babysitters refer to mythology, use potions and have a huge book on monsters. Cool gadgets alluding to spy films aside, the potions, mythology and particularly the big book of knowledge would place them into the category of teen good witches fighting monsters and evil. Popular drama series often featuring and addressed to teens feature good witches in training, relying on books of spells and potions. The book in particular could be read as a trademark of the subgenre.[25] Like all the genres used here, witch teen dramas also share the good ending convention whereby good prevails over evil.

Liz, the action heroine/good witch, becomes a co-protagonist, but her role is mainly as Kelly's helper. The scenes leading to the final battle and the final battle itself are indicative of Kelly being the main heroine, as discussed below. Liz and the other teenagers in the Order of the Babysitters function as a team that backs up Kelly. As Neale notes, in the action-adventure films, there are two tendencies: the lone hero or the hero interacting with a microcosmic group.[26] Their function in the narrative is typical of a simple narrative model that is

> both linear and additive, involving stories in which a single protagonist (or group of protagonists) sets out to achieve a particular end, encounters in the

process an indefinite number of obstacles and opponents ..., overcomes them with varying degrees of difficulty and possibly with the assistance of a helper or helpers and duly achieves the desired end.[27]

In this case, the microcosmic group of helpers has a triple function: to provide help and a safety net for the heroine, implicitly reassuring the audience that she will prevail; to help the protagonists overcome traumas; and to function as a stepping stone for Kelly's socialization, within the teen film genre. The group helps in various ways, including making the potion that will eventually kill the Grand Guignol, as explained below. Liz and the group also function as a therapy group. It is worth noting that the narrative is linear, with the exception of flashbacks to Kelly's and Liz's childhoods. Wojcik-Andrews notices that flashbacks in children's films are often used as a therapeutic process, helping the hero or heroine— and by extension the audience—to overcome traumas.[28] The *Babysitter's Guide to Monster Hunting* revisits traumas in the protagonists' childhoods and actualizes overcoming them through killing the Grand Guignol and extinguishing Jacob's nightmares. Liz and Kelly are not the only ones who have had similar traumatic experiences. All the teens in the Order of the Babysitters have been attacked by monsters, so they believe Kelly. She feels accepted and becomes part of the group. Her newly found confidence and Liz's advice will help her triumph over evil and eventually get her romantic interest's attention.

It should further be noted here that although it is Liz who is initially depicted as a stereotypical "action chick," the film's narrative focuses on Kelly. The plot towards the end of the film is exemplary of a linear narrative focusing on the main heroine. Kelly and Liz have a bonding scene (58:13–1:00:00) in which Liz, making herself vulnerable, admits that she had lost her brother to the Grand Guignol. Liz then gets taken by the Grand Guignol, leaving it up to Kelly to save the day with help from the Order of the Babysitters. The underdog becomes the main heroine who will have to save both Liz and Jacob.

When she is hypnotized by the Grand Guignol, Liz unwillingly and briefly turns into a rival, and there is a battle between Liz and Kelly that further foregrounds Kelly as the main heroine (1:13:28–1:14:48). It is Kelly who eventually defeats the Grand Guignol, using the potion prepared by the Order of the Babysitters. Perhaps more importantly, Kelly uses math calculations to execute perfectly a move she has learned from the big book at the Order of the Babysitters' headquarters. The use of math here and Kelly's use of technology, in particular light gadgets that she makes and uses to defeat the cats, need to be highlighted. Kelly's talent in mathematics and technology undermines gender stereotypes that are also common in children's films. As Wojcik-Andrews notes, "technology in children's films is often engendered,"[29] Although the film has not built up action scenes as spectacle, in this scene of the final battle, the move is spectacular, choreographed and shown in slow motion, transforming Kelly through images as well as narrative to an action-adventure heroine (1:21:00–1:22:41).

The move is executed accurately in order to put the potion straight to the Grand Guignol's heart. It is the culmination of the third act, where the Grand Guignol eventually dies. According to the big book, he is notoriously difficult to kill, a trait that links him to the undead. The need to aim for his heart strengthens his relation to zombies. As Petridis notes, a common theme in horror films is the emergence of the monster after its alleged death.[30] The undead are also key in evoking the uncanny, as they blur the boundaries between life and death.

The Grand Guignol and his relation to Jacob could be read as a reversal of a story that Freud uses in *The Uncanny*. He uses Hoffmann's story "The Sandman," in which a boy is afraid that the Sandman will take his eyes if he does not sleep. The Grand Guignol in the film, in opposition to Freud's story, will actualize Jacob's nightmares if he sleeps. Not sleeping in Freud's story, along with the fears mentioned in it, i.e. the fear of the father and the fear of witnessing and losing one's eyes, have all been linked to the primal scene and the fear of castration.[31] The reversal of the punishable act, not sleeping versus sleeping, shifts focus from witnessing the primal scene to the fear of death. Jacob's unwilling relation to the Grand Guignol who wants to enable him to make his nightmares real implies an identification with the evil character.

When Jacob, who has the power to turn nightmares into reality, gets kidnapped, he bravely refuses to go to sleep so that the grand Guignol cannot take advantage of his power. This narrative choice undermines gender stereotypes, as Jacob both undertakes the traditional role of the princess waiting to be rescued and valiantly resists falling asleep, displaying both stereotypically feminine and masculine qualities. However, he spends most of the film's duration trapped and his resistance is passive, therefore he does not partake in much of the action. It is a rather bizarre choice for a children's film to give a supporting role to the only child in it.

As we have seen, the film also uses a lot of conventions for teen dramas. It seems that there may be a degree of uncertainty as to the age of the intended audience. Another possible explanation is the stereotypical belief that kids look up to older children or teenagers. In any case, the film seems to redeem the choice to overlook Jacob when he gets to extinguish his nightmares through standing up to them. Being in control of one's fears can be seen as coming of age. Carroll and Buckingham see a "pedagogical dimension" in horror films, since they show audiences how "normal," psychologically healthy characters react to the monsters that represent "the 'dark' side of human experience" or one's fears.[32]

Jacob initially sees the monsters as threats out of his control. The audience is also invited to see them as threatening to Jacob, but they could be read as representing his fears and his dark side. The dismembered octopus tentacle could also be a transfer of his own fear of dismemberment or his castration complex. "The disturbing theme of sliced limbs is linked to the repressed castration Complex."[33] It is also important to note that Jacob is not just a victim. He is essential to Grand Guignol's plan, albeit an unwilling accessory. The Grand Guignol needs him to make monsters real and can only bring to life the specific monsters that Jacob dreams of. The characters thus identify with each other—the Grand Guignol representing Jacob's evil, dark side. It has been highlighted by Freud and others that "the uncanniness of the double [is] being intensified by the spontaneous transmission of mental processes from one of these persons to the other— what we would call telepathy—so that the one becomes co-owner of the other's knowledge, emotions, and experience."[34]

The process of telepathy is implicitly based on the omnipotence of thoughts, an omnipotence further exemplified here by the very actualization of Jacob's nightmares—the monsters in his mind becoming real creatures in the film's fictional world. The belief that we are able to control the world with our mind is central in Freud's concept of the uncanny.[35] Along with animism and superstition, we could add that bringing dreams to life is based on primary narcissism and the omnipotence of thoughts. The solution offered by the film—Jacob telling his nightmares to go away after the Grand Guignol's death—is also based on Jacob's narcissistic omnipotence. Perhaps this affirmation of the omnipotence of thoughts is considered suitable for children or maybe just fitting in this paranormal world.

Kelly helps Jacob to believe in himself just before he wills his nightmares away. She functions as surrogate mother, and their apparent affection for each other could potentially be read as a step away from the Oedipal complex for Jacob, since he directs his desire away from his mother and towards another female figure. For Kelly, taking up a mother's role, an adult role, connotes growing up.

The final sequence also focuses on growing up as well as fighting monsters. Kelly gets a message from the boy she is interested in. Although teens' romantic interests feature in horror films, the promised happy ending for the underdog fits in better with teen or school films. The romance here also undercuts the uncanny, as she is reading up on monsters in order to become a babysitter in training. She is reading up on the Spider Queen, a focus that obviously prepares a sequel yet also evokes the uncanny, as we see an image of a half spider, half woman that blurs boundaries between humans and insects to create a scary monster. The Spider Queen also fits in with conventions of horror movies—particularly sequels—that often end with the threat that evil is still out there. As in many of the film's scenes, the genre hybridity contains the uncanny.

The structure of the opening sequences as well as the last one reveal that genre hybridity contains the uncanny by providing relief from the monster theme. As analyzed above, genre hybridity along with the linear narrative structure builds expectation that good will win out over evil, based both on genre conventions and on the transformation of the nerdy teen to an action-adventure heroine supported by a group of helpers. Allusions to other media and popular culture stress performativity, highlighting the construction and reinforcing the playfulness of the audiovisual text, so that the film can provide a safe space, separated from reality, where children can explore fears and aggressive tendencies. Other aesthetic choices also play a part in containing the uncanny: obviously unreal monsters like the Toadies move away from the uncanny valley. Potentially frightening scenes, like the sofa turning into dangerous black cats, are anticipated in the dialogue, while suspense is always limited, since frightening scenes last less than a minute. By making all these creative choices with regard to narrative and aesthetics, the film can contain the uncanny while simultaneously evoking it by exposing children to blurred boundaries between the animate and the inanimate, humans and animals, death and life, self and other as well as fears of death and dismemberment.

## Notes

1. Bruno Bettelheim, "The Struggle for Meaning," in *Folk and Fairy Tales: Second Concise Edition*, eds. Martin Hallett and Barbara Karasek (Peterborough: Broadview Press, 1996), 179–183.
2. Melanie Klein, *Love, Guilt and Reparation and Other Works, 1921–1945* (New York: Free Press, 1984), 52.
3. David Buckingham, *Moving Images: Understanding Children's Responses to Television* (Manchester: Manchester UP, 1996), 69–71.
4. D.W. Winnicott, *The Child and the Family: First Relationships*, ed. Janet Hardenberg, Second Publication (London: Tavistock, 1962), 98.
5. Nicholas Rogers, *Halloween: From Pagan Ritual to Party Night* (Oxford: Oxford UP, 2002), 104–105.
6. Rogers, *Halloween*, 105–108.
7. Sotiris Petridis, *Anatomy of the Slasher Film: A Theoretical Analysis* Jefferson, NC: McFarland, 2019), 5.
8. See Catherine Lester, *Horror Films for Children: Fear and Pleasure in American Cinema* (London: Bloomsbury Academic, 2022).
9. For the conventions of teen movies, see Frances Smith, *Rethinking the Hollywood Teen Movie: Gender, Genre and Identity* (Edinburgh: Edinburgh UP, 2017), 85–187, and for action-adventure and race, see Steve Neale, *Genre and Hollywood* (London: Routledge, 2000), 48–49.
10. The Final Girl as the final survivor in horror films and the conventional representations of this character are analytically discussed in Carol J. Clover, *Men, Women, and*

*Chain Saws: Gender in the Modern Horror Film*, Updated Edition (Princeton: Princeton UP, 2015), and Petridis, *Anatomy of the Slasher Film*.

11. Andrea Ruthven, "*Other* Girl Powers: Final Girls, Super Girls and Kamala Khan's Ms. Marvel," in *Final Girls, Feminism and Popular Culture*, eds. Kataryna Paszkiewicz and Stacy Rusnak (London: Palgrave MacMillan, 20020), 194.

12. Sotiris Petridis, *The Netflix Vision of Horror: A Narrative Structural Analysis of Original Series* (Jefferson, NC: McFarland, 2021), 2.

13. For the traits of the post-classical mode of narration see Eleftheria Thanouli, "Post-Classical Narration: A New Paradigm in Contemporary Cinema," *New Review of Film and Television Studies* 4, no. 3 (2006): 191.

14. Cynthia Freeland, "Natural Evil in the Horror Film: Alfred Hitchcock's *The Birds*," in *The Changing Face of Evil in Film and Television*, ed. Martin F. Norden (Amsterdam: Rodopi, 2007), 60.

15. Nicholas Royle, *The Uncanny* (Manchester: Manchester UP, 2003), 1.

16. Royle, *The Uncanny*, and Penelope Buska, "The Uncanny—A Psychoanalytic Study in Film" (PhD diss., Aristotle University of Thessaloniki, 2016).

17. Royle, *The Uncanny*, 2–3.

18. Peter Hutchings, *The Horror Film* (New York: Routledge, 2004), 60.

19. Christian Seulin, "About Freud's 'The Uncanny,'" in *About Freud's "The Uncanny*,*"* eds. Catalina Bronstein and Christina Seulin, Contemporary Freud: Turning Points and Critical Issues series (London: Routledge, 2020), 4.

20. Seulin, "About Freud's 'The Uncanny,'" 4.

21. "Grand Guignol," *Oxford Languages and Google*, accessed December 12, 2022, https://languages.oup.com/google-dictionary-en/.

22. Petridis, *Anatomy of the Slasher Film*, 5.

23. Hutchings, *The Horror Film*, 60.

24. Anneleen Masschelein, *The Unconcept: The Freudian Uncanny in Late-Twentieth-Century Theory* (Albany: State University of New York Press, 2011), 172.

25. On the evolution of the book convention in teen witch drama, see Emily Brick, "Spellbound: The Significance of Spellbooks in the Depiction of Witchcraft on Screen," in *Terrifying Texts: Essays on Books of Good and Evil in Horror Cinema*, eds. Cynthia J. Miller and A. Bowdoin Van Riper (Jefferson, NC: McFarland, 2018), 175–185.

26. Steve Neale, *Genre and Hollywood* (London: Routledge, 2000), 49.

27. David Herman, Manfrend Jahn and Marie-Laure Ryan, eds., *Routledge Encyclopedia of Narrative Theory* (London: Routledge, 2005), 367.

28. Ian Wojcik-Andrews, *Children's Films: History, Ideology, Pedagogy, Theory* (New York: Garland, 2000), 167–168.

29. Wojcik-Andrews, *Children's Films*, 156.

30. Petridis, *Anatomy of the Slasher Film*, 51.

31. Seulin, "About Freud's 'The Uncanny,'" 1–3.

32. Carroll's and Buckingham's views are discussed in Buckingham, *Moving Images*, 111.

33. Seulin, "About Freud's 'The Uncanny,'" 3.

34. Veronica L. Schanoes, *Fairy Tales, Myth, and Psychoanalytic Theory: Feminism and Retelling the Tale* (London: Routledge, 2016), 115.

35. For further information on the omnipotence of thoughts, animism and primary narcissism see Seulin, "About Freud's 'The Uncanny,'" 2.

## Works Cited

Bettelheim, Bruno. "The Struggle for Meaning." In *Folk and Fairy Tales: Second Concise Edition*, edited by Martin Hallett and Barbara Karasek, 179–183. Peterborough: Broadview Press, 1996.

Brick, Emily. "Spellbound: The Significance of Spellbooks in the Depiction of Witchcraft on Screen." In *Terrifying Texts: Essays on Books of Good and Evil in Horror Cinema*, edited by Cynthia J. Miller and A. Bowdoin Van Riper, 175–185. Jefferson, NC: McFarland, 2018.

Buckingham, David. *Moving Images: Understanding Children's Responses to Television.* Manchester: Manchester UP, 1996.

Buska, Penelope. "The Uncanny—A Psychoanalytic Study in Film." PhD diss., Aristotle University of Thessaloniki, 2016.

Clover, Carol J. *Men, Women, and Chain Saws: Gender in the Modern Horror Film—Updated Edition.* Princeton: Princeton UP, 2015.

Freeland, Cynthia. "Natural Evil in the Horror Film: Alfred Hitchcock's *The Birds.*" In *The Changing Face of Evil in Film and Television*, edited by Martin F. Norden, 55–70. Amsterdam: Rodopi, 2007.

Herman, David, Manfrend Jahn, and Marie-Laure Ryan, eds. *Routledge Encyclopedia of Narrative Theory.* London: Routledge, 2005.

Hutchings, Peter. *The Horror Film.* New York: Routledge, 2004.

Klein, Melanie. *Love, Guilt and Reparation and Other Works, 1921–1945.* New York: Free Press, 1984.

Lester, Catherine. *Horror Films for Children: Fear and Pleasure in American Cinema.* London: Bloomsbury Academic, 2022

Masschelein, Anneleen. *The Unconcept: The Freudian Uncanny in Late-Twentieth-Century Theory.* Albany: State University of New York Press, 2011.

Neale, Steve. *Genre and Hollywood.* London: Routledge, 2000.

Petridis, Sotiris. *Anatomy of the Slasher Film: A Theoretical Analysis.* Jefferson, NC: McFarland, 2019.

Petridis, Sotiris. *The Netflix Vision of Horror: A Narrative Structural Analysis of Original Series.* Jefferson, NC: McFarland, 2021.

Rogers, Nicholas. *Halloween: From Pagan Ritual to Party Night.* Oxford: Oxford UP, 2002.

Royle, Nicholas. *The Uncanny.* Manchester: Manchester UP, 2003.

Ruthven, Andrea. "*Other* Girl Powers: Final Girls, Super Girls and Kamala Khan's Ms. Marvel." In *Final Girls, Feminism and Popular Culture*, edited by Kataryna Paszkiewicz and Stacy Rusnak, 189–208. London: Palgrave Macmillan, 2020.

Schanoes, Veronica L. *Fairy Tales, Myth, and Psychoanalytic Theory: Feminism and Retelling the Tale.* London: Routledge, 2016.

Seulin, Christian. "About Freud's 'The Uncanny.'" In *About Freud's "The Uncanny,"* edited by Catalina Bronstein and Christina Seulin, 1–5. Series: Contemporary Freud: Turning Points and Critical Issues. London: Routledge, 2020.

Smith, Frances. *Rethinking the Hollywood Teen Movie: Gender, Genre and Identity.* Edinburgh: Edinburgh UP, 2017.

Thanouli, Eleftheria. "Post-Classical Narration: A New Paradigm in Contemporary Cinema." *New Review of Film and Television Studies* 4, no. 3 (2006): 183–96.

Winnicott, D.W. *The Child and the Family: First Relationships.* Edited by Janet Hardenberg. London: Tavistock, 1962.

Wojcik-Andrews, Ian. *Children's Films: History, Ideology, Pedagogy, Theory.* New York: Garland, 2000.

# *The Hauntings* on Netflix

## Hill House *and* Bly Manor *as the Forms of the Serial Anthology in the Binge-Watching Era*

### Anna Rufer Bílá *and* Klára Feikusová

In the age of streaming and surplus production of original television shows, *peak TV*,[1] a program with a clearly defined ending might be the solution for audiences overwhelmed with content options. This is where the serial anthology seems to be an appropriate strategy. By serial anthology we mean an anthology where the transformation of setting, plot, and characters is limited not to single episodes but to seasons. *The Haunting of Hill House* (2018) and *The Haunting of Bly Manor* (2020) are examples of this narrative form and the subject of the present essay.

Within it, we discuss the general context of contemporary television, its main changes and challenges. The narrative structure of a serial anthology could represent an advantage for TV creators. It has a closed narrative that does not commit the audience to long-term viewing but also allows the story and characters to unfold. This form represents a type of narrative complexity as it works with intratextuality and, in the case of *The Hauntings*, with numerous narrative devices such as flashbacks, multiplied points of view, focalization, etc.[2] We approach the topic from the perspective of television narratology concerning the context of digitalization and streaming.

First, we provide a synopsis of the general shifts in the television industry leading up to the era of plenitude, binge-watching, and online TV. Subsequently, we present the main concepts of complex narrativity and serial anthology that are important to our analysis. This essay aims to use *The Haunting*'s example to introduce this updated form of a serial anthology and highlight its functionality in the era of plenitude.

## Context of Today's Television and Streaming Services

Antecedently, watching television was primarily defined as a coherent stream of programs, regardless of genre or format, all connected and entwined with commercial breaks. Simply put, it is the concept of flow.[3] The television flow is a central characteristic of linear television where the audience cannot choose when to watch a particular program—it was all prepared for them and served to them in a carefully planned schedule. This is not to say that such broadcasting does not exist anymore; it still is very much existent and watched. However, with the new media possibilities, the audience can stop the flow and make decisions about when, where, how, and what they want to watch. This new era of television can be defined as a post-flow era. Some authors use different terminology. For example, Jeremy G. Butler writes about network and post-network eras; John Ellis divides television history into eras of scarcity, availability, and plenty; and Mark Rogers, Michael Epstein, and Jimmie Reeves talk simply about eras of TV–I, TV–II, and TV–III. In all of these categorizations, we find similar characteristics—the first decades of television were the times of big television companies that controlled most of the market. It was the time of television flow, programming strategies, and least objectionable content designed to appeal to as many people as possible. Then the new technologies of cable and satellite television and video recorders came, and suddenly the audience had more control over what they were consuming and when. In today's world, the influence of the internet and digitalization brought new media like streaming services, where *all* the consumption control lies in the hands of the viewers—if they pay for the service. Michael Curtin describes contemporary television as a matrix era "characterized by interactive exchanges, multiple sites of productivity and diverse modes of interpretation and use."[4] Mareike Jenner even talks about the TV–IV era, "where viewing patterns, branding strategies, industrial structures, the way different media forms interact with each other or the various ways content is made available, completely shift away from the television set."[5] Either way, television is changing, and at the core stand new media.

We use the term *new media* to describe a broad set of communication technologies, from physical hardware to software, and all the applications available to distribute, store or consume media content. Digitalization is the primary process that enables this sort of change and is typical for all media types. As Henry Jenkins writes, all these changes lead to the current state of *convergence culture*. "By convergence, I mean the flow of content across multiple media platforms, the cooperation between multiple media industries, and the migratory behavior of media audiences who will go almost anywhere in search of the kinds of entertainment experiences they want."[6] For Jenkins, the convergence culture consists of three connected processes: media convergence, participatory culture, and collective intelligence. Media convergence refers to the hybridization of formerly distinct media technologies and circulation of one media content through various communication platforms. In the case of participatory culture and collective intelligence, Jenkins gives audiences a significant amount of control. He assumes that the consumers are active in their content choices, time management, or meaning making. An active audience is the kind that interacts with the media content and its creators and contributes to the formation of popular culture constantly. It is important to note, however, that while audiences certainly have the option, only some use it.

Moreover, it is also essential to reflect that all these changes are the outcome not only of technology but also of the way it is used. Either way, when publishing his book *Convergence Culture: Where Old and New Media Collide* (2006), Jenkins could only have anticipated some of the directions of changes in television production. At about the same time, we mark the birth of Netflix—the first of many successful streaming services that combine the elements of new media, convergence culture, and active audience participation.

The current era of television can be described as convergent, dynamic, and amplified. There are no new trends, but the original ones have been enhanced. We can still watch traditional, linear television that we know from the early network/flow/TV–I eras, but at the same time, we can consume the large amount that the VoD[7] platforms offer. Different types of television forms coexist. The offerings are only getting more extensive. We live in an era of plenitude:

> The condition of media culture today is a plenitude—a universe of products (websites, video games, blogs, books, films, television and radio programs, magazines, and so on) and practices (the making of all these products together with their remixing, sharing, and critiquing) so vast, varied, and dynamic that it is not comprehensible as a whole. The plenitude easily accommodates, indeed swallows up, the contradictory forces of high and popular culture, old and new media, conservative and radical social views. ... Digital technology has not eliminated any of [the traditional mass media] yet; instead, the digital realm provides reflections, extensions, and remediations of many, but not all, earlier forms.[8]

In other words, just as we stated earlier, the old and new media coexist, creating more media and content for audiences to consume. There is no longer any center that provides media content to the masses. Instead, the many different fragmented audiences search for their niche media experiences.

We argue that, in the era of plenitude, the audience seeks a certain form of stability in their media consumption. In the case of television, there are many offers from traditional linear stations, cable and satellite broadcasting, and online streaming services that sometimes are "too much." There are too many TV series, too many seasons, and too much time and emotional commitment. That is also why we talk more about the phenomenon of *comfort television*. People like to have a particular constant in their lives, something well-known and familiar. It could be their all-time favorite show they rewatch on repeat or a new TV show that brings them a sense of mental and/or physical comfort.

Another distinctive shift in both TV show production and the experiences of today's viewers relates to the phenomenon of binge-watching. As Dennis Broe writes:

> "The series are designed to be consumed over a short period. They are usually ten to thirteen episodes of an hour or less in duration for a season, taking approximately that many hours to consume, and so the ideal time to 'binge watch' is the weekend, with viewers boasting that they 'accomplished' watching the series' season in that time."[9]

Binge-watching is a strategy mainly used by VoD platforms such as Netflix, Amazon Prime Video, Hulu or HBO Max. Mareike Jenner suggests it functions on "three axes of industry-text-audience."[10] The industry uses a specific binge-model strategy to release new TV shows—usually by releasing the entire season at once. "The serial form combined with technologies that give viewers the authority to decide when to watch what, with the added benefit of avoiding interruptions by ads, seem to be what drives binge-watching."[11] Viewers' control over their own time is also a prominent characteristic of the active audience. Jenner also argues that the TV shows have a certain "binge-worthy"[12] quality to them. They are usually produced as complex narratives and labeled as quality or cult TV, thus indicating that they bring their viewers more considerable cultural capital, thereby justifying the bingeing (which is linked to the negative connotations of something excessive or unhealthy).

One of the ways to deal with the era of plenitude while also fulfilling the demand for binge-worthy shows can be the television anthology form. Because of its episodic and (in comparison) short form, anthology represents a way to stand out from the television production, overflooded with storytelling. The narrative form enables the audience to engage with the show for a particular time frame and set of characters. Such features can be an advantageous branding strategy in the era of plenitude. Shows of this kind provide a clear, brief, and straightforward idea of what to expect as a viewer, usually emphasizing an exciting topic, diverse characters, or a creative attitude toward genre expectations. For the viewer, the television anthology represents an appealing one-time event that requires little time or commitment. This is our central premise explored further in this essay.

## Complex Narrativity of Serial Anthology

Before we begin our analysis, we must address the terminology concerning the different television narrative forms. First, the anthology refers to a long-form program consisting of self-contained episodes bound together by a genre or topic. The anthology was especially popular in the 1950s and 1960s (*Playhouse 90, The Twilight Zone, The United States Steel Hour, The Outer Limits,* etc.). The form was practical as the audience was not obligated to watch all the episodes to understand the story since this was before the introduction of video recording devices. The anthology became less prevalent, probably because of its production cost as "each chapter requires a new stage, actors and plot,"[13] but never really disappeared. Serial anthology partially eschews these costs as the setting and plot change not every episode but every season. On the other hand, it can be used to boast its big budget, as in the case of *Guillermo del Toro's Cabinet of Curiosities* (2022), also created for Netflix, which features well-known horror directors (Catherine Hardwicke, Jennifer Kent) and established actors (F. Murray Abraham, Dan Stevens, Rupert Grint, Ben Barnes, Crispin Glover, etc.). Moreover, as with *American Horror Story* (2011– ) and *The Hauntings,* the creators can recycle the cast and give them new roles. The newest television show by Mike Flanagan, *The Midnight Club* (2022), uses the anthology as stories-within-a-main-story and lets the main protagonists play the characters of the stories they tell each other within the program. While García argues that the cost of an anthology is a reason why it is rare in the contemporary television landscape, there has been a slight rise in the number of productions. While some of them are traditionally stand-alone episodic shows, like *Black Mirror* (2011– ), *Amazing Stories* (2020), or *Lore* (2017–2018), others fall under the serial anthology form (*True Detective, Fargo, The Terror, Why Women Kill* and others). Serial anthology became popular with the success of *American Horror Story.* There is also a practical reason for this narrative form, as Dana Walden, then a chairman and CEO of Fox Television Group, explained in the context of the beginning of *American Crime Story*: "Miniseries are challenging business propositions because they don't really travel very well internationally. They're just sort of one-off events. And I kept saying to Ryan [Murphy], 'You can't do this because it is a terrible piece of business, because it is not an ongoing series.... We have to find a way to make it an ongoing series.'"[14]

Second, we distinguish between a series and a serial. In our understanding of these forms, we draw on Alberto N. García's definition, influenced by the writings of Sarah Kozloff: "Series refers to those shows whose characters and setting are recycled, but the story concludes in each individual episode. By contrast, in a serial the story and discourse do not come to a conclusion during an episode, and the threads are picked up again after a given hiatus."[15] Similarly, Jason Mittell differentiates between episodic and serial storytelling, even though he uses the term series more generally.[16] Both the series and serial incorporate a steady set of main characters and settings. However, in the former, the plot renews itself in each episode (like in the case of crime dramas and their case-of-the-week structure). In contrast, in the latter, the plot evolves throughout numerous episodes, an entire season, or all seasons. However, current television shows are usually more or less a combination of both episodic and serial narratives. As Dennis Broe states, "there is a continual tension between episodic closure and serial deferment."[17] According to Mittel, this tension is also one of the characteristics of narrative complexity:

> At its most basic level, narrative complexity redefines episodic forms under the influence of serial narration—not necessarily a complete merger of episodic and serial forms but a shifting balance. Rejecting the need for plot closure within every episode that typifies conventional episodic form, narrative complexity foregrounds ongoing stories across a range of genres. Complex television employs a range of serial techniques, with the underlying assumption that a series is a cumulative narrative that builds over time, rather than resetting back to a steady-state equilibrium at the end of every episode.[18]

Therefore, episodic storytelling can be used to advance the serial storytelling of a program.[19] This notion is especially important in *The Haunting of Hill House,* which combines both narratives forms, while *The Haunting of Bly Manor* mostly adheres to serial narration, with the exception of episode 5, "The Altar of the Dead," framed by secondary character Hannah's point of view, and the flashback episode "The Romance of Certain Old Clothes."

The narrative complexity cannot be defined only by the blending of serial and episodic narratives. After all, Mittell states that narrative hybridity is not reserved solely for complex television. Mittell considers the narrative complexity a narrational mode,[20] which manifests itself through self-reflexive and playful storytelling.[21] Concerning self-reflexivity, Mittell uses two crucial terms: operational aesthetic and narrative spectacle. The operational aesthetic refers to the mechanics of storytelling brought to the forefront, prompting the viewers to ask: "How are they doing this/how will they do it?" For Mittell, the operational aesthetic relates closely to the spectacular storytelling because "[t]he operational aesthetic is heightened in spectacular moments within narratively complex programs, specific sequences or episodes that we might consider akin to special effects."[22] The narrative spectacle (or narrative special effect) offers "baroque variations on themes and norms"[23] which can manifest themselves in the specific episodes (as in the "silent" episode, "Hush," on *Buffy the Vampire Slayer*) or the overall narration of a program ("real-time" narration of the serial *24*).

Complex television is more prone to dealing with the operational aesthetic and narrative spectacle because it purposefully confuses and challenges the audience, prompting them to rewatch the shows.[24] This derives from the fact that the narrative complexity is historically embedded, appearing in the late 1990s and continuing to this day. Mittell argues that this narrational mode has grown from the industrial changes in the 1980s and 1990s, such as narrowcasting; expansion of channels available; rising popularity of cable television; and technological innovations such as VHS, VCR and later DVDs, DVR, TiVo, and streaming portals. Moreover, the narrative complexity was allowed to develop thanks to "the changing perception of the medium's legitimacy and its resulting appeal to creators."[25]

Mittell's narrative complexity represents a useful device through which a serial anthology can be understood. It is also a new narrative form that combines different modes of storytelling—in this case, an anthology and serial—that usually works with the "variations on themes and norms" in each season (as neatly demonstrated on *American Horror Story*, where a horror subgenre or setting frames each season; *Murder House*, *Asylum*, *Freak Show*, *Roanoke*, *1984* and others). We define the serial anthology as the narrative form that uses continuous serial narratives throughout the season and then changes the setting, characters, and plot in the next season. Nevertheless, all seasons share unifying elements, usually genre (self-explanatory *American Horror Story* and *American Crime Story*, irreverent crime comedy *Fargo*, comedy/sitcom *Miracle Workers*, etc.), sometimes the cast but in the different roles (*American Horror Story*, *The Haunting of Hill House* and *Bly Manor*, *Miracle Workers*). The creators, mode of storytelling, and audiovisual style usually remain the same. While García suggests two terms for this distinct narrational form, series-miniseries and anthology series, we counteroffer our term, serial anthology. We consider García's terminology confusing and inaccurate. Although García differentiates between the series and serial, he uses the latter, which is imprecise because these programs use mostly serial narratives, not episodic ones.

Moreover, the miniseries describes a limited number of episodes with a definitive end (for that reason, they are sometimes referred to as limited series). Although miniseries can become regular serials (as in the case of *Big Little Lies*), they are intended to have just one season. For these reasons, the serial anthology is a more relevant and exact term. We explore three aspects of this narrative form. These are intratextual repetition of production elements, hybridization of serial and episodic narratives, and serialization and the role of the narrator.

## Intratextual Repetition of Production Elements

*The Haunting of Hill House* was released in 2018 on Netflix. It was created by Mike Flanagan and produced by Amblin Television and Paramount Television for said streaming service. This series eventually became the first of a future anthology series known as *The Haunting*. Since the beginning, then, it was created and produced with anthology storytelling in mind. *Hill House* is loosely based on Shirley Jackson's novel of the same name. It follows the Crain family, Hugh and Olivia, and their five children (Steven, Shirley, Theodora, Luke, and Nell). In the beginning, we learn that back in 1992, the family experienced paranormal encounters at the mansion they lived in. A tragic occurrence made Hugh and the children leave without Olivia, a loss that follows the family to this day. In the modern day, we follow the lives of the family members as they have to live through another loss in the family—when the youngest of them, Nell, dies back in the same house.

The second installment in the anthology, *The Haunting of Bly Manor*, was released two years after its predecessor. Similarly, it was created by Mike Flanagan and produced by the same two companies (with the addition of Intrepid Pictures) for Netflix. Furthermore, just like *Hill House*, it was based on a literary work considered a classic in the horror genre, Henry James's *The Turn of the Screw*. The story is set in 1987 and follows a young American au pair, Dani, who leaves for England to escape her past. The Wingrave family hires her to look after their two kids, Miles and Flora. The mansion's staff—housekeeper Hannah, cook Owen, and gardener Jamie—greets her. Dani is recovering from her own trauma and discovering herself while experiencing weird behavior from the kids and paranormal activity in the house.

From the basic synopses, we can notice recurring elements that build the anthology character of the shows right from the beginning. First, there is the same creator, the same production companies, and the same streaming platform, which gives *The Hauntings* a label of anthology series.

Not only are the series produced by the same team, but they also involve many of the same cast. Even though the series are not connected in narrative and the actors portray different characters, we can see a specific pattern in casting for certain types of personas. For example, the youngest Crain sibling, Nell, is played by Victoria Pedretti, the actress who portrays the main character of the *Bly Manor*, Dani. Both characters are troubled by their past, having experienced trauma and battling mental obstacles. Nell has trouble with sleep paralysis, and because of this, she saw her husband die of an aneurysm and could not move and help him. Dani also witnessed her partner dying. In both instances, the characters cannot stop the tragedy from happening, but both feel partly responsible for the deaths of their partners. Next is Oliver Jackson-Cohen, who played Luke Crain in *Hill House* and Peter Quint in *Bly Manor*. These characters are similar in that they cannot settle down and get their lives together, using others to hide their problems. Luke is battling drug addiction and using his family for money, while Peter is a chronic liar, thief, and manipulator. Henry Thomas represents the failed father figure in both series. Hugh Crain is estranged from his kids because of the lies about what happened to their mother; Henry Wingrave is an estranged uncle and foster parent to the kids who is never present. Carla Gugino represents the calm, mysterious female figure of the stories who ties them together—being Olivia Crain, the late mother and primary motivation behind *Hill House* events, and the narrator of *Bly Manor*. Lastly, Kate Siegel portrays the sharp, strong-headed characters of Theo Crain in *Hill House* and Viola Willoughby-Lloyd, the original owner of *Bly Manor* and the lead, unapologetic ghost who takes victims to the lake by the house. It is worth noting that some of these actors and the new cast from *Bly Manor* appear in other horror anthology series by Mike Flanagan, *The Midnight Mass* (2021) and *The Midnight Club* (2022).

The stories are both based on the horror genre, one historically linked to the anthology narratives (e.g., *Alfred Hitchcock Presents, The Twilight Zone, Tales from the Crypt, Goosebumps*, and others). Both are also based on literary horror classics *The Haunting of Hill House* (1959) and *The Turn of the Screw* (1898), making them adaptations, however loose. From the genre point of view, there is another uniting element: the haunted house setting—a classic horror trope. "The haunted house narrative, as the term implies, connects a ghost to a physical location. Haunted house narratives proliferated in the East in the 18th century..., and can also be found in Chinese and Japanese folklore. In the West, the haunted house narrative as a literary form derives from the Gothic ... [that] often center on haunted houses in which locales are antiquated and harbor a secret."[26] This applies to *Hill House* as well as *Bly Manor*. Both haunted mansions have a ghost inside their walls, and spectators gradually unveil the secrets of *why* and *how* the hauntings exist. Of course, this could be simply because of the adaptation process of the literary works based on this trope. However, considering the very loose nature of adaptations, Flanagan has worked with the trope by himself just as much as the original works. Both of these shows have a similar narrative style, which will be discussed further in the essay.

## Hybridization of Serial and Episodic Narratives

To better understand the storytelling in *The Hauntings*, its hybridization of serial and episodic forms must be addressed since it is a characteristic of complex television. As the term serial anthology suggests, there are at least two narrative forms. Of all multi-episode narrative forms, the most self-contained episodes can be found in the anthology. There, the main story starts and ends within each episode. With the serial anthology, the self-containment of an episode is replaced by a season. The plot is told across a limited number of episodes of the season and has a definitive conclusion. However, some space is left for intratextuality, meaning that seasons can be connected through repeated motifs (as we mention more thoroughly in the following sections). The seasonal plots use serial storytelling, but in the case of *The Hauntings*, there are also episodic narratives. This is especially evident in *Hill House,* where eight out of ten episodes combine episodic and serial narratives. Seven of these episodes are told from the point of view of a member of the Crain family. Additionally, the sixth episode is constructed around the specific spatiotemporal setting where the events unfold as if in "real" time on two parallel nights. Here, the double setting of stormy nights, one set in the past and the other in the present (during the preparation of Nell's funeral), "real" time with minimal time ellipsis, and the use of incredibly long takes together create what Mittell calls a narrative special effect. While the focalization in other episodes can also be described as the narrative special effect, it is less spectacular.

*Hill House* has two main intertwining storylines, one set in the past, when the family lived in the actual Hill House, and the present. The past is reconstructed through flashbacks, often presented from the point of view of different characters. Mittell argues that "complex narratives often reorder events through flashbacks, retelling past events, repeating story events from multiple perspectives, and jumbling chronologies—these are overt manipulations of discourse time, as we are to assume that the characters experienced the events in a linear progression."[27] However, the time in the show is not linear. It would be more accurate to describe it as circular—the future has already happened. For example, in the first season, Nell is haunted by the ghost of the Bent-Neck Lady. However, it is later revealed that it is her own ghost and always has been. Therefore, she functions as a flash-forward. While the flashbacks help to reconstruct the past and make sense of the present, they also move the plot forward. They also show differing perspectives of the characters on the same events—for example, in *Hill House*, it is revealed that the mysterious Red Room changes its interior for every character—according to their feelings and thoughts—which develops their psychological depth. According to Kaufler, the house is out of time because of its hybrid combination of architectural styles.[28] Furthermore, of course, its ghosts come from different historical eras.

The narratives that are not linear but combine multiple timelines and include flashbacks or flash-forwards serve to engage or even temporarily confuse the audience and create suspense. That is especially important with specific genres (e.g., horror, thriller, crime fiction in general) or any story with a narrative enigma:

> Mystery plotlines often play with discourse time to create suspense concerning past events, waiting until the end of the narrative to reveal the inciting incident that diegetically occurred near the beginning of the story, and many complex narratives play with chronology to engage viewers and encourage them to try to actively parse the story.[29]

*Hill House* begins with a voice-over of Steven, the oldest of the Crain siblings, now a writer of horror novels, one of them being based on his family's tragedy in Hill House. The first narrative tool is used—a story within a story, basically mapping the past events in the house. Time is not linear, there are two prominent timelines, and the characters find themselves out of time and place. Nevertheless, the program also works with time demarcations "Hill House Then" and "Hill House Now," so the viewers can comprehend the storytelling more easily.

*Bly Manor* uses the same tool, this time voicing Dani's main story through her partner's words. Flashbacks work similarly, with the eighth episode being created with flashbacks only.[30] This episode gives a background to the setting, Bly Manor mansion, and explains the origin of the Lady of the Lake, the primary and most dangerous ghost. While some episodes focus on specific characters, they are more intertwined with the seasonal arc. Thanks to more overall serial narration, *Bly Manor* uses fewer episodic plots than *Hill House*. The time is also more linear here, except for Hannah and her focalized episode (serving as a metaphor for her inability to come to terms with her death).

In both seasons, many other shorter stories build together the mythology of said haunted houses—and are also inserted in the main storyline. It is most evident concerning the ghosts trapped in the manor. After a while, their faces get erased, and they lose their identity. So, for example, Viola, the original lady of the manor, becomes the anonymous Lady of the Lake who repeats nightly her walks through the house even though she can no longer remember why. That is what the ghost of antagonist Peter Quint fears and why he wants to possess Miles, the older of the Wingrave siblings. A limited time becomes a topic for *Bly Manor*, manifested in several untimely deaths (Dani's fiancé, Peter, Rebecca, Hannah, Flora and Miles's parents) and the knowledge that Dani lives on borrowed time after she invites the Lady of the Lake to possess her. The limitation is also spatial—whoever dies on the land of Bly Manor is trapped there forever (though the Lady of the Lake haunts Dani even when she moves abroad but compels her to return). In *Hill House*, the ghosts can appear beyond the house (e.g., ghosts of Nell, Olivia, and Man in the Bowler Hat), but they are still tethered to it. Whoever dies there stays there as a ghost. So, both houses have their own spatiotemporal rules that influence the narrative. It is also correlated to the haunted house trope, as mentioned earlier.

By disrupting the linearity of a story within the story, we can also find plenty of intertextual references that fulfill the role of flashbacks while connecting the series to the source material. The references come with another set of meanings to the story, creating a new narrative tool to keep the viewer interacting with and interested in the series.

Both series also pay respect to their literary predecessors by quoting them directly in the pilot. In *Hill House*, the first quote of the book was used, making only minor changes in the means of context.

> No live organism can continue for long to exist sanely under conditions of absolute reality; even larks and katydids are supposed, by some, to dream. Hill House, not sane, stood by itself against its hills, holding darkness within; it had stood so for eighty years and might stand for eighty more. Within, walls continued upright, bricks met neatly, floors were firm, and doors were sensibly shut; silence lay steadily against the wood and stone of Hill House, and whatever walked there, walked alone.[31]

In the series, it was changed to "a hundred years before my family moved in and might stand for a hundred more."[32]

In *Bly Manor*, Mike Flanagan celebrated two sources of inspiration. The first line of the pilot recites the lyrics of "O Willow Waly," a song created for the 1961 movie *The Innocents*, which is also an adaptation of *The Turn of the Screw*. Then, in another scene at the beginning of the pilot, where the narrator takes her turn telling a ghost story to the wedding guests, she cites James's *The Turn of the Screw* directly: "If the child gives the effect, another turn of the screw, what do you say to two children?"[33]

## Serialization and the Role of the Narrator

The distribution issue needs to be addressed in terms of seriality and Netflix production. Netflix does not adhere to weekly schedules like linear television and instead releases the whole seasons of their original production at the same time. Milly Buonanno calls this distribution model a *Netflix paradigm* which she explains as "the shifts in television content distribution and consumption that allow for compressed viewing of serial narratives, acknowledging that those shifts are principally foregrounded by, but not limited to, the streaming giant."[34] However, Buonanno argues that

> the Netflix paradigm undermines defining features of narrative seriality, as historically conceptualized, enacted and experienced. Seriality is constituted in the synergic interplay between production, distribution and consumption of ongoing narratives, whose segmented articulation is purposefully designed to feed a delivery system and to elicit acts of reading/viewing that follow time dynamics of repeated and enforced interruption.[35]

In other words, for Buonanno, seriality is not just textual but also refers to distribution. In that case, the notion of seriality is complicated within the Netflix production. Because of the Netflix paradigm, some theoreticians and critics even argue that it makes its shows cinematic because they are presented as unified text, just like films are.[36] Netflix sometimes uses these claims to promote its multipart programs and differentiate them from linear television.[37] But Kozak and Zeller-Jacques assert that "the television text—even the season-dropped, made-for-bingeing television text—is far from pure and inviolate."[38] In their analysis of *Stranger Things*—often described as "pure" and cinematic[39]—they find that the program often uses episodic narratives, repetition, and retelling typical for serialized fiction.[40] *The Hauntings* conform to the Netflix paradigm as both seasons released all of their episodes at the same time. However, aside from using episodic plotlines, they also work with cliffhangers or some climaxes at the end of episodes, forming breaks in the serial narrative between episodes. It would not be accurate to describe *The Hauntings* as "pure" or cinematic. So, even though both seasons were released according to the Netflix paradigm, the storytelling is more tuned to the rules of serialized fiction.

Both *Hill House* and *Bly Manor* contain a diegetic narrator who provides the story's framing. In *Hill House*, Steven narrates the opening monologue in the first episode and the closing monologue at the end of the last episode. These two monologues are closely intertwined, with some phrasing repeated or challenged. In the opening monologue, Steven declares: "It has stood for a hundred years and might stand a hundred more." There is a sense of continuation, open-endness, and longevity, all characteristics of serial fiction. The repetition in the monologues is also a great part of both episodic and serial narratives. Episodic series are based on regularly repeated patterns and plots ("case of the week," "monster of the week," etc.), and serials often use recaps, diegetic retelling, or flashbacks to remind the viewer of the necessary information needed to understand current events. While Netflix does not use recaps for its original productions (except for new seasons but not for individual episodes), retelling of previous events is common. In their narrative analysis of *Stranger Things*, Kozak and

Zeller-Jacques list several *"recall strategy types"* the show works with (the first six of them are borrowed from Jason Mittell): (1) diegetic retelling, (2) voice-over narration, (3) flashbacks, (4) repeated emphasis on an object, (5) repeated emphasis on a setting, (6) repeated shot composition, (7) repeated musical cue, (8) repeated costume element, (9) repeated language, (10) fulfilled predicted action, (11) repeated scenarios, and (12) returning characters.[41] Both *Hill House* and *Bly Manor* work with these devices.

*Hill House* emphasizes diegetic retelling, flashbacks, voice-over narration, and repeated language (the last two are neatly demonstrated by the opening and closing monologue). Fulfilled predicted action and repeated scenarios have a prominent place in *Hill House*. The former is tragically manifested through the character of Nell and her ghost of Bent-Neck Lady, who had haunted her since childhood and predicted her death. The latter can be found in Nell's and Olivia's deaths, with the one mirroring the other. Events are often shown repeatedly through different perspectives, which helps viewers make sense of them. The topic of repetition fits neatly with the idea of time in Hill House, which is circular or cyclical—things that will happen have already happened.

In *Bly Manor*, the narration is framed as a story-within-a-story as the character of Jamie retells the happenings at Bly Manor when she was young. The story starts in 2007 at the rehearsal dinner for Flora's wedding, when Jamie tells a ghost story in the evening. Then the story shifts to twenty years earlier when the main storyline occurs. The framing narrative only appears again after the flashback ends. So, most of the story takes place in the past. Also, there are flashbacks within the main storyline flashback, mostly linked to certain characters and their backstories. Therefore, flashbacks, voice-over narration, and diegetic retelling are even more prominent here than in *Hill House*. There is also an emphasis on repetition; repeated objects (Flora's dolls, butterfly hair clip), costume elements (Hannah's checkered shirts that keeps changing even when she is dead), musical cue (song "O Willow Waly"), repeated scenarios (Lady of the Lake's ritual walk, Rebecca's and Dani's drowning) and even repeated showing of some scenes. This emphasized repetition is taken to the extreme in "The Altar of the Dead," where Hannah is doomed to relive the same scenes until she realizes she is dead. Moreover, there is a repeated emphasis on setting, which is the same for both seasons, where the titular houses are the primary locations.

## Conclusion

In the era of plenitude, the audience is presented with an overwhelming number of choices about what to watch. Selecting a program to watch can be a challenge. Not all viewers want to start a new long-form program to which they will have to commit. Choosing a limited series or miniseries can be an answer for them. As our text proposed, an anthology might work for the audiences as well; they can watch in whatever order or watch just a few episodes without needing to finish the season to comprehend the storytelling. In the era where serials constitute the dominant narrative form,[42] a definitive ending can be a welcoming aspect. As Buonanno argues, the ending brings a "satisfaction for completeness and closure."[43]

Furthermore, serial anthology is advantageous because it contains enough space to develop a story and characters without a long-term commitment. It also offers the satisfaction of ending, even if it is open-ended. Because intratextual elements between the seasons (creators, actors, narrative style, etc.) are not necessary for comprehending seasonal narratives, the audience can also decide what seasons to watch. García calls this practice *vertical viewing,* noting that it gives the viewers freedom to choose.[44] Also, while the viewers get closure, they can continue watching other seasons if they like the unifying elements (genre, storytelling, actors, premise, and others). Latecomers to a show also do not have to feel obligated to watch previous seasons.

One downside for the serial anthology is the change of setting and characters, which is often why viewers continue to watch serial narratives, as they form a parasocial relationship with them. Nevertheless, the serial anthology has its advantages for both viewers and producers. It is practical to have steady sets and cast; multi-episode seasons make it worthwhile when it comes to the costs, unlike stand-alone episodes. Moreover, it works as a reinvention, offering something familiar but new, which is how the genre works. The serial anthology can then stand out among many series or serials. Netflix has started to work with the serial anthology strategy more frequently, producing *Conversations with a Killer* (2019– ) and *Monster* (2022– ), to name a few. *The Hauntings* then represent contemporary narrative and production trends, as well as shifts in technology and distribution.

## Notes

1. Amanda D. Lotz, *We Disrupt This Broadcast: How Cable Transformed Television and the Internet Revolutionized It All* (Cambridge: MIT Press, 2018), 106.

2. Jason Mittell, *Complex TV: The Poetics of Contemporary Television Storytelling* (New York: New York University Press, 2015).

3. Raymond Williams, *Television: Technology and Cultural Form* (New York: Schocken Books, 1974).

4. Michael Curtin, "Matrix Media," in *Television Studies After TV: Understanding*

*Television in the Post-Broadcast Era*, ed. Graeme Turner and Jinna Tay (London: Routledge, 2019), 13.

5.  Mareike Jenner, "Is This TVIV? On Netflix, TVIII and Binge-Watching," *New Media & Society* 18, no. 2 (2014): 257–273, https://doi.org/10.1177/1461444814541523.

6.  Henry Jenkins, *Convergence Culture: Where Old and New Media Collide* (New York: New York Universty Press, 2006), 2.

7.  We use the term VoD as a general concept of video-on-demand services that can be subscription based (by monthly or annual payment), transaction based (one-time purchase) and advertisement based (streaming online with inserted advertisement sequences).

8.  Jay David Bolter, *Digital Plenitude: The Decline of Elite Culture and the Rise of New Media* (Cambridge: MIT Press, 2019), 8–10.

9.  Dennis Broe, *Birth of the Binge: Serial TV and the End of Leisure—Contemporary Approaches to Film and Media Studies* (Detroit: Wayne State University Press, 2019), 23.

10.  Mareike Jenner, "Binge-Watching: Video-on-Demand, Quality TV and Mainstream Fandom," *International Journal of Cultural Studies* 20, no. 3 (2015): 3, https://doi.org/10.1177/1367877915606485.

11.  Jenner, "Binge-Watching," 7.

12.  Jenner, "Binge-Watching," 9.

13.  Alberto N. García, "A Storytelling Machine: The Complexity and Revolution of Narrative Television," *Between* 6, no. 11 (2016): 7, https://doi.org/10.13125/2039-6597/2081.

14.  Ashley Dize, "Fox Nearly Rejected 'The People v. OJ Simpson,'" *mxdwn.com*, October 4, 2016, https://television.mxdwn.com/news/fox-nearly-rejected-the-people-v-o-j-simpson/.

15.  García, "A Storytelling Machine," 5.

16.  Mittell, *Complex TV*, 18–30.

17.  Broe, *Birth of the Binge*, 80.

18.  Mittell, *Complex TV*, 18.

19.  Mittell, *Complex TV*, 18.

20.  Mittell, *Complex TV*, 17–20.

21.  Mittell, *Complex TV*, 41–43.

22.  Mittell, *Complex TV*, 43.

23.  Mittell, *Complex TV*, 45.

24.  Mittell, *Complex TV*, 42–45.

25.  Mittell, *Complex TV*, 31–41.

26.  June Michele Pulliam and Anthony J. Fonseca, *Ghosts in Popular Culture and Legend* (Santa Barbara: Greenwood, 2016), 147.

27.  Mittell, *Complex TV*, 26.

28.  Melissa A. Kaufler, "The Future Isn't What It Used to Be: Hauntiology, Grief and Lost Futures," in *The Streaming of Hill House: Essays on the Haunting Netflix Adaptation*, ed. Kevin J. Wetmore, Jr. (Jefferson, NC: McFarland, 2020), part IV.

29.  Mittell, *Complex TV*, 26.

30.  Based on the short story by Henry James of the same name and thus also becoming another example of story-within-a-story.

31.  Shirley Jackson, *The Haunting of Hill House* (New York: Penguin Classics, 2006), chap. 1, Kindle.

32.  *The Haunting of Hill House*, season 1, episode 1, "Steven Sees a Ghost," directed by Mike Flanagan, written by Mike Flanagan, aired October 12, 2018, https://www.netflix.com/watch/80189222?trackId=200257859, 00:00:17.

33.  Henry James, *Turn of the Screw* (New York: Penguin Books, 2011), prologue, Kindle. *The Haunting of Bly Manor*, season 1, episode 1, "The Great Good Place," directed by Mike Flanagan, written by Mike Flanagan and Jamie Flanagan, aired October 9, 2020, https://www.netflix.com/watch/80227423?trackId=14170287&tctx=7%2C3%2C4299e37d-beeb-4805-8718-43b5804211e6-180061677%2CNES_8C8AECCBB3979A3E32DE81162B
A10A-994911DC4F528C-53CCB16633_p_1674323780435%2CNES_8C8AECCBB3979A3
E32DE81162BA10A_p_1674323780435%2C%2C%2C%2C%2CVideo%3A8123785,4 00:05:28.

34.  Milly Buonnano, "Widening Landscape of TV Storytelling in the Digital Media

Environment," *Anàlisi. Quaderns de Comunicació i Cultur* 58 (June 2018): 194, https://doi.org/10.5565/rev/anaalisi.3133.

35.  Buonnano, "Widening Landscape," 194–195.

36.  Ana Cabral Martins, "Netflix and TV-as-Film: A Case Study of Stranger Things and The OA," in *Netflix at the Nexus: Content, Practice, and Production in the Age of Streaming Television*, ed. Theo Plothe and Amber M. Buck (New York: Peter Lang, 2019), 86–88.

37.  Cabral Martins, "Netflix and TV-as-Film," 85.

38.  Lynn Kozak and Martin Zeller-Jacques, "Digressions and Recaps: The Bingeable Narrative," in *Binge-Watching and Contemporary Television Studies*, ed. Mareike Jenner (Edinburgh: Edinburgh University Press, 2021), 211.

39.  Cabral Martins, "Netflix and TV-as-Film," 89.

40.  Kozak and Zeller-Jacques, "Digressions and Recaps," 214–216.

41.  Kozak and Zeller-Jacques, "Digressions and Recaps," 216.

42.  Broe, *Birth of the Binge*, 119.

43.  Milly Buonnano, "Seriality: Development and Disruption in the Contemporary Medial and Cultural Environment," *Critical Studies in Television* 14, no. 2 (2019): 198, https://doi.org/10.1177/1749602019834667.

44.  García, "A Storytelling Machine," 17.

## Works Cited

Bolter, Jay David. *The Digital Plenitude: The Decline of Elite Culture and the Rise of New Media*. Cambridge: MIT Press, 2019.

Broe, Dennis. *Birth of the Binge: Serial TV and the End of Leisure—Contemporary Approaches to Film and Media Series*. Detroit: Wayne State University Press, 2019.

Buonanno, Milly. "Seriality: Development and Disruption in the Contemporary Medial and Cultural Environment." *Critical Studies in Television* 14, no. 2 (2019): 187–203. https://doi.org/10.1177/1749602019834667.

Buonanno, Milly. "Widening landscape of TV storytelling in the digital media environment." *Anàlisi. Quaderns de Comunicació i Cultur* 58 (June 2018): 1–12. https://doi.org/10.5565/rev/analisi.3133.

Butler, Jeremy G. *Television: Critical Methods and Applications*. Mahwah, NJ: Lawrence Erlbaum, 2007.

Cabral Martins, Ana. "Netflix and TV-as-Film: A Case Study of *Stranger Things* and *The OA*." In *Netflix at the Nexus: Content, Practice, and Production in the Age of Streaming Television*, edited by Theo Plothe and Amber M. Buck, 81–96. New York: Peter Lang, 2019.

Curtin, Michael. "Matrix media." In *Television Studies After TV: Understanding Television in the Post-Broadcast Era*, edited by Graeme Turner and Jinna Tay, 9–19. London: Routledge, 2019.

Ellis, John. *Seeing Things: Television in the Age of Uncertainty*. London: I.B. Tauris, 2000.

Epstein, Michael M., Jimmie L. Reeves, and Mark C. Rogers. "Surviving the 'Hit': Will The Sopranos Still Sing for HBO?" In *Reading The Sopranos: Hit TV from HBO*, edited by David Lavery, 15–26. London: I.B. Tauris, 2002.

García, Alberto N. "A storytelling machine: The complexity and revolution of narrative Television." *Between* 6, no. 11 (2016): 1–25. https://doi.org/10.13125/2039-6597/2081.

Jenkins, Henry. *Convergence Culture: Where Old and New Media Collide*. New York: New York University Press, 2006.

Jenner, Mareike. "Binge-watching: Video-on-demand, quality TV and mainstreaming fandom." *International Journal of Cultural Studies* 20, no. 3 (2015): 304–320. https://doi.org/10.1177/1367877915606485.

Jenner, Mareike. "Is this TVIV? On Netflix, TVIII and binge-watching. " *New Media & Society* 18, no. 2 (2014): 257–273. https://doi.org/10.1177/1461444814541523.

Kaufler, Melissa A. "The Future Isn't What It Used to Be: Hauntology, Grief and Lost

Futures." In *The Streaming of Hill House: Essays on the Haunting Netflix Adaptation*, edited by Kevin J. Wetmore, Jr., 128–141. Jefferson, NC: McFarland, 2020.

Kozak, Lynn, and Martin Zeller-Jacques. "Digressions and Recaps: The Bingeable Narrative." In *Binge-Watching and Contemporary Television Studies*, edited by Mareike Jenner, 207–223. Edinburgh: Edinburgh University Press, 2021.

Kozloff, Sarah. "Narrative Theory and Television." In *Channels of Discourse, Reassembled: Television and Contemporary Criticism*, edited by Robert C. Allen, 67–100. London: Routledge, 1992.

Lotz, Amanda D. *We Now Disrupt This Broadcast: How Cable Transformed Television and the Internet Revolutionized It All.* Cambridge: MIT Press, 2018.

Mittell, Jason. *Complex TV: The Poetics of Contemporary Television Storytelling.* New York: New York University Press, 2015.

Pulliam, June Michele, and Anthony J. Fonseca. *Ghosts in Popular Culture and Legend.* Santa Barbara: Greenwood, 2016.

Williams, Raymond. *Television: Technology and Cultural Form.* New York: Schocken Books, 1974.

## TV

*Alfred Hitchcock Presents* (1955–1965), USA: CBS, NBC.
*Amazing Stories* (1985–1986), USA: NBC.
*American Crime Story* (2016– ), USA: FX.
*American Horror Story* (2011– ), USA: FX.
*Big Little Lies* (2017–2019), USA: HBO.
*Black Mirror* (2011– ), UK: Channel 4, Netflix.
*Buffy the Vampire Slayer* (1997–2003), USA: The WB, UPN.
*Conversations with a Killer* (2019– ), USA: Netflix.
*Fargo* (2014– ), USA: FX.
*Goosebumps* (1995–1998), USA & Canada: Fox Kids & YTV.
*Guillermo del Toro's Cabinet of Curiosities* (2022), USA & Mexico: Netflix.
*The Haunting of Bly Manor* (2020), USA: Netflix.
*The Haunting of Hill House* (2018), USA: Netflix.
*Lore* (2017–2018), USA: Amazon Prime Video.
*The Midnight Club* (2022), USA: Netflix.
*The Midnight Mass* (2021), USA: Netflix.
*Miracle Workers* (2019– ), USA: TBS.
*Monster* (2022), USA: Netflix.
*The Outer Limits* (1963–1965), USA: ABC.
*Playhouse 90* (1956–1960), USA: CBS.
*Stranger Things* (2016– ), USA: Netflix.
*Tales from the Crypt* (1989–1996), USA: HBO.
*The Terror* (2018–2019), USA: AMC.
*True Detective* (2014– ), USA: HBO.
*The Twilight Zone* (1959–1964), USA: CBS.
*The United States Steel Hour* (1953–1963), USA: ABC, NBC.
*Why Women Kill* (2019–2021), USA: CBS All Access, Paramount+.

## Other Works Cited

Dize, Ashley. "Fox Nearly Rejected 'The People v. O.J. Simpson.'" *mxdwn.com*, October 4, 2016. https://television.mxdwn.com/news/fox-nearly-rejected-the-people-v-o-j-simpson/.

Isla Cameron with the Raymonde Singers. "O Willow Waly". 1962. Decca, Spotify. https://open.spotify.com/track/0x15sHgWFCMNykh1HfukkC.

Jackson, Shirley. *The Haunting of Hill House.* New York: Penguin Classics, 2006. Kindle.

James, Henry. *The Turn of the Screw*. New York: Penguin Classics, 2011. Kindle.

*The Haunting of Bly Manor*, season 1, episode 1, "The Great Good Place," directed by Mike Flanagan. Netflix, 2020.

*The Haunting of Hill House*, season 1, episode 1, "Steven Sees a Ghost," directed by Mike Flanagan. Netflix, 2018.

# On *Black Summer* and Embodied Spectatorship

FERNANDO GABRIEL PAGNONI BERNS

The power of narrative cinema lies, in part, on the construction of empathy-inducing characters who can carry the audience into any kind of adventure, world-building and fantasy. The weight on well-delineated characters is basic in film script development.[1] The emphasis on character development is especially relevant with TV seriality, where the length allows multilinear and complex storylines.[2] Shallow characters may be admissible (to some extent) in film storytelling,[3] seriality, prolonged through weeks and months, is not so deferential. Viewers have to intimately know the main protagonists (who they are, how they will react to a particular situation, etc.) to return to the story over and over on a weekly and annual basis. American TV seriality drama has been called "complex" by Jason Mittell, as to call something complex "is to highlight its sophistication and nuance, suggesting that it presents a vision of the world that avoids being reductive or artificially simplistic, but that grows richer through sustained engagement and consideration,"[4] characters included.

Further, streaming seriality came to change the rigid order of conventional TV. Rather than depending on an elevated number of episodes each season (roughly, 21–23 episodes per year as in the 1980s and 1990s), streaming allows TV series to use only the length they need to tell the story without resorting (in most cases) to padding and filling. This is a double-edged sword, since characters now must be delineated through eight to 10 episodes. It can be argued, then, that the identification between fully fleshed out characters and viewers is key for the success of complex serialized TV storytelling.

The TV series *Black Summer* (Netflix, 2019–2021) successfully plays with this new freedom while, at the same time, disrupting it. Created by Karl Schaefer and John Hyams, the series is a spinoff of *Z Nation* (SyFy), the story centered around the early days of a zombie apocalypse and the lives of those who have to live through it. It adopts a documentary style with little verbal exposition about the lives of the different characters. *Black Summer* privileges action and horror, asking the viewers to follow characters presented through brief segments with little (if any) backstory.

Provided only "bare bones" presentations with no exposition, viewers are confused about who exactly the leading characters are and what their motivations might be. Further, no one is exempt from death: characters who begin to emerge as protagonists in one episode may die in the next, leaving viewers few focal points of identification. In his book on horror and affect, Adam Daniel argues that when classical structures of narrative are de-emphasized—via emphasizing the camera's movements, out-of-frame shots, or delivering pure action rather than plot—they "activate a distinct concurrent embodied response for the viewer."[5] *Black Summer* invites viewers to a constant re-evaluation of their ideological and/or affective positions as pinning a particular moral to a particular character becomes increasingly hard. With little exposition, the viewers' sympathy starts to collapse in stories where "evil" and "good" characters shift their positions constantly. This flux of moral identification is further enhanced by the series' narrative device of using a very small temporal frame for dead humans to become zombies. With the killed victims becoming murderous zombies in just seconds, moral identification is severely disrupted: one character audiences have celebrated as heroic or empathic becomes a monster in seconds, rather than hours, days or even weeks later. Thus, *Black Summer* offers an innovation, being the only TV series based, mostly, in an embodied spectatorship of affective, corporeal response that may contradict or undermine cognitive evaluative processes where the moral is the main source of identification.

I am not arguing here that embodied spectatorship is a new phenomenon invented by *Black Summer*. What the series brings as a novelty is the emphasis on this kind of identification in a serialized narrative, while embodied spectatorship is more common in films, especially those belonging to the found-footage cycle, with its "sense of increased immediacy and alignment with the characters through various techniques associated with the diegetic camera trend."[6] With little in terms of moral identification, *Black Summer* creates a world where viewers are forced to engage in innovative ways with the different characters, using the advantages given by the new system of streaming TV and its flexibility in time span. The sharp difference between the episodes' lengths (varying from 21 minutes to one hour) further plays with expectations, as the series focuses only in the minimal structures of storytelling. Through an affective framework, this essay will investigate the disruptive nature of this (overlooked) Netflix show to identify an unusual mode of identification based more on the somatic and circumstantial empathy than in the cognitive.

## Complex Storytelling and Horror Identification

It must be stated that *Black Summer* belongs to what Trisha Dunleavy calls "complex seriality,"[7] meaning serials that "are distinguished within TV drama by their tendency to tell a complete story, the 'overarching story,' from beginning to end" (unlike sitcoms, structured around episodic storytelling). The "overarching story" spans "all episodes of the show and receives more emphasis than any other story strand."[8] Further,

> because both the overarching and lesser stories are delivered incrementally, the episodes of a high-end serial are interdependent, must be viewed in strict order, and audience knowledge of the narrative past is vital to the interpretation of new events. In high-end serials, the larger category within which "complex serials" can be located, it is possible for a single character to dominate this overarching story, core characters are less interchangeable than is possible in other long-format dramas, and the idiosyncrasies of these characters can be more fully fleshed out by writers. In the serial's narrative context of progression and change, characters remember their history which has repercussions in the narrative present.[9]

Certainly, *Black Summer* fits the politics of "complex seriality," as the horror TV show revolves around the lives of survivors of some kind of apocalypse (it is unclear what happened with the world or why the corpses have returned to life)[10] whose adventures, escapes and reunions audiences follow through the episodes. Also, *Black Summer* has "main characters" leading the episodes, a staple in "complex seriality." The "main characters" are those with whom audiences will supposedly identify the most because (1) they lead the narrative, appearing on-screen more than other secondary characters (including villains) and (2) they are the "heroes," meaning those who are ethically compatible with valuable moral principles.[11] Jaime King stars in the lead role as Rose, a mother who is separated from her daughter during a zombie apocalypse. Julius James (Justin Chu Cary) is a man (maybe a criminal) who took the name of the soldier he killed—"Spears"—and must deflect not only zombies but also suspicions about his true identity. Ooh "Sun" Kyungsun (Christine Lee) is a Korean woman who does not speak English, a fact that makes her situation more complicated. All three are what can be labeled as leading characters, with many others leading season 1 and appearing as guests in season 2: Lance (Kelsey Flower), a young survivor with no family; William Velez (Sal Velez, Jr.), a pole lineman who has a sister and children in Texas; etc. The series follows these characters and how they reunite, interact and became separated through the episodes. In other words, *Black Summer* invites viewers to identify with these characters and follow their struggles through the apocalypse. Also, as Trisha Dunleavy argues, what happened in previous episodes is of importance, as the story builds itself from the sequentiality of the different stories and adventures. Part of the engagement with the series comes from viewers wondering if the main characters will, after many episodes (weeks of viewing), escape from their horrible situation.

*Black Summer's* first episode, "Human Flow," is coherent with the politics of "complex seriality," as the story presents the series' main character, Rose, and tells a little about her life. A siren wails in the distance in what looks like a desolated town. Cut to a title card (simple white words on a black background) that says only "Rose," thus introducing the character. She is first depicted in a close shot, her eyes filled with tears and fear. She, her husband (Patrick), and their daughter (Anna) pack their things and prepare to leave the house. As they hurry down the street, they meet hundreds of other people running to an unknown destiny. An army blockage stops them, though, lining people up and checking them for signs of infection. Soldiers discover that Patrick is hiding a wound on his stomach, and he is denied entry into the truck. As chaos breaks out, the truck speeds away, leaving the remaining survivors to fend for themselves. Only Anna leaves with the soldiers, while Rose and her husband take refuge in an abandoned house. Patrick dies and returns moments later as a zombie, chasing Rose, who is saved at the last moment by a soldier.

The episode continues with its focus on the plight of the survivors. A title card tells "Ryan." The titular character, Ryan (Mustafa Alabssi), finds a dying woman on the floor. Alarmed, a Korean woman (Sun) takes him away and they keep running together. A new title card introduces viewers to "Barbara" (Gwynyth Walsh), who is approached by a man in her car. He asks if she can take him and his family to a stadium where, supposedly, survivors will meet helicopters that will take them to a safe zone. Barbara, who is also heading that way, agrees and opens her car's door. Unfortunately, the man only wants to steal her vehicle and commands her to get out of the car. As she gets out of the vehicle, another man shows up and beats him up. The next title card reads "Lance." He and his girlfriend are trying to figure out where to go when a car hits her. He leaves her as she bleeds out only to be approached by Ryan and the Korean woman whom audiences saw earlier. Lance's girlfriend changes into one of the undead and starts walking around the town looking for fresh victims. More characters follow, including Julius James, the man who saved Rose from her zombified husband.

The brief synopsis above indicates that *Black Summer* is, certainly, part of the "complex seriality," as the first episode is used to present the main characters to the audience. All the characters presented with a title card may be considered as "good" ones, as they suffer and try to help others: as such, audiences understand that these characters are the "main" ones. In consequence, audiences expect that the protagonists' lives and identities will be elaborated as the series progress, even if new characters are introduced. Following this expectation, at the end of the episode all characters converge at the checkpoint, reunited at last to begin their interactions.

Indeed, "Human Flow" addresses the logic of any TV series' first episode, presenting storylines and the main characters. Yet, the series will slightly subvert viewers' expectations in the episode's first minutes. We see Rose and her husband preparing to leave in the episode's opening scene. They do so silently, the lack of dialogue preventing an adequate comprehension of what is going on and who these people are. The show's initial credits don't add much in terms of narrative: black clouds open to reveal "Black Summer" as the only index of the story. Still, it is easy to infer that these three persons are a family, thus inviting emphatic engagement with the predicament of parents trying to do their best for their daughter. Yet, when the family hastily flees the house, a brief tracking movement from the camera reveals family portraits that depict another family, one clearly Asian. Whose house is this? Why this family lives in this house? What has happened with the previous family? Are the people depicted in the portraits the home's owners or friends of Rose and her family? None of these questions is answered in the episode—or, indeed, those that follow. In fact, the house is left behind, never to be addressed again. Basically, the show asks viewers to infer that, as an apocalypse erupted across the globe, Rose and her family, fleeing the chaos, took refuge momentarily in this home. What the series provides is not backstory, but speculation.

Further, the narrative device of presenting the different characters through the use of title cards seems to indicate the series' main characters. Still, only Rose and Sun will be revealed—and only as the series progress through its two seasons—as protagonists; all the other characters slowly or quickly fade away as the series progresses. Presenting the characters through title cards creates expectations that are later subverted, creating a crisis of affective identification. Another disruptive point is the lack of backstory: audiences know these characters by name only (thanks to the title cards), but nothing is told about them. As "Human Flow" is focused heavily in people running through the streets, avoiding zombies and desperately trying to arrive to a meeting point, there is no time left to delineate their identities and personal stories. Only Rose gets a time of rest after her daughter is taken by the soldiers; she talks with her husband, who asks her to leave him behind. Rose rejects the idea, her sacrifice (she knows her husband will become a zombie soon) creating an emotional bond with viewers. The respite is short-lived, however, as the man soon becomes a monster that starts chasing Rose through the house and the streets. The other characters are also delineated with the same lack of information. Neither does the audience know why the soldiers have arrested Julius. Is he a criminal? Are the soldiers the bad guys? Julius states to one of the soldiers that he is not the man they want, but he also argues that they already know that fact. Is he a wrongly accused man? At the end of the scene, Julius coldly kills a soldier, leaving audiences at an emotional disjunction where moral identification is kept in ambiguous terms.

Acknowledgment about seriality indicates that viewers have nothing to fear; as the series unfolds, particular stories will be explained. It is common to use action and an edgy narrative in the first episode to hook viewers, promising more relaxed episodes to come. Yet, *Black Summer* is uninterested in slowing down, as the episodes to come follow the strategy of big-action sequences with little (if any) moment of exposition used in episode 1. Episode 2, "Drive," certainly follows where the previous episode left off. The Korean woman, Barbara, and the man who beat up Barbara's hijacker continue to drive along the road. The guy's name is William and the Korean woman's name is Sun, yet neither is presented using the title cards, which still show up but now to indicate actions like "drive" or just words like "Bicycle." As William, Sun, and Barbara drive along the road, they interact, bond and even start singing. Abruptly, a black truck is upon their car, ramming them from behind, trying to force them off the road. William tells the women to buckle up and starts to accelerate. As they speed along, distracted by the race, they approach a concrete roadblock, and both cars run headlong into it. Barbara does not have her seatbelt on and flies through the windshield, dying instantly. The truck's driver also dies, and soon the surviving occupants of both vehicles join together to evade their zombified friends.

There are two elements to highlight from this second episode. First, most of the characters from "Human Flow" reunited at the end of the episode start to interact and, as mentioned, even bond. Still, viewers know nothing of their backstories yet. Rose has lost her husband and her daughter, and Julius is impersonating another person. Sun has problems with her English, and William is still an unknown. Can Sun and Barbara trust him? Basically, in terms of characterization, the series has not advanced much. Action predominates as William, Sun and Barbara fight for their lives, but the audience's knowledge about these characters is the same one they have in the first episode.

Second, Barbara was presented in the first episode as a "main" character, according to the logic of the title cards. Yet, she is killed at the end of the episode, even if her fear and open trust in strangers made her someone emotionally "relatable" to audiences. If the title cards are not an indication of who the series' main characters are, as audiences arguably presumed due to the individualized presentation in "Human Flow," then Rose and Julius can be killed as well. The question that this uncertainty opens is: how viewers can relate to these characters? They are only sketched in bare bones and they can disappear from the narrative at any point. In episode 3, "Summer School," the group formed through the first two episodes enters a large school building, looking for a safe place to spend the night. Not long later, they split up and end up being captured by an organized child army. Lance is seemingly killed by abooby trap,[12] and Ryan is shot by one of the youngest kids by mistake. Both Lance and Ryan were considered, so far, "main" characters and, as such, safe from being killed. Furthermore, Ryan is a disabled young man, his deafness positioning him as an extremely emphatic character as he is forced to fight both his disability and an army of zombies. Clearly, writers of *Black Summer* know viewers will take for granted that Ryan will survive or, at least, get a sacrificial death by, for example, giving up his life for the welfare of others. Yet, he is unceremoniously killed as early as episode 3, thus increasing the sense of uncertainty about whom to follow. Further, Ryan rises from his death as a zombie just a minute after being killed. As a monster, he hunts down his former companions through the school's cafeteria. At the climax of the episode, Julius is forced to exterminate Ryan to get out alive. At the end of "Summer School," only Sun, Rose and Julius are still alive, and they receive the help of a stranger, the latter coming so abruptly to the story that audiences cannot even get a clear look at his face. Still, the series seems to indicate he will be a new "main" character.

Viewers' emotional and ethical identification is key for seriality. Yet, *Black Summer* seems to violate some of the crucial devices of "complex seriality," as the characters are more focused on running away than on opening themselves to viewers. In his book *Horror Film and Affect*, Xavier Aldana Reyes uses affect theory to evaluate viewers' engagement and identification with the horror film. Affect theory argues vehemently for the need to consider audiences' affect as a serious approach through which to analyze cinema, a useful tool to open investigation on emotional identification, being cognitive and/or corporeal. In other words, affect theory looks for the way our emotions may be moved by what is taking place in the film. Aldana Reyes addresses the problems that come with affect theory, meaning, that this new film discipline "is not a totemic or even cogent school of thought adhering to a given number of precepts,"[13] that this analytical tool may be also known by other names such as "cognitivism" and "phenomenology"[14] and that there are many approaches "to affect, all of which vary depending on angle and discipline."[15] Yet, the author highlights the privileged place that horror cinema occupies for studies on affect theory, as this particular genre invites productive readings from almost "emotional and somatic levels"[16] as torture (both mental and corporeal), bloodshed and the dread in the screen force more direct commitments with audiences. "The Horror film is a source of negative affect that does everything it possibly can to connect the viewer with the victim and simulate moments of vulnerability dependent on corporeal intelligibility, particularly of the results and effects of pain."[17]

Aldana Reyes bases his investigation mostly in bodily reactions uniting studies on abjection and disgust. His study "places the body at the centre of critical attention at the representational, emotional and affective levels."[18] Still, the author separates reflex responses (like those born, for example, from close shots of open wounds or spilled blood) from cognitive emotions, "eminently processual and construal-based,"[19] meaning, affect that requires mental evaluation from viewers.

For Aldana Reyes, the spectator's body "can be a source of affect at a representational level when it dares to transgress the neatly delineated boundaries of inside and outside"[20] through the "instinctive reactions connected to the vicarious experience of imagined pain"[21] suffered by characters. As a horror TV show, *Black Summer* offers many manifestations of pain. It can be emotional, such as when Rose is framed in close shot screaming in anguish when Ryan is killed by a small kid. There is corporeal pain as well, as when, in episode 5, "Diner," a character called Phil (Stafford Perry) is attacked by all the other survivors via any weapon they can find (including pans and fire extinguishers) to the point of leaving the young man a bleeding pulp. The camera takes the point of view of the man on the floor, thus inviting audiences to share his physical pain. Phil is an evil man, one who has tried to plant seeds of doubt in the minds of the different survivors, suggesting that they "divide and conquer." Yet, viewers are forced to feel his pain in a double way: first, because he is brutally beaten, and second, because Phil knows the other survivors trapped with him at a cafeteria will throw him out to serve as food for zombies, thus providing all the others the opportunity to escape the place. In episode 6 from season 2, "Currency," viewers are forced to confront one of the visual examples discussed by Aldana Reyes in his book: a close shot of a broken leg, a bone protruding from the skin, blood flowing freely, creating "a form of somatic empathy that allows the viewer to empathise" with pain and "which reminds us of the vulnerability of the body."[22]

Somatic identification, especially noticeable in horror cinema, is corporeal, via pain or disgust. It produces an instantaneous affective identification. This relation with cinematic pain is what Julian Hanich calls "somatic empathy":[23] the repercussion in the viewer's body of the intense pain suffered by some character, especially when close shots are involved.

This is the capacity that horror films have "to affect bodies pre-cognitively or in ways that bypass complex thought processes."[24] For Aldana Reyes, one "of the issues at stake in this cinematic exchange is the capacity for the human body to vicariously feel for another,"[25] and, as such, he anchors his theories in Pain Studies, as this theoretical framework privileges "corporeal identification" and not "character identification"[26] in ideological terms. Aldana Reyes also engages with the study on disgust in relation with cultural abjection: "Drawing on recent scholarship on the nature of disgust, I suggest that we understand abjection, still useful as a construct that articulates the immediate rejection of certain images, as a form of fearful disgust based on corporeal vulnerability and the human capacity to assess the pain and danger in physical harm."[27] Still, Aldana Reyes is quick to point to the fact that "somatics cannot be neatly separated from cognition, as it often relies on feelings of affinity or empathy."

Besides somatic identification, another, more complex form of affective identification comes with moral alignment. It may be argued that this is the classical form of identification in cinema and TV series. The ethical identification is built on a Manichean binary that identifies who is evil and who is good in the fiction. This is constitutive of the horror film, as argued by Robin Wood in his classic essay "An Introduction to the American Horror Film." The author argues that the dominant ideology (bourgeois capitalism) cancels any potential opposition to the hegemonic power through the repression of possible alternatives to that power.[28] If the repression fails, then oppression takes its place and the subject who does not repress himself or herself is harassed.[29] Anyone who fails to fit within the hegemonic sphere is then classified as a disruptive Other,[30] a monster that comes to perturb the "natural" order of things. The monster is social and cultural difference, allegorically manifested through a distorted mirror (the horror film) as an alien menace. The (heterosexual) kiss of the main couple at the end of the film seals the destruction of the monster and, as direct consequence, the return of the status quo. The horror film invites audiences to identify with the heroes, the one who bravely fights the monstrous creature to reestablish the lost order. At least, this was the ideal in classical horror cinema. Spectatorship is more complex, however, and nothing can stop viewers from identifying with the monster. After all, the monster, as stated, embodies difference and anyone who considers himself/herself/themselves different (by being gay, proletariat, Black or Asian—in a Western country—Latinx, etc.) may find more emotional and ideological affinity with the hunted monster. Thus, even if not intentional on the part of studios, writers and directors, viewers may identify with the plight of the monster at the brink of destruction rather than with the white, heterosexual, "perfect" heroes. However, identification between viewer and monster is still built on moral ground, as viewers identify with the heroes due to their role as saviors or with the monsters because of their marginal position as pure difference with respect a hegemonic axis. As Marshall Soules argues, there is a distinction between alignment and allegiance depending on the moral and ideological: "Alignment merely places spectators in relation to characters, while allegiance depends on the moral and ideological evaluation of characters."[31] Allegiance requires evaluation, as viewers follow those they identify as closer to their respective political and ideological point of views. This requires a cognitive and judgmental position from viewers, as audiences need to evaluate, in moral and ideological terms, the main characters' actions.

As mentioned, *Black Summer* complicates the moral/ideological base for affective allegiance, as (1) there is no backstory for the "main" characters and (2) they can either die or disappear from the series for many episodes (Julius, for example, is mostly absent through season 2). Hence the quotation marks used when speaking of "main" characters. Further, characters' empathy-inducing traits—ingenuity, warm personalities, caregiving attitudes—can change from one moment to another, as with the process of zombification, or from episode to episode, as with Rose, who becomes a harsh, selfish woman in season 2.

In this scenario, *Black Summer* emphasizes the somatic identification but not, as Aldana Reyes argues, in particular brief moments of insane pain or disgust but as an integral part of the whole narrative. *Black Summer* tells its story using silence (episode 6 from season 1, "Heist," is basically free of dialogue) or a shaking camera and long takes that follow the different characters without much editing. This form of narrative invites a somatic experience, as audiences are mobilized to emotional empathy towards characters they do not know. Viewers may not identify with some characters' ideologies or subjectivities (since the series is uninterested in offering this kind of opening), but will corporeally respond, through an embodied experience of spectatorship, to characters being chased by zombies through narrow corridors or empty streets. There is a shared synesthesia taking place between characters and viewers. Aldana Reyes divided reflex responses from cognitive emotions; *Black Summer* is a rare case of study where the narrative is sustained, mostly, on reflex responses, as the audience follows a nervous camera always on the move, which in turn is always following a character (or characters) either running away or fighting. *Black Summer* proposes what Adam Daniel calls "embodied spectatorship," more present in found-footage horror cinema. Embodied spectatorship downplays the role of the gaze as the main vehicle to apprehend cinema, to discuss, in turn, a bodily identification with both the movements of the characters framed in documentary style and the kinetic camera. The bodily components experience is predicated on "intensi-fy[ing] the liminality of the division between illusionism and realism and bring[ing] to the fore the embodied experience of the viewer,"[32] charging the fictional with embodied and subjective senses. The out-of-frame, shak-ing camera and the presence of characters in constant movement highlight "the embodied response of the viewer, as it engenders an intense sensory engagement, one that the viewer may less keenly feel when watching con-tent that safely positions the frame within a larger diegetic world that is, in a sense, known"[33] in formal and moral ground. As Julian Hanich argues, following to some extent to philosopher Gilles Deleuze,[34] the experience of horror cinema involves both "affects" and "sensations," via understanding film in corporeal terms and

> as an event that is a becoming-in-movement rather than a static being which represents; that confronts us with an enveloping reality at once actual and vir-tual rather than as an illusion; that has a sensory immediacy which enables somatic experiences like kinaesthesia or hapticity rather than remaining a disembodied mental phenomenon; that is always perceived synaesthetically rather than discretely by the disjointed senses of seeing and hearing.[35]

It is possible to note, then, two major lines working on identification in horror cinema: one predicated on the corporeal (yet with a lesser degree of involvement of the cognitive) and one cognitive, including moral, ideo-logical and emotional attachment (which includes the corporeal as well). Both forms of engagement are present in *Black Summer*, but the series' complex way of telling the stories merges both branches to produce one that emphasizes embodied spectatorship via a "circumstantial physical morality" that eschews ideological allegiance but favors momentary align-ment and the somatic. In brief, *Black Summer* offers a new engagement with somatic where this kind of identification is not part of the narrative *but the main narrative.*

## Embodied Spectatorship

As previously stated, *Black Summer*'s "complex seriality" involves a narrative opacity that diminishes ethical engagement. Viewers do not, for one thing, know who the "main characters" are. They can die in the sec-ond episode, as with Barbara, or simply disappear for many episodes, thus disrupting any narrative arc. And the narrative is driven by action scenes staged in long takes filmed with a nervous camera that left little space and time for exposition but invites a bodily experience where audiences feel in their bodies part of the urgency felt by the characters, regardless of their morality.

I said that the series stands for a "circumstantial physical morality" that transcends the somatic or cognitive/moral approach, even if both poles play a role as well. I will briefly explain this mode of identification as follows.

(1) Circumstantial. With so little information about the characters and lack of development in the construction of identities, in addition to the uncertainty about who the "main" characters are, identification is problematic and, in consequence, circumstantial. Audiences may feel a momentary empathy towards the characters who are suffering the most or are in greater danger, regardless of who they are. As soon as the scene ends, the empathy may end as well. One example is the aforementioned scene in the cafeteria, where Phil, sketched briefly as an evil character, is beaten by the rest of the group. As mentioned, the camera takes his point of view, indicating to viewers that he is the victim now and audiences should empathize with him. This scene is attached with morals, albeit grayish rather than black and white: Phil is "evil" because he wants to send Sun to face the zombies, but the rest of the survivors, including Sun, do exactly that with him, throwing him away to serve as a distraction and food for zombies. In the opening episode of season 2, "Cold," Lance lets a woman into his vehicle, but it is a trick, as the woman has a partner in crime, Luke (Daniel Diemer), who shoots him and then steals the car. Lance, now a zombie, starts to follow the couple. Eventually, the car crashes. Luke gets out of the wrecked car. He finds a building, but the owner, an unknown woman, locks the door before he can get in. He begs the woman to let him in, but they end up arguing. Luke finds a working car and he is relieved. As he is about to set off, the zombie smashes through his car window. Viewers' identification fluctuates through the episode, as Luke is a thief and a cold-blooded killer. Audiences also know that the woman in the building is right in suspecting him and not letting him in. Yet, as the situation worsens, sympathies start to shift to Luke: not only is he alone in the streets, with zombies closing in, but the woman in the building is absolutely cruel in her words, mockingly taunting Luke about his misfortunes while the young man tries to reach some zone of mutual agreement that may prompt her to let him in. Luke is bleeding and pleading, inviting viewers to connect with him and his desperate circumstances. He was a victimizer a few scenes prior, but he is the victim now, and it is difficult not to identify with his dire circumstances.

(2) Physical. The series, as stated, is focused in bodily spectatorship, with the camera most of the time moving energetically through the streets, corridors or roads, inviting to a bodily interface with the image and the protagonists' bodies. Furthermore, the camera is always slightly shaking, thus deepening the sense of kinetic narrative that invites viewers to accompany,

with their bodies, the same urgency framing the characters to be always in movement. This point is favored by the streaming medium, which allows episodes to be basically "bare bones." Episodes of *Black Summer* fluctuate in length, with many clocking around 25 to 45 minutes. The final episode of the first season lasts only 17 minutes without titles. These elastic lengths give the series the opportunity to offer only the basics—the actions that take characters from one place to another, dispensing with most dialogue. *Black Summer*'s aesthetics approach that of documentary, especially the observational or direct type, which "lay closer to reality than the highly mediated films"[36] of other documentarists. Episode 4 from season 1, "Alone," is exemplary of this approach, as the episode is focused on Lance and his fight against a zombie without much in the way of subplots or character development: only physical action. Lance enters an abandoned supermarket to gather supplies, but a zombie is lurking around, and rather than patiently trying to get out of the store, he lures it towards him. He climbs on top of a school bus to escape, only to find that the zombie can also climb. In the end, a random man kills the zombie for him, but Lance notices the man is bitten; Lance thanks him then proceeds to kill the person who saved his life. The episode features basically three characters. Lance, who audiences may consider a "main" character since he is in the show from episode 1, a zombie and a random character. Lance's identity is not developed, and the other two characters are just elements added to the action. As the whole episode revolves around Lance trying to escape a zombie, audiences can only empathize with Lance's actions, any cognitive alignment attached to the only living character besides the random man at the end. The story invites a somatic reading that frames the whole episode: Lance climbs a bus, jumps, hides, runs, etc. Viewers' commitment with him is driven by physical alignment, as viewers receive/interpret the action through their own bodies and sensoria, "the indivisible integration of the senses, the body and cognition."[37] This corporeal identification, however, it is not via pain or disgust, but by a correspondence between Lance's attempts to stay alive that the audience can empathize with on a physical level. The realism is vital in the series' aesthetics, provoking an intensification of experience that resonates in the viewers' senses with an affective precognitive process.

(3) Finally, the moral plays a part in this scheme, but it is downplayed in this form of narrative. Vivian Sobchack states that reflexive exercises surrounding violence in film have an "ethical charge: one that calls forth not only response but also responsibility—not only aesthetic valuation but also ethical judgment."[38] Certainly, the series wants ethical evaluation but, at the same time, blurs the lines between good and bad characters, and, furthermore, the plot itself remains ambiguous. This is especially visible in season 2, which starts strikingly confusing and remains so through the season. The urban settings are left behind in favor of icy landscapes. There is

no indication of how the survivors from the first season arrived here. There is a fight between militia and what look like civilians. There is plenty of struggle between both groups, but it is impossible to differentiate between the "good" and "evil" characters, as each faction tries to exercise power over the other one. Further, the first two episodes of the second season go back and forth in time, thus adding to the general sense of narrative crisis. Sun is the prisoner of a militia group that is suddenly attacked by zombies. Meanwhile, Julius is by himself in the middle of the forest with a severe stomach wound. In "The Manor" (season 2, episode 3), the tension is unbearable, as Rose and Anna (Zoe Marlett) live among strangers, a family led by a cruel matriarch and paranoid members who see enemies in everyone. Yet, Rose is depicted completely detached from everything that is happening around her, a cold attitude that disrupts classical identification. When hell breaks loose within the manor, Rose takes charge, coldly securing the survivors under her own rule where everybody, except her and Anna, is disposable. In episode 5 from season 2, Rose and Anna are led by a survivor to an apparently safe place, but he has difficulty in finding it in the snowy landscape. Rose feels like he is lying, but he is insistent—Rose says if they are not in this safe place by sundown, she will kill him. After many scenes of Rose threatening the man, she decides to kill him, but Anna stops her. At this point in the series, it is hard to feel empathy for Rose, who is always manipulating or threatening people. It may be argued that Rose's character has been, certainly, developed. Yet, this evolution took place in the ellipsis between season 1 and 2, which *Black Summer* carefully left in darkness. Any form of identification with Rose comes from her status as a survivor from episode 1 from season 1, rather than any trace of humanity or warmth inherent in the character. Further, season 2 of *Black Summer* stages many fights between a militia and what looks like civilians (or are they another militia?), thus leaving viewers with different groups of unknown people (who look interchangeable) fighting for props and food and a main heroine who behaves more and more like a villain. The situation invites an instinctual moral alignment, as viewers can only identify with those undergoing the most extreme physical or psychological torture at the moment; however, this identification is always shifting as the fortunes of the different characters change from one minute to another.

In brief, *Black Summer* is adamant in presenting new ways of identification or, at least, disrupting the classic ones. The plot of each episode is basically a pattern of handheld long takes, a realistic take on the apocalypse filled with intense fight scenes and zombie chases that invites viewers to a somatic kinesthesia where sympathy is built on the basis of particular and circumstantial forms of behavior rather than by a deep cognitive and/ or moral attachment.

## *Conclusions*

*Black Summer* plays with classical forms of audiences' identification to offer a subversive story that carefully eliminates all the elements necessary for emotional engagement. "Complex seriality" needs complex storylines led by relatable characters with whom audiences can identify. *Black Summer*, certainly, provides points of affective identification, but not on the basis of moral judgment and the cognitive, but by providing an embodied spectatorship. This bodily spectatorship is recurrent in horror cinema, yet is novel in a TV series, which, due to their lengths, tend to classical forms of commitment; it is difficult to think of a TV series that will, through many episodes and seasons, base its identification mostly in the bodily; still, *Black Summer* does exactly that.

Still, in the last episode of season 2 ("The Plane"), a moral and emotional alignment is finally enthroned. All the main characters from season 2 arrive at an airport, where supposedly an airplane will take them to a safe place. A horde of zombies shows up and kill the group. An explosion blasts Rose across the ground, along with Sun and Anna. Rose's leg is broken and she tells the others to leave. Sun makes it on the plane, but Anna changes her mind and decides to return to her mother. As the season closes out, Sun greets the pilot who happens to be an American who can speak Korean. In the finale, Sun has found not only freedom from the zombie outbreak but someone who speaks her language.

Sun was the only character through season 1 who constantly trusted other people. Season 2 saw Sun as a prize of war, someone who was interchanged between factions. Still, she fought for human communication, trying, uselessly, to make people understand that all factions are in the same situation. People should be friends not enemies in this dire circumstance. At the end of *Black Summer*, Sun is rewarded for her humanity, for being the only character who, even with her downfalls, was the only one who remained "good" and, as such, morally relevant. Still, this moral judgment came in the last scene of the (up to today) last season of *Black Summer*, a series that tried to innovate audiences' affective identification with the screen.

### NOTES

1. Rakesh Sengupta, "Scripting for the Masses: Notes on the Political Economy of Bollywood," in *The Palgrave Handbook of Script Development*, ed. Craig Batty and Stayci Taylor (New York: Palgrave Macmillan, 2022), 223.

2. Yvonne Griggs, *Adaptable TV: Rewiring the Text* (New York: Palgrave Macmillan, 2018), 4.

3. For example, the slasher cycle of a group of teenagers facing a masked killer who

murders them one by one was predicated, especially through its zenith in the 1980s, on stock characters defined with just one word: the dumb, the jock, the hunk, the slut, the virgin, etc. See John Kenneth Muir, *Horror Films of the 1980s* Jefferson, NC: McFarland, 2010), 23.

4. Jason Mittell, "Vast Versus Dense Seriality in Contemporary Television," in *Television Aesthetics and Style*, ed. Jason Jacobs and Steven Peacock (New York: Bloomsbury, 2013), 46.

5. Adam Daniel, *Affective Intensities and Evolving Horror Forms: From Found Footage to Virtual Reality* (Edinburgh: Edinburgh University Press, 2020), 4.

6. Peter Turner, *Found Footage Horror Films: A Cognitive Approach* (New York: Routledge, 2019), 3.

7. Trisha Dunleavy, *Complex Serial Drama and Multiplatform Television* (New York: Routledge, 2018), 105.

8. Trisha Dunleavy, "*Mad Men* and Complex Seriality," in *The Legacy of Mad Men: Cultural History, Intermediality and American Television*, ed. Karen McNally, Jane Marcellus, Teresa Forde and Kirsty Fairclough (New York: Palgrave Macmillan, 2019), 49.

9. *Ibid.*

10. It may be argued that it is possible to find all the explanations in the "parent" series, *Z Nation*, from which *Black Summer* is a spin-off. Still, with exception of the zombies populating the earth, there is little connection. Further, being a spin-off does not mean that all viewers will follow the new story coming from the previous TV series. It looks like *Black Summer* is comfortable in its own sense of uncertainty.

11. Of course, villains may also be "main characters," but here I am proposing a reading based on identification between viewers and characters. It is possible that audiences can identify with a villain, yet most of mainstream fiction revolves around the hero/heroine as the focus of action.

12. Only in the next episode do viewers learn that he actually survived the trap.

13. Xavier Aldana Reyes, *Horror Film and Affect: Towards a Corporeal Model of Viewership* (New York: Routledge, 2016), 5.

14. *Ibid.*

15. *Ibid.*

16. *Ibid.*

17. *Ibid.*, 196.

18. *Ibid.*, 9.

19. *Ibid.*, 6.

20. *Ibid.*, 29.

21. *Ibid.*

22. *Ibid.*, 42.

23. Julian Hanich, *Cinematic Emotion in Horror Films and Thrillers: The Aesthetic Paradox of Pleasurable Fear* (New York: Routledge, 2010), 83.

24. Aldana Reyes, *Horror Film and Affect*, 150.

25. *Ibid.*

26. *Ibid.*, 164.

27. *Ibid.*, 16.

28. Robin Wood, "An Introduction to the American Horror Film," in *Planks of Reason: Essays on the Horror Film*, ed. Barry Keith Grant and Christopher Sharrett (Lanham, MD: Scarecrow Press, 2004), 109.

29. *Ibid.*

30. Wood, "An Introduction," 111.

31. Marshall Soules, *Media, Persuasion and Propaganda* (Edinburgh: Edinburgh University Press, 2015), 145.

32. Daniel, *Affective Intensities*, 38.

33. *Ibid.*, 54.

34. Hanich criticizes Deleuze's opaque language predicate on metaphors taken from "biology, neurophysiology, physics and engineering" that may "suggest a scientific understanding of the physiological body that can be objectively analyzed and measured." See Hanich, *Cinematic Emotion*, 14.

35. *Ibid.*
36. Anna Grimshaw and Amanda Ravetz, *Observational Cinema: Anthropology, Film, and the Exploration of Social Life* (Bloomington: Indiana University Press, 2009), 24.
37. Daniel, *Affective Intensities*, 47.
38. Vivian Sobchack, *Carnal Thoughts: Embodiment and Moving Image Culture* (Los Angeles: University of California Press, 2004), 284.

## Works Cited

Aldana Reyes, Xavier. *Horror Film and Affect: Towards a Corporeal Model of Viewership.* New York: Routledge, 2016.

Daniel, Adam. *Affective Intensities and Evolving Horror Forms: From Found Footage to Virtual Reality.* Edinburgh: Edinburgh University Press, 2020.

Dunleavy, Trisha. *Complex Serial Drama and Multiplatform Television.* New York: Routledge, 2018.

Dunleavy, Trisha. "*Mad Men* and Complex Seriality." In *The Legacy of* Mad Men: *Cultural History, Intermediality and American Television*, edited by Karen McNally, Jane Marcellus, Teresa Forde and Kirsty Fairclough, 47–62. New York: Palgrave Macmillan, 2019.

Griggs, Yvonne. *Adaptable TV: Rewiring the Text.* New York: Palgrave Macmillan, 2018.

Grimshaw, Anna, and Amanda Ravetz. *Observational Cinema: Anthropology, Film, and the Exploration of Social Life.* Bloomington: Indiana University Press, 2009.

Hanich, Julian. *Cinematic Emotion in Horror Films and Thrillers: The Aesthetic Paradox of Pleasurable Fear.* New York: Routledge, 2010.

Mittell, Jason. "Vast Versus Dense Seriality in Contemporary Television." In *Television Aesthetics and Style*, edited by Jason Jacobs and Steven Peacock, 45–56. New York: Bloomsbury, 2013.

Muir, John Kenneth. *Horror Films of the 1980s.* Jefferson, NC: McFarland, 2010.

Sengupta, Rakesh. "Scripting for the Masses: Notes on the Political Economy of Bollywood." In *The Palgrave Handbook of Script Development*, edited by Craig Batty and Stayci Taylor, 217–228. New York: Palgrave Macmillan, 2022.

Sobchack, Vivian. *Carnal Thoughts: Embodiment and Moving Image Culture.* Los Angeles: University of California Press, 2004.

Soules, Marshall. *Media, Persuasion and Propaganda.* Edinburgh: Edinburgh University Press, 2015.

Turner, Peter. *Found Footage Horror Films: A Cognitive Approach.* New York: Routledge, 2019.

Wood, Robin. "An Introduction to the American Horror Film." In *Planks of Reason: Essays on the Horror Film*, edited by Barry Keith Grant and Christopher Sharrett, 107–139. Lanham, MD: Scarecrow Press, 2004.

# The Many Faces of Thomas Hewitt

## A *Streaming Approach* *of* The Texas Chainsaw Massacre

### Giuseppe Previtali

Among the classic slasher sagas that began between the 1970s and the 1980s, the one inaugurated by Tobe Hooper's *The Texas Chainsaw Massacre* (1974) is without a doubt one of the most intriguing and complicated when it comes to narrative expansions, rewritings, and readaptations. If John Carpenter's *Halloween* (1978), Wes Craven's *A Nightmare on Elm Street* (1984) and Sean S. Cunningham's *Friday the 13th* (1980) gave birth to what we may label an additional and paratactic set of sequels, in which new installments show further iterations of the same plot with minimum changes, Hooper's horror was at the center of a very complicated operation of continuous rewriting, in a far more complicated sense. If it is undoubtedly true that the original *Texas Chainsaw Massacre* easily became a cult film in the context of the renovation of horror films in the direction of what Freeland identified as "realist horror,"[1] the subsequent installments were not so easily recognized by film critics and scholars as relevant works and were often dismissed as derivative iterations or parodic experiments. In an attempt to systematize the analysis of *The Texas Chainsaw Massacre* movie series taking into account both the narratological aspects and the ways in which the retelling of the story has been influenced by the sociocultural context, this essay will move from remake theory[2] and "political" horror studies[3] in order to see how the franchise relocates[4] itself (from a narrative, aesthetical and political point of view) in a wide variety of contexts, from the original "modern horror" setting of the 1970s to the streaming and data-driven environment of the Netflix version released in 2022.

Before proceeding in this direction, it is worth summarizing the general physiognomy of the franchise, in order to build a road map that can serve as a general orientation for the following analysis. The original *The*

*Texas Chainsaw Massacre* (1974) offered for the first time a glimpse into the murderous life of a family in rural Texas, while also helping to canonize the structure of the slasher subgenre. *The Texas Chainsaw Massacre—Part II* (1986) worked both as a sequel in continuity with the original film and as a parody of the models and structures of the slasher itself, adopting a very self-reflexive attitude that, indulging in camp and funny moments, helped to differentiate it from the gloomy atmosphere of the original. In 1990, to revamp the series following the long-term serialization of other slasher series, *Leatherface: The Texas Chainsaw Massacre III* was released. The movie was a first attempt to reboot the saga, adapting it to a new cultural sensibility and focusing more specifically on the figure of the killer, who becomes, rather than an anonymous and destructive force,[5] a specific character with a name and more defined background. Released in 1995, *Texas Chainsaw Massacre: The Next Generation* further complicates the series, because while it works as a canonical sequel, it is once again explicitly parodic towards the more serious installments (*The Texas Chainsaw Massacre* and *Leatherface*) and also dismiss both the sequel and the reboot as "minor incidents."

At the beginning of the 21st century, then, Hooper's creature already has a very specific physiognomy, and it was one of the first to be affected by the emerging trend of "upscaled remakes." In 2003, with the involvement of several members of the original crew (such as Tobe Hooper himself as a co-producer), *The Texas Chainsaw Massacre* was finally released, and it was probably the most critically discussed movie in the whole series. Acting both as a remake and a reboot, working on the tension between faithfulness to the original model and innovation, the film presented a sordid and sleazy portrait of Texan countryside, where the bloody and crude slaughter of a group of youngsters seems to finally fulfill Hooper's hope for a cinema that needs first of all to be felt: "It is important for a movie today to do more than tell a story. You've got to send a physical sensation through the audience and not let them off the hook."[6] The same goes for *The Texas Chainsaw Massacre: The Beginning* (2006), a prequel to the remake that maintains the franchise's tradition of continuously reworking the same elements and ideas in a quasi-Warholian manner,[7] where every scene looks at some sequence of the past while updating it to some extent.

While John Luessenhop's *Texas Chainsaw 3D* (2013) makes no exception in this sense, Maury and Bustillo's *Leatherface* (2017) is more radical in its retelling of the same story, abandoning the aesthetics of the so-called torture porn and producing a strange but fascinating hybrid between a typical U.S. horror and the so-called New French Extremity.[8] The final installment of the movie series (*Texas Chainsaw Massacre*) came out in 2022 under the direction of David Blue Garcia and was released directly on

Netflix, making it the first movie of the franchise to be distributed solely on streaming platforms. It is unclear if the movie will make a case for a new trend of what we may call "streaming horrors," but the recent release of David Bruckner's *Hellraiser* (2022) on Hulu seems to provide a first confirmation for this hypothesis. In any case, *The Texas Chainsaw Massacre* franchise seems the perfect case study to see the ways in which, under different productive, cultural and political circumstances, a same story can be (potentially infinitely) retold in order to highlight different aspects of it. In the following pages we will address the various strands of serialization based on the original movie, focusing distinctively on the first sequels (1986–1995), on the remake and its prequel (2003–2006), on the experimentations with 3D and different visual styles (2013–2017) and on the Netflix movie (2002), in order to produce a more nuanced and in-depth understanding of this complex filmic franchise.

## Parodies and Reboots

As already mentioned, the original *Texas Chainsaw Massacre* acquired a specific cultural relevance precisely because it was capable of renovating horror filmic language and aesthetics, working on a more realistic dimension of terror that had lot to do with American culture and politics. Robin Wood was probably one of the first to recognize the explicitly political value of the movie, highlighting the ways in which the classic conflict between urban and rural spaces was intertwined with issues of class segregation and economical exploitation.[9] According to Wood, Hooper's grotesque and alienated family stands for a whole subaltern proletariat that was progressively territorially secluded and socially excluded by the circulation of wealth provided by capitalism. This overtly political interpretation contributed to define the cultural identity of modern horror as a deconstruction of American middle-class utopia, built on the exclusion of suburban and rural areas and of their uneducated laborer.[10] More recent approaches have also pointed out the ways in which the filmic form itself contributed to enhance this political discourse working on specific elements of cinematic language, such as the composition of the shots and the relationship between foreground and background.[11] What these two different but not necessarily contradictory strands of research tell us is that *Texas Chainsaw Massacre* represented a milestone for horror cinema due to its capacity to encapsulate a specific set of anxieties, social tensions, and cultural problems, also thanks to a set of very peculiar intertextual link with classic horrors.[12]

If in the original movie the formal minimalism contributed to generate a sense of fear that is probably still unmatched, *The Texas Chainsaw*

*Massacre—Part II* has acquired a quasi-cult status due to its very personal approach and strangely camp attitude. Where the first movie was gloomy and disturbing, *Part II* becomes self-reflexive and parodic, to an extent that it is almost impossible to not catch the very explicit sexual metaphor that has to do with Leatherface's use of the chainsaw.[13] If *Texas Chainsaw* prefigured the canonical structure of the slasher movie, *Part II* already appeared a postmodern meditation on that specific subgenre and is very self-aware of its essential codes and mechanisms. The exaggerated monstrosity of the family members, their grotesque corporeality that draws into question what can be labeled as human, and the parody of American values and economical abundance encapsulated by the absurd chili cookoff competition are all signs of a black humoristic approach. It is precisely this new disposition towards the same narrative universe that makes the relationship between *Texas Chainsaw* and *Part II* so complex and intriguing: while still being a very "epidermic" movie,[14] the sequel acts both as an homage, a narrative extension and a quasi-theorical reflection on the original installment and the mechanisms of rewriting.

In both movies, the character of Leatherface was almost undefined: he didn't have a specific identity or background and worked as an obscure force, designed to punish and kill an urban and "degraded" group of youngsters (in the first movie) or a couple of "alien yuppies" (at the beginning of the sequel). *Leatherface: The Texas Chainsaw Massacre III* was more explicitly focused on the character of the killer, thus following a tendency that was common in later installments of slasher sagas (I think, for instance, of movies such as *A Nightmare on Elm Street 5: The Dream Child* or the *Halloween* movies devoted to the character of Jamie Lloyd). This element becomes immediately clear during the title sequence, in which the names of cast and crew's members are punctuated by close-ups of Leatherface cutting and sewing parts of human skin in order to produce a version of his iconic mask. As I have argued elsewhere,[15] this focus on the mask and on the act of covering the face will progressively become quintessential, while the issue of Leatherface identity will gain more and more importance. Junior (as he is called in *Leatherface*) is continuously trying to acquire a new face through the *quasi*-sacrificial killing of his victims: as both psychiatry and cultural anthropology taught us, the skin (and especially the skin of the face) is extremely relevant because it works as an osmotic surface and has relevant implications in the construction of one's identity.[16] It is thus hardly coincidental that in the films more overtly devoted to the exploration of Leatherface's identity and background, the act of sewing skin to create masks is more openly depicted, as we can also see in the 2003 remake.

However, it is not just Leatherface that changes in this rethinking of the original story: where in 1974 the role of victims was played by a group of youngsters who encapsulated the late spirit of youth contestation, the violence of the Sawyer family is here directed towards a couple of young adults who happen to accidentally pass within Texas. Their entrance in this land of primitive violence, sexual perversity and bodily degeneration is immediately marked by death when they are forced to stop not far from a mass grave full of decomposing and mutilated corpses. This explicit depiction of the Sawyers' violent actions is typical of this reboot: instead of a slow buildup of tension that explodes with the first appearance of the killer, here everything is immediately made explicit for the enjoyment of a well-aware public. The spectator knows, while the characters do not, that nothing pleasing is going to happen in this western-like landscape, where sexual depravation is celebrated and where the female body is literally chopped up (not just by Junior/Leatherface, but also metaphorically and visually by Alfredo, the owner of a gas station). While in Hooper's movie the killer appeared (at least initially) as a nihilistic force, a pure evil entity designed to punish the aberrations of modernity,[17] Jeff Burr's Leatherface is immediately framed within the power dynamics of a larger group, a family in which he is accepted and encouraged.

This crucial issue is made explicit when, in a remake of the similar sequence of the original *Texas Chainsaw*, the female protagonist is introduced to the members of the family. If in that instance the focus was mainly on the dysfunctional depiction of the various individuals, here their distance from common values does not automatically imply the lack of any kind of affection or bonds between them. Leatherface immediately brings his chainsaw to the dining table, and the other Sawyers react normally, as if this commitment to an instrument of death was no more than one of Junior's personality traits. Immediately after, the youngest member of the Sawyer family (known just as "the Little Girl") asks to be granted the honor of finalizing the killing of Ryan, the other main character of the film. This rite of passage is celebrated with great happiness by all the relatives, and her older brother (and *de facto* householder) Edward "Tex" Sawyer instructs her on how to do it. Tex's character is probably one of the most interesting of the movie, because it encapsulates the predatorial masculinity of Texas (recalled even by his nickname) through the adoption of a western-style iconography,[18] but in this scene he wears a cooking apron that points out his maternal role towards his relatives, thus producing a peculiar effect of queerization. Gender fluidity is here represented not solely by Leatherface's depiction[19] but, more interestingly, in the whole representation of the nuclear family as a social institution.

If the main point of *Leatherface* was to update the narrative of Hooper's original, adapting it to a different productive and aesthetical context, the subsequent installment of the series (*The Texas Chainsaw Massacre: The Next Generation*) represents another crucial turning point for the franchise. From the beginning, the desire to distance the movie from the previous two is quite explicit; we hear a voice-over reading a chart in which the murderous actions of Leatherface and his family are recalled.[20] The intention to connect this movie directly with the original film, thus dismissing both Hooper's parodical sequel and Jeff Burr's reboot, is evident here, and the whole movie is filled with direct visual nods to *Texas Chainsaw Massacre* (think, for instance, of the final shots of Leatherface, which perfectly mimic the ending of the movie). However, *The Next Generation* is anything but a remake: rather, it is a new update of the saga into the realm of mid–1990s teen movies. Following a new interest for teen horrors that dated back to the previous decade[21] and just before the release of Wes Craven's *Scream* (1996), *The Next Generation* already presents both the prototypical elements of the subgenre and the self-reflexive attitude that will characterize postmodern horror films.

The whole first part of the movie is a canonical representation of American youngsters, and the iconic school ball is the catalyst for a nocturnal exploration of rural Texas, in which the main characters end up meeting a new iteration of Leatherface's family. If compared with the previous films, *Next Generation*'s Leatherface seems to retreat into the background, to leave all the members of the group to do their part: far from being the manifestation of an irrational killing force or a character in search of an identity, here the main antagonist is just part of a larger setting that, according to a new paranoid subplot, serves the purposes of a local (but maybe bigger?) secret society. It can be argued that this narrative arc can be used to problematize the role of the film within the political framework of the saga, but the point seems not particularly relevant here. Rather, the peculiar rewriting of Leatherface as a character is worth further reflection. It is undoubtedly true that at least since *Texas Chainsaw Part II* Leatherface appears as a problematic character from the point of view of gender identity, but his transvestitism becomes explicit and narratively relevant in *Next Generation*. It is well-known that transvestite characters have been a staple of horror imaginary,[22] but here the female aspect assumed by the main antagonist has the effect of ridiculing it, transforming the once bloody killer into a parody of himself, as visually stressed by the finale.

## Politics of Remaking

What we may label the "original tetralogy" of *Texas Chainsaw Massacre* proved to be already complex, presenting not just a series of additional sequels but rather a continuous form of rewriting and re-appropriation that both innovated, honored and betrayed the original cult movie. The poor critical reception of *The Next Generation*, however, ended up producing disaffection in the public, that was unable to find the old, aggressive fascination of Hooper's film in the later installment of the series. At the beginning of the new century, Leatherface's saga seemed at a dead end, and this destiny was shared by all the other slasher franchises: the plots started to become more and more absurd, and the killing scenes were no longer perceived as something scary, mainly due to an outdated aesthetics. An innovative approach to horror was provided by the new wave of Japanese cinema, where from the late '90s new stylistic and dramaturgical experiments were made: Hideo Nakata's *Ringu* (1998) and Takashi Shimizu's *Ju-On* (2000) opened a new season for spiritual horrors, acting as game-changers in an industry in which the lack of new expressive solutions was condemning a whole genre to be residual.[23] American directors and producers immediately perceived the potential of this new trend and thus rapidly started producing more less faithful remakes, such as Gore Verbinski's *The Ring* (2002) or Takashi Shimizu's *The Grudge* (2004). Besides the complex nature of these operations,[24] it is precisely in this circumstance that we can identify the starting point of a new interest in remaking, which soon enough started to interest the canonical figure of modern American horror cinema.

Way before Rob Zombie's *Halloween* (2007) or Samuel Bayer's *A Nightmare on Elm Street* (2010), it was Marcus Nispel who started this trend with his remake of *The Texas Chainsaw Massacre* (2003), a very interesting re-imagination of Hooper's original movie. Like *Leatherface*, Nispel's *Texas Chainsaw* was designed precisely to promote a rebranding operation, useful to wipe out the camp, queer and parodic aspects of the killer in order to update the whole aesthetic of the film to make it more contemporary. It is not that Nispel deliberately rejected Hooper's aesthetics, but he has decided to re-mediate it for a new public, a different generation of young spectators for which *The Texas Chainsaw Massacre* was probably no more than a name or a title that vaguely evoked the past[25]; after all, in the early '00s we were still far from the possibility granted by peer-to-peer platforms or streaming sites, and was therefore often difficult to gain direct knowledge of old movies.

The differences between the two movies are already evident in the prologue, which mimics the original scene in which four youngsters give a ride to a hitchhiker. While in Hooper's version this moment marked the first encounter with the cannibal family, Nispel presents us with a female victim who luckily escaped from them. After realizing that the van of the protagonists is going back to where she escaped from, she pulls out a gun and shoots herself, granting Nispel the possibility of a highly spectacular and grotesque shot of the exploded cranial cavity. We are poles apart from any form of filmic philology here: the raw and unpolished images that Hooper cut together in an extraordinarily creative way are here replaced with glossy, high-quality, and precise shots.[26] More than remaking, Nispel's film is enhancing the original source,[27] stressing the gory, degraded, and nauseating aspects that have to do both with the depiction of characters (like the old amputee Monty) and settings (the Old Crawford Mill and the Hewitt mansion).

Much happened in American culture following the rise of the so-called American Gothic in the late '60s, and the 20th century began with the symbolic and physical downfall of the Twin Towers, producing a climate of paranoia and insecurity that was uncannily similar in some sense to the one in which the original *Texas Chainsaw* was released. After the great claims about the end of history and the collective security brought by New World Order, the World Trade Center collapse and the subsequent conflicts in Afghanistan and in some sense to the ignited a sense of uncertainty and fear that re-infected old wounds and cultural removals. Nispel's *Texas Chainsaw* goes precisely in this direction, producing a perverted portrait of rural America where the constitutive exclusions of capitalism continue to generate degradation and deformity, like a never-ending cancer.[28] The "clash of civilizations" diagnosed by Huntington in a well-known and problematic essay, then, is not just between a coherent image of the West and an obscure representation of an Orientalized (Middle) East, but *also* between the West and its "heart of darkness," a residual form of wilderness that seems to resist any form of civilization. With its sole existence, the Hewitt family proves that the comforting narrative of America's key values is fragile and questioned from within. This element is continuously stressed by Nispel's remake especially from a visual point of view: his Texas is as rotten and repulsive as it can be, as the persistent focus on secretions, organic fluids and dirt make immediately clear. Sheriff Hoyt's character is quintessential in this respect: gross and grotesque, he represents the perversion of law at the borders of civilization, and he is probably one of the best examples of contemporary Texan hillbilly.[29]

This political-ideological subtext, that both updates and betrays Hooper's, is perfectly encapsulated by Leatherface, here finally named as Thomas Hewitt. This character, granted a more developed personal background, is once again the surface on which the many tensions of the movie are inscribed. This is even more explicit in the prequel movie *The Texas Chainsaw Massacre—The Beginning* (Jonathan Liebesman, 2006), whose prologue shows both how Thomas was born and how he started to kill. From a narrative point of view, the prequel aims at working in perfect continuity with Nispel's remake, thus providing a more complex background for characters we already know, and in Thomas/Leatherface's case this is particularly evident. The first sequence of the film goes back to 1939 and shows how Thomas was born in a slaughterhouse to a mother exploited by her supervisor; the shots are designed to underline the unsanitary and dirty aspect of this workplace, and the newborn child is seen on a dirty floor, covered in blood and organic fluids. We are immediately granted a close-up of his face, deformed by a skin disease, and the uniqueness of this shot exemplifies the process of familiarization with the killer the film is trying to develop.[30]

Left in a dumpster, the child is found by the matriarch of the Hewitt family, and it is at this point that the opening credits begin. Here, both pictures and medical reports of the young Thomas are shown, focusing both on his desire to conceal his disturbing aspect and on his tendency to mutilate himself and others, skinning animals to create masks of some sort. Besides providing the spectator with a more nuanced understanding of Leatherface, the opening titles also tell the story of an abandoned city, of a dying economic business (unautomated animal slaughtering) and of a new cultural climate (the slaughterhouse will be closed, significantly, in 1969) that is relegating the Hewitt family (and many others, we may presume) to extreme indigence. Once again, we see here that the Hewitts' killings and their cannibalistic tendencies are somehow motivated by the urgent need to survive when every authority is absent and when the whole society becomes unrecognizable.[31]

After two narratively coherent movies, the franchise was reignited and rewritten once again in 2013, with the release of Luessenhop's *Texas Chainsaw 3D*. Even without extensively taking into account the critical reception of the film, it has to be said that *3D* is probably the least interesting installment in the series, if we exclude the opening sequence. For our purposes it is relevant to notice that this movie is intended to be a direct sequel to Hooper's *Texas Chainsaw* and is thus designed to ultimately dismiss all the events depicted both in the sequels and the remakes. During the opening titles we see well-known shots from the 1974 version, and the film begins in perfect continuity with its conclusion, showing how the Sawyer family was hunted and eliminated by a group of vigilantes, in an eruption of collective violence that explicitly resembles (especially in the way it is photographically documented) the lynching of African Americans. Even if the critical reception of the movie was quite uneven, *Texas Chainsaw 3D* proved to be a financial success, so the release of *Leatherface* in 2017 hardly came as a surprise. However, the choice of directors was rather interesting: Julien Maury and Alexandre Bustillo were already a renowned duo, especially thanks to the success of *Inside* (2007) and *Among the Living* (2014). Their movie shows how Jedidiah Sawyer ultimately became Leatherface after being separated by his family and secluded in a mental institution, from which he will manage to escape. This new incarnation of Leatherface is rather interesting, because Maury and Bustillo decide to focus on his coming-of-age story, showing how both his family background (the Sawyers are depicted since the beginning of the film as a group of killer and kidnappers) and the failure of social institutions contribute to his transformation into a killer who is more violent and brutal than ever before (see the beheading scene at the end of the movie).

## Leatherface Goes to Netflix

Although *Leatherface* was well-received and Lionsgate had plans for a whole new series of installments for the franchise, the long time needed to produce the movie cost the loss of the rights, which were then re-acquired by Legendary. Kim Henkel, who wrote the original *Texas Chainsaw Massacre* with Hooper back in the 1970s and had variously contributed to many rewritings of the saga,[32] figures here as one of the producers, somehow granting a canonicity sign to the movie, directed by David Blue Garcia and released on Netflix in February 2022. As already said, *Texas Chainsaw Massacre* is the first case of a new installment of a slasher saga to be shown directly on demand on a streaming platform, following an interest in horror films and TV-series that is becoming more and more evident.[33] The success of a series like *The Haunting of Hill House* (2018) was just the beginning of a new focus on the horror genre that involved not just Netflix but also other platforms, such as Hulu and Shudder, this latter being one of the main fields of formal experimentation for contemporary horror. As for some other installments in the franchise, Blue Garcia's movie suffered from a poor critical reception, but the film is nevertheless an interesting example of how a movie saga can rethink and re-rewrite itself in the new ecology of streaming platforms.

As noted by Gaynor, on demand platforms offer to horror the possibility of "an expansive exploration of the story or universe, character development ... and the maintenance of tension,"[34] thus promoting stylistic experimentations that would be impossible (or at least very difficult) in other industrial contexts. Also, as Lotz rightly pointed out, one of the reasons why Netflix was a game-changer in the industry is its hybrid nature that blurs the definition of television while also presenting itself as a library and a reflection of the habits and preferences of its users.[35] It could be then argued that the whole production and marketing of a horror movie could be rethought considering the importance that algorithms now play in the ecology of the platform, helping to detect emerging and recurring trends in the public and therefore to design successful and potentially viral products; however, the exploration of this issue—while crucial—will go far beyond the aim of this essay, which is rather to see how the main elements of *Texas Chainsaw Massacre* have been redefined in the later installment of the series.

The film opening presents mediated images from a documentary that recalls the story of the original *Texas Chainsaw*, retelling it through the canons of contemporary true crime TV,[36] a genre that—it is worth noticing here—has some popularity on Netflix. This form of hyper-mediation is not new to the franchise, which had already experimented with the forensic documentation that opens Nispel's remake and with intertextuality at the beginning of *Texas Chainsaw 3D*, but becomes more significant here, given the positioning of the movie in the contemporary media ecosystem and the fact that the false documentary is screened in a drugstore in rural Texas on a series of DVDs, thus stressing the difference between the setting and the main characters. Once again, the catalyst of the movie is provided by the reciprocal extraneousness between the protagonists and the inhabitants of a new wilderness; however, this dynamic is here embodied by a group of young digital entrepreneurs whose intentions are to buy an abandoned town in Texas to transform it in a gentrified and cool area for the new creative upper-middle class of the digital world. This act of depredation is made possible and legally proved by bureaucratic papers, but the situation will begin to collapse when the protagonists will force an old woman named Ginny to leave her house despite her being still in possession of its property. This element further problematizes the relationship between the protagonists and the landscape, because we end up discovering that the expulsion of this lady (which will lead to her death) was ultimately unlawful and it is certainly not coincidental that Leatherface's homicidal rampage begins just after this moment.

Leatherface is here depicted as an agent of vengeance, a son deprived by the presence of his mother; if in all the other installments he was the central point of a family setting, here he appears almost always alone and is thus more similar to other slasher killers, such as Freddy Krueger and Michael Myers. The introduction of this theme is functional to the reignition of the political reading of the franchise, which has to do mainly with class issues. This idea was already evident in some of the earlier installments but becomes here one of the main elements of the plot: Ginny and Leatherface (and Richter, who constitutes an intriguing subversion of the prototypical hillbilly character) represent the last heritage of an economic and social past that somehow resisted despite all, while the small group of protagonists embodies the contradictions and the predatorial aspects of a new young, creative and always connected social class. Gentrification is here depicted as a predatorial act perpetuated to the detriment of previous inhabitants, whose stories, memories, and legitimate demands are foreclosed and violently suppressed.

The well-known scene of the bus massacre is, in this sense, extremely clear. After the first couple of killings, the remaining protagonists head to a bus that is filled with young potential investors for the urban regeneration of the Texan ghost town. Here, the two girls of the group try to tell everyone what is going on, while the rest of them carelessly continue to celebrate, in what seems a nightclub on wheels. They are almost immediately stopped by Leatherface, who first chops the head of the driver off and then proceeds to the back. Here, in a scene that has been often dismissed as ridiculous if compared to other massacres he perpetrated, everyone takes out their smartphones and starts to live stream the event on platforms like Instagram or TikTok just before being murdered. Some shots of the smartphones are provided as well, with a focus on the comments, showing a range of different and prototypical reactions to the sharing of violent content ("ehh, I've been to more intense haunted houses before. 4/10," "wait WTF is this actually real?!?," "who hired this clown?," "THAT LOOKS SO FAKE"). The scene is rather interesting, because it visually epitomizes the irreconcilable contrast between two different worlds that the film (and the whole franchise) continuously stress. Leatherface has always been the insuppressible incarnation of all the things that are categorically excluded by modernization and always reappears when society is experiencing moments of change, whether it's social, political, cultural, or technological. Leatherface's gaze never changes; it stares at us silently behind a mask that reinvents itself while always staying the same. The ways in which we (as characters in the movie or spectators at home) look at him may change, but the uncanniness of his looks will stay the same, even if we are watching a movie that a streaming platform randomly suggested to us.

## NOTES

1. Cynthia A. Freeland, "Realist Horror," in *Philosophy and Film*, ed. Cynthia A. Freeland (London: Routledge, 1995), 126–42.

2. Christian Knöppler, *The Monster Always Returns: American Horror Films and Their Remakes* (Bielefeld: Transcript verlag, 2017).

3. Such as Adam Lowenstein, *Shocking Representation: Historical Trauma, National Cinema and the Modern Horror Film* (New York: Columbia University Press, 2005); Antonio José Navarro, *L'impero del terrore: Il cinema horror statunitense post 11 settembre* (Milan: Bietti, 2019).

4. In the sense outlined by Francesco Casetti, *The Lumière Galaxy: Seven Key Words for the Cinema to Come* (New York: Columbia University Press, 2015).

5. As noted by Phelps, the original *Texas Chainsaw Massacre* made "no explicit attempt

to offer explanations for the behaviour of the killers, beyond simple bloodlust …. It's a film about meat, about people who are gone beyond dealing with animal meat and rats and dogs and cats. Crazy, retarded people going beyond the line between animal and human," Guy Phelps, "Family Life," *Sight & Sound* 45, no. 2 (Spring 1976): 84.

6. Quoted in L.M. Kit Carson, "Saw Thru," *Film Comment* 22, no. 4 (July/August 1986): 12. In this sense, both Hooper's hope and the 2003 remake seems to confirm the well-known reflections of Williams concerning body genres; see Linda Williams, "Film Bodies: Gender, Genre and Excess," *Film Quarterly* 44, no. 4 (Summer 1991): 2–13.

7. Vincent Malausa, "Massacre à la tronçonneuse: le commencement," *Cahiers du Cinéma* 620 (February 2007): 60–61.

8. Both torture porn and New French Extremity are nowadays well recognized critical categories, with an ingrowing amount of dedicated literature. See at least Steve Jones, *Torture Porn: Popular Horror After Saw* (Basingstoke: Palgrave Macmillan, 2013), 13–56; Aaron Michael Kerner, *Torture Porn in the Wake of 9/11: Horror, Exploitation and the Cinema of Sensation* (New Brunswick: Rutgers University Press, 2015), 22–55; Alexandra West, *Films of the New French Extremity: Visceral Horror and National Identity* (Jefferson, NC: McFarland, 2016).

9. Robin Wood, "An Introduction to the American Horror Film," in *Planks of Reason: Essays on the Horror Film*, eds. Christopher Sharrett and Barry Keith Grant (London: Scarecrow Press, 1984), 164–200.

10. This concept was theoretically codified as "urbanoia" in Carol Clover, *Men, Women & Chainsaws: Gender in the Modern Horror Film* (Princeton: Princeton University Press, 1992), 124–137. On the case of *The Texas Chainsaw Massacre*, see also Kim Newman, *Nightmare Movies* (New York: Harmony Books, 1989).

11. "When we shift away from trying to identify the subject position, radical or otherwise, of [an] horrible content, we find the basis for a new kind of political reading, one sensitive above all to how films refract an economic and social order that constantly produces swelling mass of the unwanted pressing up against the edges and into the foreground. It is this horror, that of the secondary material the refuses to quint the scene or do its job, that deserves to be defended and elaborated," Evan Calder Williams, "Sunset with Chainsaw," *Film Quarterly* 64, no. 4 (Summer 2011): 33.

12. Larrie Dudenhoeffer, "Monster Mishmash: Iconicity and Intertextuality in Tobe Hooper's *The Texas Chainsaw Massacre*," *Journal of the Fantastic in the Arts* 19, no. 1 (2008): 51–69.

13. Clover, *Men, Women & Chainsaws*, 28.

14. Alberto Pezzotta, "Subire l'orrore," *Filmcritica*, no. 379 (November 1987): 630–2.

15. Giuseppe Previtali, "Dietro la maschera e sotto la pelle. Alcune osservazioni sul divenire altro nel filone slasher," *Cineforum*, no. 583 (April 2019): 44. See also Judith Halberstam, *Skin Shows: Gothic Horror and the Technology of Monsters* (Durham: Duke University Press, 1995).

16. Didier Anzieu, *The Skin-Ego* (London: Routledge, 2016).

17. See Naomi Merritt, "Cannibalistic Capitalism and other American Delicacies: A Bataillean Tase of *The Texas Chain Saw Massacre*," *Film-Philosohpy* 14, no. 1 (2010): 202–31.

18. Carl Freedman, "Post-Heterosexuality: John Wayne and the Construction of American Masculinity," *Film International* 5, no. 1 (2007): 16–31; Brian Baker, *Masculinity in Fiction and Film: Representing Men in Popular Genres 1945–2000* (London: Continuum, 2008), 124–57. See also Walter F. Bell, "Westerns," in Bret E. Carroll, ed., *American Masculinities: A Historical Encyclopedia* (New York: Sage, 2003), 489–91.

19. Clover, *Men, Women & Chainsaws*, 27.

20. "August 18, 1973. News of a bizarre, chainsaw wielding family—reports which were to ignite the world's imagination—began to filter out of central Texas. Regrettably not one of the family members was ever apprehended and for more than ten years nothing further was heard. Then, over the next several years, at least two minor, yet apparently related incidents, were reported. Then again nothing. For five long years silence…"

21. Timothy Shary, *Teen Movies: American Youth on Screen* (London: Wallflower, 2005), 60–61.

22. Julie Tharp, "The Trasvestite as Monster: Gender Horror in *The Silence of the Lambs* and *Psycho*," *Journal of Popular Film and Television* 19, no. 3 (Fall 1991): 106–13.

23. For a comprehensive overview, see Mitsuyo Wada-Marciano, "J-Horror: New Media's Impact on Contemporary Japanese Horror Cinema," in *Horror to the Extreme: Changing Boundaries in Asian Cinema*, edited by Jinhee Choi and Mitsuyo Wada-Marciano (Hong Kong: Hong Kong University Press 2009), 15–38.

24. See Valerie Wee, *Japanese Horror Films and Their American Remakes: Translating Fear, Adapting Culture* (New York: Routledge 2014).

25. Alessandro Bertani and Alberto Soncini, "Texani brava gente. *Non aprite quella porta* 1974–2003. Da Toobe Hooper a Marcus Nispel," *Cineforum*, no. 431 (January/February 2004): 48–51; Mark Kermode, "What a carve up!" *Sight & Sound* 13, no. 12 (December 2003): 12–16.

26. Kermode, "What a carve up!" 13; see also Vincent Malausa, "Soleil noir," *Cahiers du cinema*, no. 705 (November 2014): 66.

27. "Faced with such a wide-eyed, unknowing crowd, the creators of the new *Texas Chainsaw Massacre* clearly felt little need to deconstruct or re-examine their source. Instead, they have simply turbo-charged the original, glossing up the gore, needlessly expanding the backstory and cranking up the action set-pieces," Kermode, "What a carve up!" 14. See also Nathan Lee, "The Return of the Return of the Repressed! Risen from the Grave and Brought Back to Bloody Life: Horror Remakes from *Psycho* to *Funny Games*," *Film Comment* 44, no. 2 (March/April 2008): 25.

28. For a general overview on how 9/11 influenced American horror cinema see Kevin J. Wetmore, *Post 9/11 Horror in American Cinema* (New York: Continuum International, 2012).

29. Although *The Texas Chinsaw Massacre* is not a canonical example of hillbilly horror, I do believe that this ideological identity can be helpful to understand the ways in which the characters of Nispel's remake are depicted; on this topic, see Anthony Harkins, *Hillbilly: A Cultural History of an American Icon* (New York: Oxford University Press 2004).

30. This tendency is common in the '00s horror remakes; Rob Zombie's *Halloween* is another quintessential example of this trend, as the long sequence devoted to the exploration of Michael's childhood and psychological background shows. See Knöppler, *The Monster Always Returns*, 230–33.

31. It is non-coincidental that, according to the Italian scholar Franco La Polla, this same problem is at the core of the New Hollyood and represents a key aspect of all American cinema in the period between the end of the 1960s and the first half of 1970s, regardless of genre dynamics and production values; see Franco La Polla, *Il nuovo cinema americano* (Venice: Marsilio, 1978).

32. Before his involvement in *Texas Chainsaw Massacre* (2022), Henkel was writer and director of *Texas Chainsaw Massacre: The Next Generation*, co-producer of Marcus Nispel's remake in 2003, producer of *Texas Chainsaw Massacre: The Beginning* and executive producer of *Texas Chainsaw 3D*.

33. Stella Marie Gaynor, *Rethinking Horror in the New Economies of Television* (Cham: Palgrave Macmillan 2022), 97–124.

34. Gaynor, *Rethinking Horror*, 12.

35. Amanda D. Lotz, *Portals: A Treatise on Internet-Distributed Television* (Ann Arbor: Maize Books, 2017).

36. See chapters 4 and 5 of Jean Murley, *The Rise of True Crime. Twentieth Century Murder and American Popular Culture* (Westport, CT: Praeger, 2008).

## Works Cited

Anzieu, Didier. *The Skin-Ego*. London: Routledge, 2016.

Baker, Brian. *Masculinity in Fiction and Film: Representing Men in Popular Genres 1945–2000*. London: Continuum, 2008.

Bell, Walter F. "Westerns." In Bret E. Carroll (ed.), *American Masculinities. A Historical Encyclopedia*, 489–91. New York: Sage, 2003.

Bertani Alessandro, and Alberto Soncini. "Texani brava gente. *Non aprite quella porta 1974–2003. Da Toobe Hooper a Marcus Nispel." Cineforum*, no. 431 (January/February 2004): 48–51

Calder Williams, Evan. "Sunset with Chainsaw." *Film Quarterly* 64, no. 4 (Summer 2011): 28–33.

Carson, L.M. Kit. "Saw Thru." *Film Comment* 22, no. 4 (July/August 1986): 9–12.

Casetti, Francesco. *The Lumière Galaxy: Seven Key Words for the Cinema to Come*. New York: Columbia University Press, 2015.

Clover, Carol. *Men, Women & Chainsaws. Gender in the Modern Horror Film*. Princeton: Princeton University Press, 1992.

Dudenhoeffer, Larrie. "Monster Mishmash: Iconicity and Intertextuality in Tobe Hooper's *The Texas Chainsaw Massacre." Journal of the Fantastic in the Arts* 19, no. 1 (2008): 51–69.

Freedman, Carl. "Post-Heterosexuality: John Wayne and the Construction of American Masculinity." *Film International* 5, no. 1 (2007): 16–31

Freeland, Cynthia A. "Realist Horror." In Cynthia A. Freeland (ed.), *Philosophy and Film*, 126–42. London: Routledge, 1995.

Gaynor, Stella Marie. *Rethinking Horror in the New Economies of Television*. Cham: Palgrave Macmillan, 2022.

Halberstam, Judith. *Skin Shows: Gothic Horror and the Technology of Monsters*. Durham: Duke University Press, 1995.

Harkins, Anthony. *Hillbilly: A Cultural History of an American Icon*. New York: Oxford University Press, 2004.

Jones, Steve. *Torture Porn. Popular Horror After Saw*. Basingstoke: Palgrave Macmillan, 2013.

Kermode, Mark. "What a carve up!" *Sight & Sound* 13, no. 12 (December 2003): 12–16.

Kerner, Aaron Michael. *Torture Porn in the Wake of 9/11: Horror, Exploitation and the Cinema of Sensation*. New Brunswick: Rutgers University Press 2015.

Knöppler, Christian. *The Monster Always Returns. American Horror Films and Their Remakes*. Bielefeld: Transcript Verlag, 2017.

La Polla, Franco. *Il nuovo cinema americano*. Venice: Marsilio 1978.

Lee, Nathan. "The Return of the Return of the Repressed! Risen from the Grave and Brought Back to Bloody Life: Horror Remakes from *Psycho* to *Funny Games." Film Comment* 44, no. 2 (March/April 2008): 24–8.

Lotz, Amanda D. *Portals: A Treatise on Internet-Distributed Television*. Ann Arbor: Maize Books, 2017.

Lowenstein, Adam. *Shocking Representation. Historical Trauma, National Cinema and the Modern Horror Film*. New York: Columbia University Press, 2005.

Malausa, Vincent. "Massacre à la tronçonneuse: le commencement." *Cahiers du Cinéma* 620 (February 2007): 60–61.

Malausa, Vincent. "Soleil noir." *Cahiers du Cinéma* 705 (November 2014): 66–68.

Merritt, Naomi. "Cannibalistic Capitalism and other American Delicacies: A Bataillean Tase of *The Texas Chain Saw Massacre." Film-Philosohpy* 14, no. 1 (2010): 202–31.

Murley, Jean. *The Rise of True Crime: Twentieth Century Murder and American Popular Culture*. Westport, CT: Praeger, 2008.

Navarro, Antonio José. *L'impero del terrore. Il cinema horror statunitense post 11 settembre*. Milan: Bietti, 2019.

Newman, Kim. *Nightmare Movies*. New York: Harmony Books, 1989.

Pezzotta, Alberto. "Subirel'orrore." *Filmcritica*, no. 379 (November 1987): 630–2.

Phelps, Guy. "Family Life." *Sight & Sound* 45, no. 2 (Spring 1976): 84–5.

Previtali, Giuseppe. "Dietro la maschera e sotto la pelle. Alcune osservazioni sul divenire altro nel filone slasher." *Cineforum*, no. 583 (April 2019): 42–7.

Shary, Timothy. *Teen Movies. American Youth on Screen*. London: Wallflower, 2005.

Tharp, Julie. "The Transvestite as Monster: Gender Horror in *The Silence of the Lambs* and *Psycho." Journal of Popular Film and Television* 19, no. 3 (Fall 1991): 106–13.

Wada-Marciano, Mitsuyo. "J-Horror: New Media's Impact on Contemporary Japanese Horror Cinema." In *Horror to the Extreme. Changing Boundaries in Asian Cinema*, edited by Jinhee Choi and Mitsuyo Wada-Marciano, 15–38. Hong Kong: Hong Kong University Press, 2009.

Wee, Valerie. *Japanese Horror Films and Their American Remakes. Translating Fear, Adapting Culture.* New York: Routledge, 2014.

West, Alexandra. *Films of the New French Extremity: Visceral Horror and National Identity.* Jefferson, NC: McFarland, 2016.

Wetmore, Kevin J. *Post 9/11 Horror in American Cinema.* New York: Continuum International, 2012.

Williams, Linda. "Film Bodies: Gender, Genre and Excess." *Film Quarterly* 44, no. 4 (Summer 1991): 2–13.

Wood, Robin. "An Introduction to the American Horror Film." In *Planks of Reason: Essays on the Horror Film*, eds. Christopher Sharrett, Barry Keith Grant, 164–200. London: Scarecrow Press, 1984.

# About the Contributors

Christina **Adamou** is an associate professor of film and television studies in the School of Film, Aristotle University of Thessaloniki, Greece. Her research interests include the representations of genders, children's films and television as well as contemporary television studies. She co-edited with Sotiris Petridis *Television by Stream: Essays on Marketing, Content and Audience Worldwide* (McFarland, 2023).

Anna Rufer **Bílá** is an assistant professor in the Department of Theatre and Film Studies (TV and Radio Studies Programme) at Palacký University in Olomouc, Czech Republic. Her research program includes fan studies, gender representation in audiovisual popular culture, and new media phenomena, such as bookstagrams.

Klára **Feikusová** is an assistant professor in the Department of Theatre and Film Studies at Palacký University in Olomouc, Czech Republic. Her main area of interest is television studies, especially television aesthetics, media convergence, television horror and media representation of minorities. She has published on colorblind casting and queerness and television horror.

Sony **Jalarajan Raj** is an assistant professor in the Department of Communication at MacEwan University, Edmonton, Canada. He is a professional journalist turned academic who has worked in different positions as a reporter, special correspondent, and producer in several news media channels including the BBC, NDTV, Doordarshan, AIR, and Asianet News.

Ivan **Jaramillo** is a doctoral student in Japanese culture at the Graduate School of Humanities, Nagoya University. He received his master's degree from Nagoya with a thesis on the translation of children's literature during the Meiji period. His research examines the transmedial affects of Japanese horror with a focus on the works of manga horror artist Itō Junji.

Neelima **Mundayur** has a background in modern South Asian studies. Her graduate research mapped the *Saptaham* ritual in Kerala, considering patterns of celebritization, commodification and resignification as central to understanding caste and gender relations within it. Her interests include media and cultural studies, focusing on topics of caste, gender, queerness, and neoliberalism. She has also worked as a journalist and filmmaker.

Fernando Gabriel **Pagnoni Berns** is a professor at the Universidad de Buenos Aires in the Facultad de Filosofía y Letras (Argentina). He teaches courses on international horror film. He has co-edited books on horror and philosophy (McFarland, 2023), director James Wan (McFarland, 2022), and the Italian *giallo* film (University of Mississippi Press, 2023).

Sotiris **Petridis** is an adjunct professor at Hellenic Open University, Greece. His research interests include film and television genres, audiovisual horror, screenwriting theory and practice, viral marketing, and new ways of film and television promotion. He has written books and articles on cinema and audiovisual narrative and is a member of the European Film Academy and the Greek Film Academy.

Giuseppe **Previtali** is an assistant professor at the University of Bergamo, where he teaches film and visual studies. His main research interests concern the extreme form of contemporary visuality, visual literacy and the critical epistemology of digital humanities. Published books include *Educazione visuale* (McGraw-Hill, 2020) and *Che cosa sono le digital humanities* (Carocci, 2023).

Adith K. **Suresh** is a research assistant in the Department of Communication, MacEwan University, Edmonton, Canada. He received his master's degree in English language and literature from Mahatma Gandhi University in Kottayam, Kerala, India. His has published on a variety of topics including film studies, literary criticism, and South Asian cultural studies.

# Index